S0-AID-902

# THE
# SCAVENGER'S
# GUIDE
# TO
# HAUTE CUISINE

# THE
# SCAVENGER'S
# GUIDE
# TO
# HAUTE CUISINE

## Steven Rinella

**miramax books**

**HYPERION**

N E W   Y O R K

Copyright © 2005 Steven Rinella

All rights reserved. No part of this book may be used or reproduced in
any manner whatsoever without the written permission of the Publisher.
Printed in the United States of America. For information address
Hyperion, 77 West 66th Street, New York, NY 10023–6298

Library of Congress Cataloging-in-Publication Data

Rinella, Steven.
    The scavenger's guide to haute cuisine / Steven Rinella.
        p.    cm.
    ISBN 1-4013-5237-5
        1. Cookery.    2. Escoffier, A. (Auguste), 1846–1935.
Guide culinaire.    3. Hunting.    4. Rinella, Steven.    I. Title.

TX651.R55    2006
641.5—dc22

                                              2005058058

First Edition
10    9    8    7    6    5    4    3    2

# Contents

*For my mom and dad*

# Acknowledgments

Without the help of the following people, this book would not be in your hands. Thanks to Marc Gerald at The Agency Group for knowing what he's talking about; Ian Frazier for his guidance and advice; Jillellyn Riley at Miramax Books for her careful reading; Mary Turner at *Outside* for taking a few chances on me; Deirdre McNamer and Fred Haefele for putting me on the right path; and Mr. Heaton for telling me that there was a path in the first place. Thanks also to Floyd Van Ert, Ray Turner, and the Leightons of Saltry Cove—I enjoyed learning how to do what you do. Thanks to all of my family and friends who were pulled into this story, especially Matt and Danny. And, finally, thanks to Diana Spechler for her endless love and made-up songs.

*One can but deplore the arbitrary proscription which so materially reduces the resources at the disposal of a cook, more particularly at a time when the universally imperious cry is for novelty and variety . . .*

—AUGUSTE ESCOFFIER

# THE
# SCAVENGER'S
# GUIDE
# TO
# HAUTE CUISINE

# Prologue

IT'S ALMOST TIME FOR THANKSGIVING DINNER AND I'M JUST NOW beginning to stuff the bird. But no matter how hard I stuff, I can't get it to fit inside the bladder. I'm following a recipe from French master chef Auguste Escoffier's 1903 magnum opus, *Le Guide Culinaire*, a 5,012-recipe compendium on haute cuisine. The book is pinned open on the counter with a one-quart jar of stingray marinade. Technically, the dish I'm making calls for a duck to be poached inside a pig's bladder. But when I killed a wild boar in northern California last summer, I accidentally nicked its bladder with my skinning knife. So I'm trying to forge ahead with an antelope bladder and half a duck. I push and pull and stretch, but it won't go.

The poached bladder is just one of the courses from *Le Guide Culinaire* that I'm attempting to construct tonight. All together, I have the ingredients for fifteen dishes scattered throughout the kitchen here in Miles City, Montana. Or, I should say, I have the ingredients for thirteen dishes scattered around; the makings of the other two courses are still wearing their feathers and fur.

My two squabs, or baby pigeons, are cooing and preening

in the coop that I built last summer. The birds' names are Red and Lil' Red, and I'll be using them in Escoffier's *pigeonneaux crapaudine.* In an hour they need to be plucked, flattened, dipped in butter, grilled, then served with gherkins and Escoffier's *diable,* or devil sauce.

The remaining dish is a pâté of cottontail rabbit. For all I know, the key ingredient for that is still hopping around south of town. My two brothers, Matt and Danny, left this morning with a group of our friends to hunt pheasants and rabbits along the Powder River, but it's getting dark and they still haven't returned.

I keep busy as I wait for the rabbit. After lifting some strips of black bear fat out of a bowl of brandy, I refill the bowl with a handful of wild boar sausage. Then I begin prepping the fixings for a freshwater matelote, a soup made from white wine, stock, and a medley of fish. I've already peeled the crayfish tails, so I trim some fillets of smallmouth bass, walleye, and bluegills and remove the long, serpentine spine from an eel.

If everything goes right, I will prepare forty-five courses from *Le Guide Culinaire* over the next three nights. I have at my fingertips a collection of the book's ingredients that I gathered from all corners of the country. As I work along, converting raw material to food, the last year of my life literally passes through my fingers. The stingray marinade takes me back to a Florida beach, where my buddy Kern and I wrestled in a stingray amid a throng of hostile tourists. The black bear fat makes me remember the glaciers of Alaska's Chugach Range, which turn the eerie blue color of gel toothpaste when the sun breaks through the clouds. The eel makes me think of Ray Turner, a self-proclaimed "old hairbag by the river" who operates an eel weir in upstate New York, keeps an emu for company, and once built a fireplace from a rock that he found by the grave site of an Indian princess.

Back when I first discovered *Le Guide Culinaire,* I knew I'd stumbled into a strange, lost world. In his day, Escoffier was known as the King of Chefs and the Chef of Kings; he cooked for the likes of Kaiser Wilhelm II, Frederick VIII, the Duke of Orleans, Queen Victoria, the Prince of Wales, the Khadid of Egypt, the emperors of Austria and Brazil, the shah of Persia, and the king of Greece. If Escoffier's list of clients just sounds like a bunch of people who figured into World War I, you might approach Escoffier through the more familiar lens of American music:

*Now, if you're blue*
*And you don't know where to go to*
*Why don't you go where fashion sits*
*Puttin' on the Ritz*

That ditty from 1929 was written by Irving Berlin, the same dude who wrote "God Bless America." In "Puttin' on the Ritz," Berlin is referring to the Swiss hotelier César Ritz, whose name is synonymous with taste and class and ostentatious display. In large part, Ritz's reputation rested on his long partnership with Auguste Escoffier. Ritz ran the hotels; Escoffier ran the kitchens in the hotels. When Escoffier collected his methods in *Le Guide Culinaire,* he produced a work that singlehandedly revolutionized French *haute,* or "high," cuisine.

As old as it is, the book didn't seem to me like a historical document when I found it. Instead, I saw it immediately as a scavenger's guide, an inventory of all that is bizarre and glorious and tantalizing about procuring your own food and living off the wild. I tore into the book, hell-bent on recreating as much of it as I could. I allowed myself a year, and now all that time has come down to these moments, these three nights, and I'm filled with overwhelming giddiness. And an equal dose of anxiety. I've got friends here from all over the country tonight. If I can't pull off this feast, this last year of my life will seem a little less extraordinary.

I go outside to see if my brothers are back yet with some rabbits. They're not. I take a peek into the pigeon coop. It's dark out, and the two squabs are sitting on their perches, oblivious to what lies ahead. The older pigeon, Red, has one of the younger pigeon's feathers stuck in his bill. There's plenty of room for the two to spread out, but they make a sport of pecking at each other in a ritualistic sort of dance. They usually shadowbox, but now and then Red connects. I'm visited by this weird sense of guilt that I get every time I look at them. Catching the squabs required almost a year's time and several near-death experiences. When I first started chasing pigeons with the thought of trying some of Escoffier's thirty-four squab recipes, I thought of the birds as dirty pests. But after catching a few pigeons and raising the squabs by hand, I came to see the birds as a metaphor for the contradictions of a society that has distanced itself from the production of its food. Now that I'm moments away from "prepping" the birds, I lament that it's going to be an awfully abrupt ending for such a long story. In Escoffier's day, people killed squabs by smothering them. The ancient Romans drowned their squabs in red wine. I might use a hatchet.

I go back to the kitchen to finish plucking a box of twenty English sparrows that I got in Iowa. The birds are so small, I can hold four or five of them in my palm at once. Plucking the little things is delicate work. I lift one from the box and pinch a tuft of feathers from its breast just as my girlfriend, Diana, walks into the kitchen. At the sight of her, I reflexively drop the sparrow back into the box and kick the lid closed. At the same time, I toss a scrap of cheesecloth over the plate of wild turkey bones that will go into tomorrow's game stock. Escoffier often recited the maxim, "If you want to keep your appetite, stay out of the kitchen." I'm trying to enforce Escoffier's advice on Diana, because she's a struggling vegetarian. I'm hoping that this feast will serve as a rite of passage for her, and that she'll emerge from the experience as a full-on carnivore. She's agreed to try as much of the food as physically possible tonight. I'm counting on her getting blown away by the beauty of the finished products and I don't want her to get turned off prematurely.

Once I shoo Diana from the kitchen, two of my buddies from childhood, Kern and Drost, come running through the front door in their hunting boots and then go out the back door. As they disappear, I yell, "Hey, did you get the rabbits?" But they don't hear me.

I go outside and see that my brothers and Drost are helping Kern pin down one of his hunting dogs. The dog got hung up on a barbed-wire fence. Kern's wife, Deirdre, is a doctor. She's got a curved needle and a long thread, and she's sewing the dog back up.

When she finishes tightening the last knot, I look at Danny. "Rabbits?"

"Two. I'll skin 'em for you."

When Danny comes in with the rabbit loins, I have what I need to finish the fourteenth dish. I slice the loins in long, thin strips and put them to soak in the brandy. Fourteen down. Now there's just one dish left.

I step outside with the hatchet. Someone's turned on the yard light, so Red thinks the sun has risen. I can hear him cooing.

# CHAPTER ONE

# Free Range

I SPEND A LOT OF TIME THINKING ABOUT FOOD. IF I'M NOT THINK-ing about food, there's a good chance that I'm out collecting it. I scrounge around in the mountains for huckleberries and I search riverbanks for wild asparagus, though mostly I hunt and fish. I suppose you could say that getting my own food is a hobby of mine, but I've never looked at it that way. When I'm packing an elk down off a mountain on my back, and it feels like my knees are going to crack open and my shoulders are going to strip away like banana peels beneath the weight, I certainly don't feel like I'm pursuing a hobby.

Don't get me wrong, though, I love scavenging for my own food. I suppose it's important to clear that up right away—that I think it's exciting to hunt and fish. People will happily pay good money for dead animals, so long as the animals are killed by proxy executioners and sold in grocery stores. But many of those same people are suspicious of folks who enjoy killing their own food in the wild. So let this serve as a warning about what kind of guy I am, and what kind of book this is.

However, it's an oversimplification to say that I enjoy killing for the sake of killing. I enjoy killing in the same way that I enjoy cooking and eating and doing all the other things that it takes to stay alive. One time, I spent a couple of days shitting my brains out on a riverbank in northern Alaska because I ate some wild mushrooms that I could have sworn were safe. I actually enjoyed getting poisoned by these unpredictable fungi, because I was living out an experience that usually only happens to characters in fairy tales. Another time, my brother Matt and I were hunting elk and heading up a mountain trail at the same time that a five-hundred-pound grizzly and her two cubs were heading down it. The sow stood up on her back feet as easily as a human rising out of a chair. She held her arms out, paws down, like she was showing us an engagement ring. She was *right* there, within striking distance. I enjoyed the hell out of that too. I guess I just like the whole package of wild food: eating, almost being killed, and, yes, killing.

Still, I can't look at that statement of mine—that I enjoy killing my own food—without cringing. I'm surprised that I came right out and said that. Even hunting and fishing magazines avoid saying that. Which is odd, because hunting and fishing are, fundamentally, methods of food procurement. One would think that a hunting and fishing magazine would be all about killing and eating. The thing is, publications like *Outdoor Life,* America's most venerable sporting magazine, try hard to distance themselves from anything that might be distasteful or insensitive to whoever thumbs through their magazines in the waiting rooms of the nation's dentists. Outdoor writers discuss "taking" turkeys, "collecting" trophies, and "harvesting" pheasants, but no one ever "kills" anything. Instead, the magazines help create and portray a type of dude who is so obsessed with trucks and chewing tobacco and guns that he doesn't have any energy left over to think about food. In the minds of many hunters, especially those who subscribe to the alarmist reckonings of the National Rifle Association, the primary threat to hunting is not suburban sprawl or wilderness destruction or the poisoning of our air and water. Rather, they believe that the primary threat to hunting lies within the government's desire to take all the guns away. Animals will be running around everywhere, elk and bears will be banging down our doors, and there won't be a thing we can do about it because of those damn liberals with their gun-control laws.

Fishermen have developed an even more thorough separation from their barbaric parent, the hunter-gatherer. Basically, catch-and-release fishing is a weird, paradoxical sort of game where you try to poke a hook through a fish's face without causing it unnecessary harm. Catch-and-release anglers "play" the fish and then toss it back. There's a reasonable chance that the fish will die from stress-induced increases in lactic acid within hours or days of its release, but by then the angler will be gone and he won't have to worry about what to do with a dead fish. Catch-and-release has endowed trout fishing with an aesthetic not unlike country-club golf, with vacation resorts, private lessons, boutique clothing shops, and cliquey social organizations. The most notable distinction between catch-and-release and golf is that the plaything being knocked around in catch-and-release is a sentient being. Catch-and-release bass fishing has hijacked the aesthetic of NASCAR, with ultrafast boats and brightly colored uniforms bearing sponsors' logos on the sleeves. The most notable distinction between NASCAR and bass fishing is that instead of racing across a black asphalt track, you're racing across fragile wildlife habitat.

The stated goal of all this sanitization is to preserve hunting and fishing rights. Hunters and fishermen need a more modern, improved image, the argument goes; they need to be more like "sportsmen." Ironically, though, most of the nonhunters I know believe that killing for sport is an abomination, and that hunting and fishing are only justifiable if the meat is being used thoroughly and responsibly.

I grew up in western Michigan, on an isthmus amid a cluster of four small lakes called North, West, Middle, and Twin. For some reason, the lakes are known collectively as Twin Lake. If you tell someone in Muskegon, the closest city, that you're from Twin Lake, he'll ask, "Oh yeah? Which one?"

I'm from Middle Lake.

In my parents' living room, an aerial photograph of the four lakes hangs on the wall. The lakes look like the watery footprint of a three-toed dog, stamped into a canopy of oak and pine. The angle of the photograph is just right, the leaves just thick enough, to hide most of the houses. Twin Lake is a summer-cottage area making a slow transition into a bedroom community, but if you only had the photograph to go by, you'd think it was a wild, woodsy place.

My brothers and I are just a couple of years apart in age. Matt's the oldest and Danny's in the middle. Growing up, the three of us were inseparable. We devoted much of our time and energy to scavenging food, though back then we would have never thought to call it that. We thought we were "messing around." Food was just something that happened as a result of whatever else we were doing. One of my first memories is of walking along the shore in front of our house and finding a large northern pike, over a couple of feet long, floating in the shallow water. It was still alive, with a speckled bass's head sticking out of its mouth. The speckled bass was still very alive too, but wedged supertight inside the pike's throat. Despite the hot sun and the obviously agonizing predicament, the two fish just floated in a sort of peaceful resignation, slowly opening and closing their gills. My brothers and I scooped the fish up in a net. It was like a two-for-one special. My dad fried the fish for dinner.

Another time, we watched a pregnant whitetail doe swim across the lake and run on to the beach, where she snapped her neck on a cyclone fence. The death of the doe and her fetuses seemed tragic to me, but I felt better when we had a party and cooked the animal in a charcoal roaster that my neighbor welded out of an old oil tank. I couldn't stand to bury the doe's unborn fawns. They were both males, with belly-button-sized bumps where their horns would someday be. The fetuses were fully developed, except for the white tips of their hooves, which still seemed too soft for walking. I put them into the chest freezer we kept in our garage. Over the next several years, I'd often pull the fawns out to admire them. Eventually the bodies were so caked in frost that I decided to give them a formal burial in the woods across the street from our house.

My brothers and I were tight hunting partners as kids, taking our bicycles out to hunt squirrels, rabbits, muskrats, and ducks. We owned a small armada of dented-up canoes and rowboats that we used for fishing. We caught bluegills on their shallow-water spawning beds. The meat was white and flaky, and sometimes my dad would also cook the sacks of spawn cut from their bellies. We caught bullheads by diving down to their hiding spots at the bottom of the lake and jiggling lures in their faces. At night, we'd hunt bullfrogs with spears.

I can see now that my childhood was a little unusual. But compared to the stuff I liked to read when I was a kid, my childhood seemed pedestrian. I used to like stories about the Ice Age Clovis hunters, who preserved their mastodon meat by weighing it down to the bottom of ponds with intestines packed full of gravel. And stories about the Comanche Indians, who would drink the warm and curdled mother's milk from the stomachs of freshly killed buffalo calves. And stories about the Great Lakes Indians from where I grew up, who would tether live sturgeon to the shore and cut off steaks as needed. What I liked about those stories was the immediacy and physical intensity of the meals. I found that I could get hungry from reading about foods that would make me sick as hell if I tried them. I used to dream of clawing my way back into the past, back to a time when things were more *real*.

A historian could make a good argument that human history is just a long story about the depersonalization of food production. Up until ten thousand years ago, every human being survived by hunting and gathering. Two thousand years ago, only one-half of the world's population survived by hunting and gathering. Over the last three to four hundred years, the number of hunter-gatherers has shrunk to just a couple of isolated pockets, located in the remotest corners of the globe.

I watched with interest a few years ago when a major international news story erupted from the small town of Yakima, Washington. In December 2003, a Holstein dairy cow in Yakima County suffered injuries while birthing a calf. Because the cow was a "downer," or nonambulatory, it was tested by the U.S. Department of Agriculture before slaughter: the cow was carrying the United States' first case of bovine spongiform encephalopathy, or mad cow disease. The discovery precipitated a temporary crash in beef markets and forced Japan and Mexico, the largest importers of U.S. beef, to halt shipments across their borders. A herd of 450 calves linked to the smitten cow were quickly destroyed. For weeks, the nightly news was dominated by images of destroyed, potentially diseased livestock. For the first time in their lives, many Americans found themselves using the phrase "food safety."

The public reaction to the mad cow scare vividly illustrates a growing apprehension among the mainstream about what people are eating and where it comes from. Consumers pressure livestock producers to adopt free-range and organic animal-husbandry methods that better simulate a life in the wild; wild salmon usually sell for three or four times as much as farm-raised salmon; and so-called wild game restaurants are surging in popularity.

I say "so-called" because one of the primary accomplishments of the American conservation movements of the 1920s and 1930s was the permanent ban on the selling or trading of flesh from wild birds and animals. The grub served up in today's wild game restaurant is no more free and wild than a Holstein. It's farm-raised and fenced in. Game ranchers sometimes whack off the antlers of bull elk so they don't damage their fellow stock. Deer and antelope are selectively bred for docility. Ironically, the production of farmed game is working directly against the health of the real thing. The deer and elk version of BSE, known as chronic wasting disease, has been spread to wild animals in several states, including Colorado and Wisconsin, by infected game farm animals that escaped holding pens. Meanwhile, the percentage of Americans who are willing to kill their own food in the "real" wild goes down every year. On top of that, the last decade has seen an unprecedented proliferation of antihunting laws.

So, if someone were watching America from a distant planet, our beliefs might look like this: domestic animals should be more wild; wild animals should be more domestic; and wild meat is good, so long as someone else kills it.

* * *

I WENT TO THREE COLLEGES BEFORE I GRADUATED. FIRST I WENT
to a community college. Then I went away to college in Sault
Sainte Marie, on Michigan's Upper Peninsula. The Soo, as locals know it, is a defunct, rundown town. Living up there, I experienced being totally broke for the first time in my life. That's
when I started to see myself as a serious hunter-gatherer. I
lived in a house with my brother Danny and our buddy Drost.
It was an amazing shithole. We only paid a hundred bucks
apiece in rent, and the place had four bedrooms, a living room,
and a smoking room. Water from the bathtub poured through
to the living room below until we caulked it with a gallon of
roofing tar. A hobo lived in a trailer in our yard and poached
electricity from an outside outlet. We practiced archery inside
the house. We'd stand in the smoking room and fire arrows
through the living room and kitchen and into a target in the
pantry. In the winter, icicles would form on the faucet. We'd
eat breakfast sitting side by side on top of the heater.

Most fall afternoons, my roommates and I fished for
salmon in the rapids of the Saint Maries River, which form
where water spills out of Lake Superior on its way down to
Lake Huron. Pink salmon and king salmon come out of Lake
Huron to spawn in the falls, and we'd fish for them from the
Canadian side of the river. Fishing the Sault Rapids could be
pretty hairy. The rocks were slippery and the water was fast.
We'd travel all over the rapids in felt-soled chest waders while
casting flies into deep holes and runs. When we hooked a big
salmon, we'd have to chase it downstream through treacherous water to land it. Several times I wiped out while battling
fish and washed downstream, still reeling line, with my rod
held up over my head. If I hung on to the fish, I knew we'd be
eating salmon that night. It was either that or potatoes, liter-

ally. During that time in my life I had an epiphany. Realizing that my actions and skills would directly affect how well I'd eat on any given night gave me a deeper sense of deliberate living than I'd ever experienced. I knew from then on how I'd live my life.

I traveled around a bit after college, at least as much as I could afford. I found that my favorite places to hang out were those places where I could help support myself on the local foods. After graduation, I hitchhiked along Mexico's Yucatán Peninsula, collecting conch in the shallow waters to simmer in fresh coconut milk, and fishing for barracuda and bonefish, which I wired to sticks and roasted over burning coconut husks. I traveled in northern Argentina and ate piranha just minutes after catching them. When I was doing some magazine reporting in the Philippines, I spent my mornings collecting freshwater crabs and shrimp with two Kalinga tribesmen. We cooked the shellfish on a smoldering log, popping them into our mouths the moment they stopped wriggling.

I eventually wound up living in Montana. I supposedly moved here for graduate school, but I knew I'd stick around because Montana is one of the three all-around best hunting states (Wyoming and Alaska are the other two). Grad school took me an extra year because I was also learning how to hunt elk and antelope, which ain't easy. But there was a reward for figuring it out, because now I can sit down to a plate of free-range steaks any time I want.

However, after a few years, as good as those steaks—and roasts and burgers and rib chops—are, they became a little humdrum. So I got creative; now I've experimented with just about everything I can get my hands on, from chipmunks to porcupines to various sorts of so-called junk fish, such as creek chubs and redhorse suckers. Well-meaning friends have often thought to purchase wild game cookbooks to give me as presents, thinking, I suppose, that I could use a little help and inspiration. The trouble with wild game cookbooks, though, is that they tend to be so tame.

So I've always relied on my crew of buddies for new recipe ideas. My brothers and I, along with a few of our friends, make up a sort of disparate and far-flung tribe of hunter-gatherers. Whenever one of us ends up living somewhere for a while, we usually converge on the place to do some scavenging and eating together. We trade stuff back and forth: red meat for fish, game birds for mushrooms. We make plans for future trips and adventures just sitting around and talking about things we'd like to eat someday.

One night, not long ago, I was having one such conversation in Missoula, Montana, with my buddy Matt Moisan. Moisan and I were talking about different things we ate as kids, and the conversation reminded me of something about my dad. My dad was married twice, but he stayed with each woman at least twenty-five years. Growing up, I considered him to be an exemplar of fidelity. For instance, he didn't believe in removing his wedding ring, no matter what. Whenever he washed his hands, he would thoroughly scrub his right hand, then align his two ring fingers tip to tip, slide the ring from his left ring finger to his right, then scrub his left hand.

I thought of that peculiar habit because I was talking about the only time he ever lost his wedding ring. He had just caught a snapping turtle. The turtle was as big around as a bushel basket. When he got the turtle home, he made me and my brothers help him "clean" it, which is a word we used for getting something ready to eat. My dad was always teaching us useful skills. How to butcher a turtle was one such lesson, and it turned out to be a difficult chore involving an axe and an oak stump. When we got done with the turtle, we put the meat in a plastic tub.

When my dad was washing his hands after the butchering job, he went to slip the ring from his left hand to his right hand—but the ring was gone. We searched and searched, even dug up the turtle's entrails from the hole in the woods where we'd buried them. Nothing. We scrambled through my mother's rosebushes, where we had dumped the water we'd used to wash the meat. We scoured the driveway. We combed the yard. My mom cried when we gave the ring up for lost.

At suppertime, my dad took the tub of trimmed meat to the garage, where he kept an industrial-sized deep fryer. When he pulled the last piece of turtle meat out of the tub, he noticed his gold wedding band lying at the bottom, covered by a shallow pool of pink water. He came out of the garage, waving the ring triumphantly in the air.

As I was relating this story to Moisan, out in Missoula, Montana, he interrupted me to say that he'd never eaten a turtle.

"I didn't know you could catch and eat turtles out in Michigan," he said.

"You can if you've got a valid fishing license," I told him.

That night, I called my mom in Michigan. I was planning on going home for a visit, because my dad had been diagnosed with lung cancer, and the doctors thought he had maybe six months left. I told my mom that, coincidentally, I was just talking about the wedding ring/snapping turtle incident, and I asked her to keep an eye out for a turtle that I could pick up on my visit.

# CHAPTER TWO

# Very Fleshy and Full of Life

THOUGH MY RELATIONSHIP WITH *LE GUIDE CULINAIRE* WOULD ultimately lead to a forty-five-course feast, it began like an old joke: with a turtle crossing the road. The road ran through a cattail marsh near Twin Lake, where I grew up. My dad happened to be driving down that road at the same time the turtle was crossing it. He stopped and grabbed the turtle's tail and wrestled it up into the trunk of my mother's car. My mom called later that day and said she had a live one, a fifteen-pounder. I instructed her to keep the turtle in the storage shed, well fed and watered, until I got there.

Though I'd eaten a few snapping turtles before, I didn't really have a clear idea what they tasted like. When I was growing up, my dad's wild game cooking did not exactly highlight the subtleties of different ingredients. He did literally all of his cooking in the industrial-strength deep fryer, which he purchased in the 1960s at a restaurant liquidation auction in Chicago. The deep fryer played as much a role in our daily lives as did the family car. We referred to it as, simply, The Fryer, but we might as well have called it The Equalizer.

The fryer held a volume of oil that would be sufficient to

flash-fry an ox's head, if you felt like it. The electric cord was as big around as a person's thumb. My mother would not allow the deep fryer in the kitchen, because it threw off enough heat and smoke to jack the mean temperature of the house about ten degrees and set off the smoke alarm. Instead, the fryer lived in the garage. My dad kept the reservoir topped off with refined peanut oil, purchased wholesale in three-gallon containers from a food service distributor. He kept a stash of the jugs in a tool cabinet next to the fryer. On the other side of the fryer was a tall white freezer full of fish and game and a case or two of Fryin' Magic, a breading of corn meal and standard seasonings. The way my old man used Fryin' Magic, you might have thought it was called Huntin' and Fishin' Magic, because he believed quite firmly that it was suitable for any item that died by way of a hook or bullet.

I thought it would be cool to try something different with this new turtle that I was about to take possession of. I'd never eaten turtle soup, and I had no idea how to make it, but I did like the sound of it. It sounded sophisticated, like a good way to honor a turtle. A friend of mine from Missoula, Dee, said that, coincidentally, she'd just found this crazy, hundred-year-old cookbook with a couple of turtle soup recipes in it. She thought it might be helpful, so she lent it to me. It was called *Le Guide Culinaire,* by a dude named Auguste Escoffier.

I flew out to get the turtle about a week later. I brought along my girlfriend, Diana, who'd never met my parents before. I was a little nervous about the introduction, because I hadn't told my folks that she was a vegetarian. The night Diana and I met, at a party, I found her to be very attractive and smart and a lot of fun, so at first I chose to overlook her vegetarianism the way parents might overlook the condoms they find in their teenager's dresser drawer. By the same token, when I told Diana that I hunted a lot, she chose to imagine me going off with my grandpa every couple of years to sit in a cabin and play cards, watching for deer out the window. She didn't really grasp that hunting was basically what I do and how I get by. Because I almost instantly fell in love and couldn't stand to be without her, I knew that the only logical course of action was to convert her to a meat eater. After months of dating, though, I had made only meager progress. Just once, I talked her into nibbling a fillet from a yellow perch that I caught through the ice in Montana. After that, I upgraded her status from pure vegetarian to 99.9 percent vegetarian. I felt that a visit to my folks might better explain to her what I'm all about and fully convince her of the merits of the hunter-gatherer lifestyle.

I didn't want to break the awful news to them over the phone, so I figured that I'd tell my parents about Diana's vegetarianism once we got there. Because I met Diana out in Montana, my dad was under the impression that I was in love with some badass hunter and fisherwoman. Even knowing that Diana was actually from Boston and was only in Montana for a two-year graduate program didn't alter his expectations.

When Diana and I got to my parents' house, I was at first surprised about how good my dad looked. The fact that he'd be dead pretty soon seemed preposterous. I didn't have time to tell my dad about the whole vegetarian situation before he greeted Diana with a hug and said, "I've got a rod and reel set up just for you, sweetheart." Then he went down to the dock and fired up the pontoon boat for some fishing in front of the house.

As we walked to the dock, Diana was panicky. "Steve," she whispered. "I don't want to kill a fish. I don't even want to catch a fish. Tell him. Quick."

"I can't just come out and tell him you won't go fishing," I said. "Besides, you eat fish now."

"I ate fish once! But *you* killed that fish, not me."

"That's pretty fucked-up logic, if you think about it," I said. "Just come out on the boat, then act like you're sunbathing."

As soon as we pulled into deeper water, my dad cut the engine and walked up to the front of the boat. He set up a chair on the deck, baited a rod with two small hooks and live worms. He dropped the bait to the bottom, then said to Diana, "Sit down, girl."

She looked at me nervously. I looked away. She sat down. My dad handed her the rod. Within seconds, something was bucking on the end of the line.

My dad was yelling, "Reel it in! Go! Reel it in!"

She reeled. Two hand-sized bluegills came rising out of the water, and my dad grabbed the line and pulled them into the boat. "Good job," he said. He threw the fish in a bucket, dropped the baits back to the bottom, and handed her the rod again.

I thought that I should intervene and maybe throw the fish back in the water. But I was paralyzed by indecision. Was it worse to upset Diana or upset my dad?

I said, "Dad, maybe Diana wants to relax for a while."

He gave me a dismissive gesture with his hand and looked at Diana. "Never mind him," he said to her. "You go ahead and fish."

In the end, I didn't intervene. I could tell my dad was quite pleased with the situation. In his mind, it seemed to me, there was no greater reward in life than watching his son's girlfriend catch dinner in front of his own house. I could understand his revelry. He was born in Chicago's South Side in 1924 (he had me when he was fifty) and was raised by his immigrant Sicilian grandparents, Rosa and Anthony Rinella. Anthony ran a produce delivery business; he had a wagon and a horse named Pete to pull it. In the mornings, Anthony would crack an egg into a glass of red wine and have that for breakfast, along with a piece of bread, and then he'd leave the house before sunup and head to the downtown markets.

Because my dad's grandparents were so poor and had to work so much, my dad didn't get to travel outside Chicago until he dropped out of high school after Pearl Harbor, enlisted in the army, and shipped out to Biloxi, Mississippi, for basic training. If he wanted to fish as a kid, he'd walk down to the Lake Michigan piers with a cane pole and a bucket of worms to catch perch. He'd usually sell his perch to passersby and give the money to his grandma. Now, standing in his own boat with an accumulating bucket of bluegills, he might have been looking back on his life as a tremendous accomplishment.

After the fishing trip was over, Diana went inside the house, lay down on the guest room bed, and cried. I tried to console her as best I could. "My dad and I would have caught those bluegills anyway," I told her. She promised me that she wasn't crying about the bluegills specifically. She was just overwhelmed by the whole experience: by my dad's illness and the beauty of the lake and, yes, the bluegills gasping in the bucket.

Whatever solace I could provide to Diana was cut short, because my dad was waiting for me outside. He was ready to clean the fish and butcher the turtle. I knew better than to tell Diana what was going down, but at the same time, I didn't want her to come looking for us and find me beside a tree stump, wielding an axe over the neck of a turtle.

"You can take it easy for a while," I said. "I've got to help my dad with some chore or another."

My parents had stashed the snapping turtle in a storage

shed beneath the screened-in porch that we built when I was a kid. The porch overlooked Middle Lake. When I went down to retrieve the turtle, my dad came up from the boat with the fish. "What happened to her?" he asked. "She'd probably get a charge out of this turtle."

"She's just resting, Dad. We can take care of this ourselves." I opened the door of the shed. I had to be careful in grabbing the turtle's tail, because a big snapper can strip your finger down to the bone. Once I caught it, I lugged the turtle up the hill and around to the west side of the house, so I wouldn't have to walk past Diana's window with it. When I got to the top of the hill, up by the road, I tried to run with the turtle so I could get it to the barn before any cars came along. My fear of drawing attention to myself was totally irrational; with a valid fishing license, you're allowed six snapping turtles a year. It was well into the afternoon of a late-summer Saturday. All around the lakes, weekend visitors were lighting up their charcoal grills and throwing on the hot dogs and hamburgers and chicken breasts they'd bought at the grocery stores in Muskegon. The smell of meat hung in the air. It seemed ironic that I should feel sheepish about dragging around my own piece of meat, but I usually try to practice discretion. I transport dead deer in the back of the truck, not tied to the roof. After I butcher a kill, I clean the blood off my knees and hands before going into a gas station. Stuff like that.

I placed the turtle in a large galvanized washtub in the barn. Then I remembered Escoffier. I told my dad that I had this old cookbook that I was going to use to make some turtle soup, and I ran down to the house to get it. I hadn't looked through the book yet, so I wasn't sure if I was supposed to butcher a turtle for turtle soup differently from how I'd normally butcher a turtle. I carried the book up to the barn and flipped through the index. I found the entry for "turtle" and turned back to a page with the heading "Particulars of the Operation." Beneath that, a subheading: "The Slaughtering of the Turtle."

Now, it didn't take me long to realize that *Le Guide Culinaire* was a pretty weird cookbook. I've read a few cookbooks with turtle recipes before, but those books always assume that you've purchased processed turtle meat from a supplier or store. This was the only cookbook I'd ever read that assumed the cook would kill his own turtle. And I could see that this Escoffier fellow didn't mince words. He first advises that the turtle be "very fleshy and full of life." Then he gets into the chore at hand. He doesn't seem to be concerned about any squeamishness or sensitivity that a cook may have about performing such unsavory duties. He writes:

> To slaughter [the turtle], lay it on its back on a table, with its head hanging over the side. By means of a double butcher's hook, one spike of which is thrust into the turtle's lower jaw, while the other suspends an adequately heavy weight, make the animal hold its head back; then quickly as possible, sever the head from the body.
>
> Now immediately hang the body over a receptacle, that the blood may be collected, and leave it thus for one and one-half or two hours.
>
> Then follows the dismemberment . . .

Escoffier's vivid description of turtle slaughtering was shocking to me. It was even more shocking than the descriptions of Native American eating habits that I used to read when I was a kid. The difference was that this passage in *Le Guide Culinaire* wasn't directed at some passive, armchair history buff. Instead, it was directed at a guy like me, who likes to make his own food.

My dad and I flipped through the book, remarking on various oddball passages. We read about how to sew ducks inside mammal bladders to prevent dryness while cooking; how to properly stun a live trout in the preparation of *truite au bleu*; how to extract marrow from animal bones; how to make a red paste from crayfish innards and cooked crayfish shells; and how to kill a rabbit in order to retain its blood for a nutritive additive in soups. I admired the way his recipes demonstrated a frontier sense of thrift and economy. However, *Le Guide Culinaire* wasn't written as a survival manual for shipwreck victims; it's more like the *Kama Sutra* of food, packed full of truffles, caviar, champagne, and recipes named after the famous actresses of fin de siècle Europe. I envied Escoffier. I was jealous that he got to live at such a cool time in history, when it was fashionable and esteemed to eat all this bizarre stuff. And here I was, stuck in a time when collecting and eating such things would be considered hickish and repulsive.

As I perused the book, I felt as though I were examining the last hundred years of culinary evolution. I'd flown to Michigan on a passenger jet, traveling thirty thousand feet over the United States, carrying a cookbook that was published the year Orville and Wilbur Wright made their first sustained flight in a heavier-than-air vehicle. Ideas about food have changed as much as aircraft since the Wright brothers' maiden voyage, perhaps more. From my perspective, Escoffier seemed incredibly far away in space and time. But it was interesting to think of how tightly connected Escoffier's life was to my father's.

In the front of the Cracknell and Kaufman English translation of *Le Guide Culinaire,* there are a series of four separate introductions that Escoffier wrote for the updated and revised versions of his book. The last introduction was written in 1921, three years before my dad was born. In that introduction, Escoffier discusses the disastrous effects that World War I had on French haute cuisine. The war had been over for several years, but postwar food rationing was still being enforced. Escoffier had lived through the Franco-Prussian War as a young soldier, and he would live long enough to see the menace of German aggression rise for the third time in his life; when he died from uremia at his family home in Monte Carlo, in 1935, the Germans had already elected Adolf Hitler to a position of absolute national power.

And here's where things get interesting: My old man, Frank J. Rinella, was part of the Allied invasion of Europe, which would eventually land him in the restaurants of Paris. After boot camp in Biloxi, he was shipped out to Casablanca. In January 1944, he landed on the Anzio beachhead, in Italy. He was twenty years old, dark-skinned, just under six feet tall, 150 pounds, and relatively fluent in the local language. As the Allies moved up the Italian Peninsula, my dad worked as a forward observer, directing firepower against the German front lines with a code book, binoculars, and a backpack radio.

To his last day, my dad would refer to Germans as "Krauts." During the war, he often slept in abandoned German foxholes and swore that he could still smell sauerkraut days after the Germans had moved on. German cigarettes had a peculiar odor as well. My dad told me that the smell of German cigarettes caused the hair on the back of his neck to stand up. Moving north, he sometimes went days without eating. He was given a Purple Heart for freezing his feet, and a Bronze Star for repairing some communications wires while under fire. He was eventually hospitalized for what he sometimes described as "the thousand-mile stare" and other times described as "shell shock."

After Germany's surrender, my dad got the best assignment he could hope for. He was stationed at an equipment depot in Paris. Everything from motorbikes to tanks came through the depot, and my dad helped to sort out what should be sent back to the States, what should be destroyed, and what should be sold off as surplus. As a side business, he pilfered a lot of stuff from the surplus warehouse and sold it on the black market. He was getting good money for motorbikes, and he also ran a successful business moving wholesale-volume shipments of contraband cigarettes. One particularly lucrative deal involved selling cigarette cartons packed with sawdust.

He later admitted to me that his entrepreneurial endeavors would have rendered him a fairly rich man if he hadn't discovered the pleasures of French-style wining and dining. To a kid from the South Side of Chicago, who'd been living for a year on military C-rations and the half-rotten food found in bombed-out German fortifications, the food of Paris was mind-boggling. Because he had so much money to burn, my dad hung out in the nicest places he could find. He got his first tastes of escargot and sweetbreads, and of wine that wasn't made in the same bathtub that he bathed in. Surely my dad's culinary wanderings would have brought him into contact with Escoffier's colleagues and protégés, and probably even some of the very establishments Escoffier influenced and helped create.

Eventually, the Yankee Go Home movement caught up with my dad. Parisians became less hospitable to vagabond GIs out looking for good times and cheap wine. Excited by his knack for business and love for French grub, my dad made plans to head back to Chicago and attend the Berlitz School of Languages. He wanted to study French and get back to Paris in

some kind of respectable capacity as an international busi-
nessman. The problem was, my dad had gotten his girlfriend
pregnant before he left for Europe. He was greeted at home by
a two-year-old standing on a chair. It was my half brother,
Frank Jr., who's a full thirty-one years older than me. With a
family to support, my dad gave up on the idea of school and
got a job as a soda jerk at a drugstore, then opted into a position as a door-to-door insurance salesman, peddling term life
policies for the Metropolitan Insurance Company.

If I'd made a dollar every time my old man told me that in
Paris they eat salad *after* dinner, I'd have enough money to fly
to Paris and live on salad for a week. For the rest of his life, he
would cite his experiences in Paris most every time the topic
of food came up. Once he was back home for a while, he realized that his developing tastes for new and peculiar foods
were not going to be financed by an international trading cor-
poration's expense account. Instead, he'd get interesting food
by hunting and fishing.

In one of my photo albums, I have a picture of my dad with
the first deer he killed, a little doe slung over his shoulders.
He was on a farm in southern Illinois. In the picture, he still
has that emaciated look from the war—his fighting weight, he
called it. He's wearing his pea green combat fatigues. After
running around Europe in those clothes for a couple of years,
my dad said, it was difficult to imagine wearing anything else.
He fished perch in his fatigues. He'd wear his fatigues down
to Lake Michigan to net smelt, which the French call *éperlans*.
He hunted with other vets who all wore the same getup. My
dad often told me about a day in the late 1940s when he and
some of his friends were walking through a harvested cornfield outside Chicago. They were all dressed in their ratty fatigues, looking for rabbits. When someone fired a shot, my

dad panicked and hit the deck. When he looked up, all the hunters except the shooter were lying on their bellies in the dirt, guns ready, scanning the tree line for enemy positions. In a few seconds, they all started laughing at themselves.

In the barn, my dad and I followed Escoffier's instructions through the slaughtering of the turtle. Once it was dead, I started cutting it up. My dad gave me a hand as needed, holding this and pulling that. Escoffier had us pick clean the inside of the turtle's carapace, or shell, and the plastron, which is the cross-shaped undershell. These parts, he says, "constitute the only portions wherefrom the gelatinous flesh, used as the garnish of the soup, are obtained." He also had us collect all the fat. Though reading Escoffier's method of turtle slaughtering caught me by surprise, the actual act of butchering the turtle felt perfectly organic and natural to me. The turtle grew up by killing and eating ducklings and muskrats and fish and smaller turtles and the occasional piece of vegetation. My eating habits weren't much different from the turtle's, and my methods of procuring my food were no more crass.

My brother Matt's girlfriend, Jen, wanted a turtle shell to use as a candy dish. I cleaned and dried the shell, lacquered the top, and painted the inside bright yellow, like the binding on a *National Geographic* magazine. It looked cool. I froze the deshelled turtle meat in a couple of one-gallon milk jugs with the tops cut off. My dad helped me pack the meat and the shell into a cooler and then wrap the cooler shut with duct tape.

On the day Diana and I flew back to Montana, my mom and dad drove us to the airport. My dad gave Diana a big hug goodbye outside the terminal. Throughout our visit, Diana had done me a huge favor: she had eaten plate after plate of fresh fish. I had made sure that we kept catching those fish, in order that our evening menus never included red meat. The ruse worked; when my dad hugged Diana, he thought he was hugging a suitable hunting and fishing companion for his youngest son. I didn't know it yet, but he and Diana would never see each other again. We walked into the airport when we finished with our good-byes. The security guy cut the tape and opened the cooler for inspection. He examined the turtle shell and the Turtle Meat labels on the jugs very carefully but didn't comment.

I WAS BACK IN MY DAD'S BARN ABOUT FIVE MONTHS LATER, SIFTING his ashes through a metal screen. I was looking for some shotgun pellets that had been blasted into his foot in a hunting accident. A couple of years after the war, he'd gone hunting with his nephew. His nephew was walking beside him on a farm lane and accidentally blasted a load from a 12-gauge shotgun through my dad's boot and into the arch of his foot. A doctor dug out a few pellets, but most of them were out of reach and had to stay where they were. While he was laid up, my dad got around on the same crutch that his uncle had used after getting shot in the leg by a cop during the Chicago race riots in 1919. My dad loved the pellets in his foot, mainly because he loved the irony of the fact that he had survived two years of combat without a scratch from a bullet, only to come home and get shot in the foot by his own goddamn nephew. Years ago, shoe stores used X-ray machines to see if a new shoe fit the client's foot properly. My dad used to take friends into the stores and use the X-ray machine to show off the pellets.

When it looked as though my dad didn't have much time left, I put my stuff in storage in Montana and went home to help my mom take care of him. His mind was slipping. I still hadn't cooked the turtle, and he asked me about it several times.

"Did you eat that turtle?"

"Not yet, Dad."

"Did you eat that turtle?"

"Not yet, Dad."

The Friday before he died, I bundled him up and helped him out to the screened-in porch. The lake was frozen, and I set a couple of tip-ups out on the ice and baited the lines with live minnows. Tip-ups get their name from the spring-loaded flag that pops up when a pike grabs the minnow. Whenever a flag popped, I'd run out from the porch to the lake as quickly as possible to get the fish and rebait the line. I was afraid that my dad might pass away while I was out on the ice, so each time I caught a pike, I would run back in to check on him. He was dozing off all the time, and I'd shake him awake to make sure he was all right. He'd sometimes seem annoyed when I woke him, so I'd act as though it was urgent that I give him a fishing report.

Sometimes he'd wake up and he wouldn't know where he was, either in place or time. Once he woke up on the porch and said, "I want to go on a nice, smooth ride."

"Where to?" I asked.

"Middle Lake."

"We're on Middle Lake," I said. "The next flag is yours, man."

That was our last day of fishing together. The next day we started him on morphine, because the lack of oxygen to his lungs would cause him to panic. He wouldn't let me put his oxygen mask on him, but he liked the morphine and it worked. I sat next to him through his final hours, placing drops of it into his mouth with an eyedropper, the way he'd once taught me to care for a baby purple martin that fell from its nest and landed on our beach.

My dad's ashes came back from the crematorium in a white

cardboard box with his name printed in a black, prosaic font. My brother Danny had come down from Alaska, where he lives. He and I spread the ashes on the workbench and started sifting them. After sifting all the ashes through the screen, we found staples from a recent surgery, pieces of dental work, and unidentifiable little bits of metal, but nothing that looked like a shotgun pellet. The cremation pyre must have melted the lead down.

When I left Michigan after the memorial service, I had the few frozen pike fillets in my cooler. I was still carrying around *Le Guide Culinaire,* which I was intending to read once I had the time. I flipped ahead to look for pike recipes in the book; Escoffier often cooked with freshwater pike from the rivers and lakes of France. In his description of the fish, he laments their loss of popularity in the "modern" kitchens of his day. "However," he says, "certain of the classical preparations of pike are worthy of being preserved and because of this they are included here." He then describes a full sixteen preparations.

I was intrigued by the fact that on my last two trips to Michigan I'd flown back to Montana with ingredients from *Le Guide Culinaire.* It made me wonder how much of that stuff I'd find if I were actually trying. I looked through the book and found plenty of things that a fellow could probably find for himself if he tried: kidneys, frog legs, carp semen, pig's tongue, songbirds, caul fat, pigeon nestlings, eel, bird nests, and on and on.

In fact, the *only* way to get most of those things would be to find them yourself. This realization struck me as I flew along. It was strange. Here was this big ol' fantastic cookbook and most people wouldn't even be able to buy this sort of stuff anymore. A lot of it would take a guy like me to make it. A guy who could find it himself. Looking through this seemingly random cookbook, I realized that I was looking at a version of my own world reflected back at me. As a twenty-first-century hunter-gatherer, I'd found my own sort of manifesto inside a one-hundred-year-old compendium on haute cuisine. By the time I landed, I knew what I wanted to do. I wanted to build an entire feast from *Le Guide Culinaire.*

# CHAPTER THREE

# What Would Escoffier Do?

THE *AMERICAN HERITAGE DICTIONARY* DESCRIBES HAUTE CUISINE as "elaborate or skillfully prepared food, especially that of France." However, haute cuisine came to resemble its modern form in Italy, during the Italian Renaissance. The elaborate preparation of food was considered to be a creative art among the wealthy classes of Milan, Florence, and Naples, and the enjoyment of the food was a sophisticated pastime. The art was transported from Italy to France by Catherine de Médicis, the great-granddaughter and only legitimate heir to Lorenzo the Magnificent, a statesman and spice trader and the patron of such artists as Botticelli and Michelangelo. When she was fourteen, Catherine was sent to Marseilles, in southeast France, to marry the duke of Orléans. As part of her dowry, Catherine brought along Tuscan chefs. Fourteen years later, the duke became King Henry II of France, and French society was enchanted by Queen Catherine's court. Her banquets enlivened an otherwise monotonous national cuisine, and she turned the French on to a new world of food: artichokes, sweetbreads, truffles, olive oil, carp, songbirds, and an array of sweets.

Haute cuisine flourished in France over the next two hundred years except for a brief remission following the French Revolution. (The proletariat considered the eating habits of the aristocracy to be excessive and indulgent. After receiving his death sentence from the revolutionary regime in 1793, King Louis XVI sat down to six cutlets and a roast chicken before napping and then having his head chopped off in a new invention created by the French physician Joseph Guillotin.) The culinary arts were resuscitated after the revolution by Antonin Carême, who is known as the Moses of haute cuisine. Carême was born in France in 1784. When he was eleven, his father took him to Paris and abandoned him on the street with a poetic farewell: "Go, little one. There are good trades in this world. Let the rest of us languish in the misery in which we are doomed to die." Carême got a job in a tavern, where he studied and advanced as a chef. Around 1805, he was hired as the personal chef for the French statesman Talleyrand, a self-styled gourmet and a minister in Napoleon's Consulate. Carême thrived under Talleyrand's patronage. He proved to be an innovative genius, and his own greatest fan. "From behind my stoves," he later wrote, "I contemplated the cuisines of India, China, Egypt, Greece, Turkey, Italy, Germany and Switzerland. I felt the unworthy methods of routine crumble under my blows."

Auguste Escoffier was Carême's most illustrious successor. Like Carême, Escoffier became a chef through circumstance, not choice. In his autobiography, *Memories of My Life,* Escoffier admits that, as a kid, he never wanted to be a cook. "I was attracted by the world of fine arts and wanted to become a sculptor," he writes. There was a fat chance of that. His father, Jean-Baptiste Escoffier, was a second-generation blacksmith; he didn't have the economic luxury of indulging his kid's frivolous desires. Escoffier was only thirteen years old when his father sent him off to work in an uncle's restaurant in Nice. "I was given no option but to obey," recalls Escoffier.

At the time, chefs were generally regarded as little more than highly skilled servants. Escoffier writes that his apprenticeship was a nightmare, but he was able to pull it off "without the slightest outward manifestation of unhappiness." He was so small in physical stature that he had to wear platform shoes to keep from burning his face while standing at the range. He washed pots, waited tables, got slapped around and yelled at—your basic old-school apprenticeship. From then on, his only break from restaurants would come during the Franco-Prussian War, when he served as a cook for the army of Napoleon III.

When the war was over, Auguste settled into his first position as head chef, at the Hotel Luxembourg in Nice. The next year he took the head position at Le Petit Moulin Rouge, a swanky Paris restaurant where he first met many of his later clients and friends, including the Prince of Wales and the actress Sarah Bernhardt. Not long after, in 1884, he became partners with César Ritz. Their alliance lasted for eighteen years, until 1902, when Ritz suffered a bizarre mental breakdown upon receiving the news that King Edward VII's coronation ceremony had been postponed because the king needed an appendectomy.

Escoffier would probably be a completely obscure figure today if he had dropped out at the same time that Ritz did. Instead, he capitalized on his reputation within highbrow European society and put the finishing touches on his masterpiece, *Le Guide Culinaire*. One year after Ritz's breakdown, *Le Guide Culinaire* was published as an encyclopedic codification of French haute cuisine.

In the back of *Le Guide,* Escoffier includes almost sixteen pages of menus. The menus are from some of the more memorable meals he created—receptions at Westminster, dinners for kings and famous people, holidays—and most of them number between twelve and twenty courses, some even more. The menus became interesting to me as I read about Escoffier and his book, because I was curious about what the King of Chefs, Chef of Kings classifies as a "memorable" meal. Apparently, a memorable meal means a shitload of food.

That he was juggling such enormous numbers of recipes in his head at any given time explains an important aspect of Escoffier's personality. Friends and colleagues thought he was a private man. When he was working, which was nearly always, he refrained from alcohol and often ate alone in his office. For his breaks, he would take private strolls down the street, stopping only to hand tips out to the crossing guards. But to me, it doesn't seem like the man was private. He was probably just trying to avoid distractions because he had a lot to keep straight in his head.

No matter how much work a complete Escoffier meal entailed, who was I to argue with Escoffier's ideas? If I wanted to make a true Escoffier meal, and I did, I'd have to collect enough stuff for a complete meal. But I couldn't just do *one* meal.

Here's why: For me to produce an Escoffier feast would require a lot of help from my five main hunting and fishing partners, who are spread out around the country. Most of them are named Matt. Together, Matt Drost, Matt Moisan, and Matt Rinella form the Matmosphere. To keep things simple, I just call Drost and Moisan by their last names, and I call my brother Matt. My other two partners are Eric Kern and my brother Danny.

If all of my hunting partners helped me with the scaveng-ing—and I knew they would—then I'd have to invite them all to the feast. And if they all flew out to Montana, they'd damn well expect more than one night of feasting. I wanted to offer them three meals. Fifty or so courses.

I began studying *Le Guide Culinaire* with Talmudic thor-oughness. I made a list of every ingredient found in the book. It was sort of like conducting a feasibility study. I wanted to de-termine what I needed, and what was possible. Then I imposed two restrictions on myself: 1) I would give myself one year to garner the necessary ingredients, so that nothing would have time to go bad. 2) Because hunting and fishing in other coun-tries pose enormous legal, logistical, and financial problems, I would limit my search to the United States.

Then I realized that I had a major geographical problem on my hands.

The problem was, haute cuisine is so deeply and historically European that its base ingredients, naturally, are the sorts of ingredients that one finds in and around Europe. Escoffier's recipes deal largely with fish of the eastern Atlantic Ocean, such as dover sole. Here in the United States, we have a variety of soles and flounders, but not that one. Escoffier recommends the meat from the European stag. We have great herds of elk in Montana, which are a close cousin of the stag, but certainly not the same thing. Another factor that concerned me had to do with threatened and endangered species lists. In Escoffier's day, people didn't worry about that sort of thing; they'd just keep on catching and eating something until it was completely wiped out. *Le Guide* includes recipes for hosts of songbirds that are now protected. As a hunter and environmentalist, I cer-tainly couldn't go out and contribute to the problems of a van-ishing species.

Luckily for me, Escoffier did occasionally recommend American counterparts to his European ingredients. For example, while Escoffier did not cook with the wild rabbits of America (he liked the Belgian hare), he does go out of his way in *Le Guide* to recommend specific substitutions for his American followers. He disguises this endorsement of American rabbits within a mild snub: "As a result of one of those freaks of taste, hare is not nearly so highly esteemed as it deserves in the United States; and the fact seems all the more strange when one remembers that in many of her states excellent specimens of the species can be found." The list of excellent specimens he recommends includes the cottontail rabbit.

It was nice to know that I could go just about anywhere in the country and get a rabbit that Escoffier gave his wink and nod to, but other things were going to be much more complicated. A quote I found in the beginning of *Le Guide* added to my anxiety about using substitutes. Escoffier offers his readers the following warning: "It is just as absurd to expect excellent cooking from a chef whom one provides with defective or scanty goods, as to hope to obtain wine from a bottled concoction of logwood."

I started to worry that I'd have to follow a strict, fundamentalist interpretation of *Le Guide Culinaire* if I wanted success, but then I started to read between the lines of Escoffier's biography, so to speak, and I realized an important element of his credo.

Escoffier was fond of the story of François Vatel's death. François Vatel was the chief steward of Chantilly, the estate of the French nobleman the Prince du Conde. On a Friday in 1671, the prince was expecting King Louis XIV for dinner. The prince was in great need of the king's favor, and the path to the king's favor led through his stomach. (When Louis XIV died, his physicians reported that his stomach was three times normal size and he had a tapeworm.) The Prince du Conde entrusted Vatel to organize an elaborate and impressive banquet. Vatel placed an order for fish, to serve for the Lenten meal, but the fish didn't show up on time. Rather than face professional embarrassment, Vatel fell on his own sword three times, the third time puncturing his heart.

Escoffier thought that Vatel had overreacted.

"Quite simply," he said, "I would have fabricated some fillets of sole using the breasts of young chickens."

This response is somewhat surprising, considering what a stickler for details Escoffier was. He used to stand in the doorway of his kitchens, readjusting the placement of garnishes as they went out to the dining room. How could a man of such exacting standards recommend a quick-fix substitution? The answer to that question lies amid the chaos of the Franco-Prussian War.

In 1870, Escoffier was plucked from Le Petit Moulin Rouge to serve in the French forces under Napoleon III. Napoleon thought Prussia's influence was becoming too strong in Europe, and he wanted to set them back militarily. Escoffier was assigned as a field cook for the officers of the General Headquarters of the Rhine Army. This was a dangerous, demanding position. As battles raged between French and German armies, Escoffier stalked rabbits with a rifle and scrounged abandoned farmyards for eggs. At the Battle of Gravelotte, he prepared hors d'oeuvres while six thousand men were slaughtered just one mile away. After making a hasty retreat under the cover of darkness, Escoffier found himself with a side of beef that might go bad if left uncooked. "My decision was quickly taken," he later recalled. "Great dangers give birth to great solutions." He then chopped some trees down and roasted his side of beef. While it cooked, he and another cook had to draw their sabers to defend the beef when their own marauding troops tried to steal a hunk.

Then came the Siege of Metz. After suffering humiliating defeats, French forces were surrounded by the Prussians in northeastern France. The conditions in the city of Metz were horrible. There was hardly anything to eat. Escoffier rustled up whatever chickens and goats he could find or purchase and assembled them in a makeshift farmyard that he established in a private courtyard. At an exorbitant price, he managed to acquire some small pike that were fished from the Moselle River. As conditions worsened, he had to slaughter the officers' horses and serve them the meat. In his autobiography, Escoffier writes, "Certainly, I reached heights never before attained when it came to using up scraps."

While Escoffier was eating braised horse flesh in Metz, Paris too had fallen under Prussian siege. But the Parisians had it worse than the citizens of Metz. As if the Prussians hadn't created enough problems by surrounding the city, a violent insurrection of the Paris Commune was broiling amid Paris's own population. Meat and vegetables were vanishing fast. Rats went on sale for three francs apiece. A chef was selling a terrine, or casserole, of rats called *rats à la parisienne* for fifteen francs. Two cookbooks were published with recipes for dogs and cats. A restaurant was selling cocker spaniel, and cats were going for a market price of ten francs. The zoo located within Paris's botanical gardens ran out of feed, so restaurants bought the zoo animals for use as fresh meat. On Christmas Day 1870, the Café Voisin menu included bear steaks, donkey, kangaroo, wolf, a house cat garnished with rats, and the trunks of two elephants named Castor and Pollux.

Rather than feeling disgusted, Escoffier found great inspiration in such improvisations. He became convinced that resourcefulness was the mark of a true chef. Forty-five years later, during World War I, a number of young French chefs working in London complained to Escoffier that the rations and wartime food shortages had rendered French haute cuisine an impossibility. Escoffier implored them to make do and carry on. Then he showed the chefs his 1870 Christmas menu from Voisin's, which he had kept as a memento for his personal records.

After considering this aspect of Escoffier's legacy, I felt that a strict adherence to authenticity might actually be an insult to Escoffier's sensibilities. In my effort to emulate him, I didn't want to overlook one of his most admirable traits.

Instead, I decided to familiarize myself with his food, in order to get an idea for what works and what doesn't work as far as substitutions go. In the soup section of *Le Guide*, I found a recipe for bird's nest soup. The soup is made from swallows' nests. Swallows use their sticky saliva to hold their nesting materials together. By simmering the nests, you can extract the saliva. Escoffier says that it lends the "characteristic viscidity," or thickness, to his consommés. To make his bird's nest soup, Escoffier used the nests of tropical swallows, from southeastern Asia. I was pleased to learn that Escoffier wasn't morally opposed to the ingredients of other continents.

As I was reading about bird's nest soup, I remembered some swallows' nests that I'd seen under a bridge in downtown Missoula. The summer before, it had been hotter than hell. In the afternoons, Diana and I would take an inner tube down to the university campus and launch it into the Clark Fork River. She'd ride in the tube and I'd swim along next to it, until we hit the Orange Street Bridge. One day we sat under the bridge in the shade and watched some cliff swallows. The birds had nests under the bridge. They'd fly from the nests to catch insects. The insects were so low to the water that the swallows' wingtips would leave a series of twin dimples along the river's surface when they swooped in to catch them.

When I went down to the bridge to look for one of these nests, the swallows were all gone. It was wintertime, so they were probably down south somewhere. The nests were the shape of bulls' scrotums and about that size. Most of them were all busted up and falling apart from neglect. I chucked a couple of rocks at a broken nest and caught some of the chunks that fell off. Tropical swallows build their nests out of sticks. These cliff swallow nests were made from mud. At the time, though, I figured swallow spit was swallow spit. I took the mud home and boiled it in a pot. I was left with nothing but hot muddy water and a dead floating bug. Nothing remotely gelatinous appeared. The water had zippo "viscidity." So if I was going to make a pot of bird's nest soup, cliff swallow nests would not cut it. This made me fret that American ingredients were not up to the task.

The next thing I tried was making a sauce out of fish semen. Escoffier recommends carp milt. Carp are pretty nasty, so I thought it would be an improvement to use milt from yellow perch. But when I cooked some perch semen and seasoned it, it looked and smelled suspiciously like, well, semen.

After these two failures, I began to think this cookbook was a hoax. I decided to thaw my turtle out and try some of that. After all, I could always get another turtle by alerting my mom to keep an eye out. I started cooking the turtle and my whole apartment began to smell like a boiled Loch Ness monster. As it was cooking, Diana walked into my apartment, covered her mouth, said, "Oh. My. God. Steve." And walked back out. I had a couple of friends over to sample the turtle and only two of them dared taste it. One friend of mine, a painter, said she wanted to try it just to see if it tasted as bad as it smelled. She dipped the ladle in and sipped. "It does," she said.

But even after my third cooking failure, I was still reluctant to dismiss the cookbook. I had a nagging belief that I wasn't following the directions carefully enough. For instance, my snapping turtle had been fed ground venison while in captivity. Escoffier doesn't say to feed meat to captive turtles. Instead, he says to flush them repeatedly in clean water before slaughtering. I hadn't flushed my turtle. Maybe that was the problem.

I decided to try one more experiment with substitutions; if this didn't work, I would either forget the whole project or move to France for a year. The dish I selected for the experiment was *truite au bleu,* or blue trout. To make it, Escoffier says you need a live trout, "procured in mountainous districts, where the clear water they inhabit is constantly refreshed by strong currents." Living in Montana, I was in the perfect place to find such a trout. Escoffier probably cooked with the European brown trout. For my *truite au bleu*, I would use a brook trout, a distinctly wild and North American fish. Other than that, I would follow Escoffier's advice to the letter, right down to the *live* trout. I waited for a warm weekend, then went to a stream up in the mountains that is open to fishing in the winter. I took Diana along with me and we set up camp and made a fire. I had all the ingredients in my pack, and I got them ready: water, vinegar, salt, thyme, bay leaves, carrots, onions, parsley, peppercorns. Diana and I took my fly rod and walked along the stream. Brook trout are aggressive fish, and they'll hit good even when it's cold. We found some trout holding beneath a rock ledge that hung over the river. I pasted out a cast and landed the fly along the rock ledge. A fourteen-inch trout rose up and grabbed the fly. I pulled the fish on to the bank and we walked it up to the fire. I thumped it and plunged the trout immediately into a pan of simmering vinegar and seasoning. Its skin turned a brilliant blue. It was beautiful, like a chameleon. It almost seemed a shame to eat something so cool-looking. The vinegar tasted subtle on the fish's flesh, and gave it a pleasing light and springy texture. It was the best trout I ever ate. So Escoffier was right, I thought. This stuff does work.

But I still couldn't completely shake my concerns about substitutions versus authenticity until later in the winter, when I was down in Florida fishing with my brother Danny and our buddy Kern. We were staying for the week in a rental house on the Gulf of Mexico. The house was made of limestone rocks. It sat low and inconspicuously among lush vegetation and palms. Little greenish brown lizards crawled around on the rocks of the house, eating ants. A small path began at the foot of the porch and led through some type of grass that would slice up your ankles when you walked through it. The path terminated on the beach and there was the ocean.

The three of us were right in front of the house, catching fish like crazy. We caught pompano, whiting, black drum, redfish, gulf flounders, sand perch, hand-sized blue runners, and a small crab of indeterminate species.

Not that we immediately knew what all those fish were. We had a copy of *Le Guide Culinaire* with us, along with a Florida fishing regulation. We also had a book called *Sport Fish of the Gulf of Mexico,* by Vic Dunaway, which I'd nabbed off my dad's bookshelf after he died.

Danny works as an ecologist for the University of Alaska; he's a whiz at identifying fish. He was operating a triage center for our catch. He would first identify each fish by species and then measure it to see if it was of a legal size to keep. If we were allowed by law to keep the fish, I would determine whether or not the specimen was a good fit for Escoffier's cooking. If it was, such as a whiting, I claimed it as my own and set it aside for the freezer. If it was unlike the fish used by Escoffier, such as a blue runner, I designated the fish as that night's supper.

That evening, as the sun set, we were talking about something that happened the last time the three of us fished together in salt water. We'd been standing alongside a barrier reef in Mexico, up to our waists, when a poodle-sized reef shark started zipping back and forth in front of us, dashing all around, as though mad about our walking into its yard. Almost impulsively, Kern slapped a fly down in front of the shark's nose as it passed just four feet away from us. The shark grabbed the fly and freaked out. It pulled all the line off Kern's reel and then busted off. When Kern turned to look at me, his eyes were wide, the way people in movies look after they get stabbed. Then, oddly, he bounced on one foot in the water, lost his balance, and impaled his hand on the innumerable spikes of a black sea urchin that was clinging to a rock. The spikes dissolved in his flesh. It caused excruciating pain and nerve damage, and his hand didn't work properly for a year after that.

We were laughing about that as Kern cast a shrimp into the Gulf of Mexico. Within moments, the rod arced into a sharp bend. His line zinged off the reel.

"Holy shit," I said, "it's that shark from Mexico." But judging by the way the fish was pulling line, it seemed more like Kern had snagged into the setting sun.

Whatever it was, it headed out past the sandbar and then hung a left and began traveling south. The way it swam, it didn't jerk the rod tip; instead, it sort of glided along like a rolling bowling ball. Kern reeled in some line, then the thing pulled the line back out.

Beaches must be boring as hell for people who don't fish, because just about anything can divert them away from what they're doing, which I guess is nothing. The sight of Kern's rod bobbing up and down against the purplish aftermath of the sunset quickly drew a crowd. A family of four came over to watch; the parents wanted to see the fish, and the two kids wanted to play with our bait. A gang of college-aged guys with cans of Budweiser gathered beside us too. Then two fellows from the condominiums next to our house walked down to the beach, swirling red wine in matching gold-rimmed glasses and trying to act very bored by Kern's fish.

By this time, it was getting pretty dark. I cracked Kern a beer. He sipped it with one hand while stabilizing the butt of the rod against his belly. One of the wine-drinking guys started getting jealous about all the attention that Kern was getting, and he began talking as though this just happened to be the one night when he wasn't the one battling a fish.

"Could be a black-tip, could be a ray," he said. "Maybe a big redfish. It's hard to say at this point. Whatever it is, it'll tire out. If that line don't break. He's just gotta keep the pressure on it. I hope he's got good line."

I tried to tune the guy out. The speculations were annoying. There are so many things in an ocean, and so many of those things eat shrimp, it seemed futile to make guesses about what it was and how strong it might be. However, I was secretly worried about it being a ray. When I was a kid, my dad and I watched some fishermen in the Florida Keys catch a couple of rays, chop the tails of the fish off, and leave them for dead. I asked why they did that, and the fishermen said rays weren't any good.

After a half hour passed, Kern finally got whatever it was reeled in close to the shore. Once it was beneath the breaking waves, it started acting more like an anchor than a fish. It wouldn't budge. I walked into the darkness of the water, following the line out, and peered into the waves. I could see a dark shape, and I poked it with my rod tip. It went ripping back out toward the deep in an explosion of silt, making a wake along the surface. I about shit my pants, then went dashing back to the shore.

After another twenty minutes or so, the fish was back up near the shore again and anchored in place. I went out and gave it another poke. As it took off, Kern walked the rod backward and, with the help of a big wave, dragged it up to shore. Our crowd let out a simultaneous sigh, an "aahhgg" that lasted a couple of seconds. The fish was a stingray, like a giant underwater moth with a bullwhip for a tail. With the identity of the fish revealed, the onlookers quickly dispersed, acting like their patience had not been adequately rewarded, as though Kern had pulled in some old car tire. They wanted a shark, something with teeth, something more . . . dramatic.

Danny determined that it was an Atlantic stingray and that we're allowed as many of them as we want. I felt a tad let down. What the hell would we do with this thing?

Curious, I sat down in my folding chair and aimed my headlamp at the index in *Le Guide.* I was surprised to find the word *raie.* I flipped back to recipe numbers 1,824 to 1,828. There I read about poached ray with brown butter, poached ray livers with croutons, ray wings gratin, and marinated ray with onion rings.

Except, I realized, the french word *raie* translates to skate, not ray. In his description of *raie* cookery, Escoffier says that he likes the thornback skate of the eastern Atlantic.

Thornback skates and Atlantic stingrays look pretty damn similar. Both have wings and long tails and blunt noses and hang out in shallow water near soft bottoms. They're both batoids, with cartilaginous skeletons. But there are significant differences. The Atlantic stingray is viviparous (gives birth to live young) and the thornback skate is oviparous (lays eggs). The Atlantic stingray has a nasty serrated spike on its tail, and the thornback skate doesn't. The Atlantic stingray ranges up and down the western Atlantic, from New Jersey to Brazil. The thornback skate ranges up and down the eastern Atlantic, from Norway to the Mediterranean Sea.

Now I was feeling especially attached to it. And I was curious about it. Here was something that many people thought you couldn't eat, but Escoffier's book suggested otherwise. I'd learned that Escoffier's recipes worked when I made *truite au bleu,* but trout always taste good. By cooking this ray, I would be putting the book to a test. And so what if it didn't taste so great? This Escoffier feast was supposed to be fun. It was supposed to be an eye-opener. If Escoffier had to make do with a stingray instead of a skate, he surely wouldn't throw himself on his own sword. He'd go for it. From then on, I had my operating theory. My modus operandi. I'd do the best I could to fulfill Escoffier's recipes, and leave the rest to chance.

# CHAPTER FOUR

# *Columba Livia*

I WAS STANDING ON THE TOP RUNG OF A RICKETY OLD EXTENSION ladder, trying to get my hands over the ledge of a concrete support beneath the Higgins Street Bridge, in downtown Missoula, Montana. While I was primarily worried about falling and dying, I was also afraid of getting in trouble with the cops. The area beneath the bridge serves as a parking lot for the Wilma Building, an eight-story mound of brickwork that houses apartments, a movie theater, and about a trillion pigeons. For whatever reason, police cars stalk through the parking lot every ten minutes or so. I couldn't imagine something that looked more like suspicious terrorist activity than the sight of two dudes in dark clothes climbing around beneath a bridge at night. Moisan was stabilizing the ladder and keeping an eye out for trouble. He was urging me to hurry up before someone came along.

"Come on, man," he yelled. "You just know there's a bunch of pigeon eggs up there. Get your ass up that ladder."

I had my cheek pressed against the bridge's concrete girders, but I just couldn't reach. Looking down, I could just see the top of Moisan's head. He's got this crazy hair; every couple of months he gets a crew cut, but it seems to morph almost overnight into a pompadour. He and I became friends through a strange set of circumstances that involved both of us having the same girlfriend at the same time. Eventually the girl dumped us both and moved away. Rather than holding grudges, he and I started a friendship and he eventually became hunting partners with my brothers and me. I climbed back down and we propped the ladder on top of a stack of busted-up shipping pallets, so that it was now blocking the underpass. I scurried back up the ladder.

"Now hurry the hell up," said Moisan.

"Just hold that ladder," I whispered back. I stood on my tippy-toes, reaching up as far as I could. I got my hands over the top ledge and dug my fingertips into a mat of pigeon shit and something that felt like drinking straws. I pulled myself up like I was doing a gym class exercise. I got one elbow over the top of the support, and then the other. I had my penlight between my teeth, and I tried to get the beam pointing in the right direction. When I did, I was looking into a pigeon nest that was indeed made of drinking straws, both the big kind and the little ones you get in mixed drinks. I yelled this piece of information down to Moisan. Then I noticed that the base of the nest was formed by two mummified pigeons and a mound of droppings the size and shape of a deflated basketball. "Oh, jeez," I shouted, "and it's also built out of shit and dead pigeons."

There were two eggs in the nest. I'd heard that pigeons will nest in the winter, and here was proof. The eggs were whitish, with slight off-color markings. They were about the size of big olives. I deposited the eggs into the hood of my sweatshirt. By waddling along the edge of the support on my elbows, I managed to check out another five or six nests. No more eggs. I wriggled back down until I was again hanging from my fingertips. Moisan adjusted the ladder to meet my dangling toes. Back on the ground, I arranged the eggs in a Cool Whip container lined with toilet paper. Moisan tucked the container inside his jacket to keep it at body temperature. Then we shouldered the ladder and lugged it along to the next bridge support.

We were collecting the pigeon eggs because I had been trying for weeks to get my hands on a baby pigeon. After several failed attempts, I came up with the idea that I could gather eggs from nests and use surrogate parents to hatch them. This would later prove to be a stupid plan, for a variety of reasons, but I was feeling desperate. When I first started collecting ingredients, it seemed that pigeons would be the easiest thing on my list. But getting baby pigeons quickly turned into a near-impossible feat.

As I was coming to my conclusions about authenticity, I was always looking forward to catching some pigeons. The common street pigeon (*Columba livia*), which Escoffier himself used, was actually introduced to North America by real live Frenchmen. What could be more authentic than that?

I'd eaten a few adult pigeons over the years and I never really considered them to be top-shelf table fare. The ones I'd eaten had always been mature adults that I shot while I was out hunting for other stuff. I'd usually pop the breasts out and toss them in the oven for ten minutes. I found the meat of the birds to be dry and tough, like a thick slice of dark turkey meat if you overcooked it and then left it uncovered in your fridge for a couple of days.

According to Escoffier, I'd gone about my pigeon eating all wrong. "Young pigeons are not very highly esteemed by gourmets," he lamented, "and this is more particularly to be regretted, since when the birds are of excellent quality, they are worthy of the best tables." But, he cautions, "those older than one year should be viewed as being old and should be completely excluded from use except for the preparation of forcemeat."

Escoffier referred to young pigeons, or squabs, as *pigeonneaux*. Technically, a squab is a fattened, flightless pigeon less than one year old. The only way to get a truly legitimate squab is to keep it in a cage; otherwise they start flying around when they're about thirty days old. While Escoffier was adamant about serving only *pigeonneaux* as a main dish, he used the older birds as thoroughly as the Plains Indians used buffalo. He pounded the flesh into forcemeat for use in soups and stuffings. He used the hearts, gizzards, and livers in pies. He used hard-boiled pigeon eggs to garnish crayfish soup.

I called the Montana Department of Fish, Wildlife, and Parks to check on the legal aspects of pigeon collecting. Because the birds are nonnative, they can be taken at any time with any method, and their eggs and nests may be legally destroyed. When I first called Moisan and proposed that we get together some night and catch a bunch of pigeons, he agreed that it would be a piece of cake. We met up at the house where I was living, a scuzzy old shithole that was divided into four apartments. I lived in the basement, a dark, cellarlike pit with one-half of a window and a steep, narrow staircase that made me feel like I was emerging from a foxhole every time I came outside. Above me, on the ground floor, were two regular apartments. Above those was a small loft-type apartment with a long, rickety staircase terminating at an entryway shelter that brought to mind a gigantic doghouse. This upper apartment was occupied by a peroxide-haired white guy in his midtwenties, who fancied himself some sort of inner-city rap gangster. This is a hard image to pull off in a cushy mountain town, but he did his best by wearing loads of gold chains and athletic suits, investing heavily in car stereo equipment, and flashing menacing hand signals at kids passing to and from the local high school. Diana and I referred to him simply as Gangsta.

When I first moved into that apartment, I witnessed three interesting Gangsta-related events: he rigged his own staircase with motion detector lights; a gang of thugs destroyed his van with baseball bats; and two pigeons built a nest outside his window. Every morning, the two pigeons would flutter to the top of the roof to engage in explicit sexual acts, punctuated by explosive bouts of cooing. Afterwards, the birds would circle the house like stars orbiting the head of a cartoon character who's been bonked by a hammer, then they'd fly off. Judging by their sexual appetites, I suspected that they would handily produce a clutch of squab, so I wanted to catch them.

You might say that Moisan's and my attempt at the rooftop pigeons was unnecessarily complicated. After securing trespass permission from Gangsta (who had offered to kill the cooing pigeons with a high-powered handgun), we waited for the pigeons to fly off. Then we climbed to the peak of the roof. Moisan held my ankles and I hung my body over the edge so that I was looking under the eaves at their empty roost. I screwed the top of a square-shaped minnow net to the side of the house, below the roost. Next I fastened a dowel to the free-hanging end of the net. I tied a long piece of parachute cord to each end of the dowel, then looped the cords through screw eyes driven into the eave of the house.

Moisan climbed down to the ground. He rigged his end of the lines through two more screw eyes driven into the house near ground level. The cords were adjusted so that pulling them from the ground lifted the net, blocking the escape of the pigeons from their perch. As a last step, Moisan pounded a nail into the house, so that once the net was engaged, the line could be secured and the operator could climb up and retrieve the birds.

I was convinced that this device would work, given a chance. The problem was, the pigeons wouldn't go near the roost with that net hanging there. It seemed as though they'd eventually get used to it and return. But they never did.

Moisan suggested that we start going downtown to look for pigeons at night. Downtown pigeon hunting proved to be much more fun than trying to trap pigeons at my house; it had all the excitement and secretive tactics of vandalism or graffiti, without the negative moral ramifications. And it was much more productive.

It turns out that the Achilles' heel of a pigeon is its proclivity to spend the night tucked behind air-conditioning units. We discovered this while cruising alleyways behind rows of bars and restaurants. The units are mounted a few inches away from each building, forming little nooks. It seemed as though a fellow could easily climb up to these units and block off the exits with a net.

The next night we set off wearing dark clothes, toting along one of those boxes people use to transport pet dogs on airplanes. We started out behind an Irish pub. A car full of old blueprints and newspapers was parked beneath the AC unit. I used the car's trunk as a foothold to climb up the wall, and Moisan used the hood. He had a blocking mechanism, a pizza box taped to a long pipe. I had a net, also taped to a long pipe. With the box, Moisan blocked one end of the unit. Simultaneously, I thrust the net over the other exit and a nearly black pigeon flew squarely into the net. I lowered the net down and transferred the bird to the cage. Satisfied with ourselves, we hid the cage and nets and moseyed into the pub for a drink. After a few nights of this, I was sharing my apartment with six pigeons.

Bringing the pigeons into my home did not make Diana very excited about coming over. She found the idea of keeping pigeons in your apartment so you could eat their babies repugnant. The pigeons cooed a lot, which I interpreted as a sign of contentment. Diana thought the cooing sounded desperate and sad. As we argued about this, I told her about my desire to adhere to a strict interpretation of *Le Guide Culinaire* whenever possible.

"And since I'm being so strict," I said, "I have to keep these pigeons until they produce squab. I can't settle for anything less than the real thing on this particular ingredient."

"Steve," she said, "if you're so concerned with authenticity, you shouldn't talk so much about a cookbook that you can't even pronounce. It's annoying."

This was something I hadn't even considered. I pronounced the book's title like this: For *Le*, I said "la" to denote the Frenchness of the title. I pronounced *Guide* just as you would in English. I pronounced *Culinaire* phonetically, because I hate when people who speak regular American English come to a word like *croissant* and suddenly affect a phony French accent. Whenever I defend my stance on this subject, I point out that I don't pronounce my last name with an Italian accent, which, if I did, would bug the shit out of everybody.

Diana dialed her best friend, Julie, who lives in Boston, where Diana grew up. Julie speaks fluent French because her mother is French. Diana spelled the book's title to Julie and asked her to pronounce it to me. I wasn't too far off on the *Le* part, which is supposed to sound like an *l* sound without the accompaniment of a vowel. *Guide* is "Geed," with a hard *g*. *Culinaire* is some tangled-up mess and my efforts to say it made me sound ultrapretentious and stupid, though coming from Julie's lips, the word sounded beautiful. I decided that I might start calling the cookbook *Le Geed* in conversation, depending on the sensibilities of the person I was talking to.

But I was way more concerned about my pigeons than I was about my French. As my apartment filled with the aromas and sounds of pigeons, I felt inclined to study up on the birds, to learn about their care and breeding. It made sense that pigeons would be easy to take care of, because they were probably the first bird domesticated by man. The common pigeon is a descendant of a Eurasian cliff-dwelling bird. Representations of pigeons appear on figurines, mosaics, and coins dating back to 4500 BC, in Mesopotamia. In an Egyptian tomb dating from the third millennium BC, archaeologists found a vat of preserved pigeon stew. Ever since the Egyptians, people have been carrying pigeons around from place to place. The French introduced the common street pigeon to North America before North America had streets. In the sixteenth and seventeenth centuries, French settlers brought flocks of domesticated pigeons across the Atlantic Ocean to supplement the often scanty supplies of wild food found near their settlements along the Saint Lawrence River. Many of the birds escaped captivity or were released, and the flocks thrived and spread southward across the whole continent. I learned that a pair of pigeons with adequate food and water will produce up to four clutches a year. As for my pigeons, no two birds had taken even the slightest romantic interest in each other. I waited weeks for this to happen, but it didn't. Aside from that, they seemed perfectly comfortable. They ate and drank and cooed and preened and perched. But no sex. No eggs.

And that is how, one night, I found myself beneath the Higgins Street Bridge, standing on my tiptoes atop an extension ladder with my fingertips sunk into a loaf of pigeon shit. Since my birds didn't want to lay eggs, I'd give them some eggs. When I got back to my apartment with the kidnapped eggs, I fashioned a nest out of a soup bowl and toilet paper. I nestled the eggs into the bowl and placed them into the cage. The pigeons just sat on their perch. In the morning, they were still sitting on their perch. I gave them a day to think it over, but still no one opted to care for the eggs. I pulled the eggs back out of the cage and hard-boiled them.

A few days later, while I was vacuuming pigeon feathers and fretting over the birds' blunt refusal to foster the eggs, I got to thinking about something I'd read. The ancient Romans—who ate their own fair share of squab—believed that captive birds were capable of homesickness. The Romans built their aviaries with very small windows and no good views. They thought that if the birds could see trees, they'd be sad and wouldn't get fat. I'd put my pigeon cage next to a small half-window. I took a peek out the window, and sure enough, there was an apple tree out there. Maybe that's why they wouldn't care for the eggs.

I was fixing to move the cage when a buddy of mine, Fred, stopped by my apartment. Fred took one look at the birds and said, "Personally, I think pigeons are disgusting."

This upset me. "Sure, they make a mess everywhere and eat people's garbage, but that's what any animal would do if you turned it loose in town," I said. "If chickens were pecking around in the streets, you'd think they were gross too."

"No, I wouldn't."

"Yeah, you would."

"Crows run around in the streets," he replied, "and I don't

think crows are gross. Same with sparrows. But pigeons carry bubonic plague."

Fred has often told me that squirrels carry bubonic plague. He's a tree surgeon, so he's naturally disposed to despise squirrels.

"You think everything has bubonic plague," I said.

"Well," said Fred, "pigeons do carry a lot of diseases. I don't know about that one, specifically, but wait and see."

I studied a little more about why exactly pigeons are considered pests by so many people. I found that pigeons can carry aspergillosis, avian tuberculosis, coccidiosis, cryptococcosis, encephalitis, histoplasmosis, Newcastle disease, salmonellosis, thrush, toxoplasmosis, West Nile virus, and a nasty little mite that can cause skin irritations in humans. As for bubonic plague, which wiped out one-third of Europe in the fourteenth century, Fred must have been thinking of the Norway rat.

With the pigeons living in my apartment, I became paranoid about mites. If my arm had an itch, I just knew it was mites. When I woke up in the middle of the night, I would lie there quietly, trying to feel mites crawling on me. I didn't mention any of this to Diana, but when I saw her scratch her head a couple of times one day, I knew that the pigeons had to go.

Luckily I knew a guy named Cody who had an empty chicken coop. He had recently complained to me that something, perhaps a weasel, had gotten into his coop and murdered the occupants. Cody's about forty but seems way older. He looks like one of those bearded, hollow-eyed Confederate soldiers lying dead on the battlefield after Gettysburg. Cody lives up the Bitterroot River. The Bitterroot River drains the Bitterroot and Sapphire Mountains and dumps into Missoula from the south. Whenever Cody comes down into Missoula, he talks about how much more severe conditions are up the Bitterroot. It's colder and snowier and windier up the Bitterroot; the roads are icier. In the summer, he always says it's hotter and drier up the Bitterroot, with a much greater risk of things like wildfires and bear attacks. To his credit, Cody actually did get attacked by a bear in his own yard.

I went to Cody and explained that I couldn't keep the pigeons in my apartment because of my worries about getting in trouble for infecting the place with skin mites. I told him that I'd like to move the birds into his vacated coop, while I waited for them to pair up and produce a dozen or so squab. He took my request as an admission from me that Missoula is a fainthearted place for the weak and overly civilized.

"Yup," he agreed, "those pigeons would be better off up the Bitterroot. You're going to laugh"—Cody always precedes information with the prophecy that you will laugh upon hearing it—"but I've been wanting some pigeons to train my dogs with."

"Well," I said, "if this all works out, maybe we'll see about that."

So Cody took the pigeons up the Bitterroot. I was feeling pretty good about the whole situation. I pictured myself, off having a good time while my captured birds cranked out a perpetual stream of authentic genuine flightless squab. At that moment, it would have been next to impossible to spoil my happiness and my sense of accomplishment. In fact, the only thing that could have spoiled it would have been Cody's admitting that he planned on screwing me over and stealing my squab. But he kept quiet about that, so for the moment I was truly, deeply content.

## CHAPTER FIVE

# Flying Pie

UNTIL I FOUND MYSELF IN THERMOPOLIS, WYOMING, MY SEARCH for the ingredients of *Le Guide Culinaire* had been all fun and games. Chasing street pigeons in downtown Missoula was exciting (if unproductive), and it was relaxing to hang out on the beach in Florida catching all sorts of fish and a ray, but there was nothing exciting or relaxing about being stranded in an unheated house in minus-thirty-degree weather, trying to trap English sparrows while my girlfriend was lying on the floor in a sleeping bag with her arm in a sling and her head wrapped in bandages.

As I sat by the window, waiting for sparrows to find the two bird feeders I'd tied to a lilac bush, I busied myself by blowing warm air on a frozen bottle of Pepsi. I couldn't help but wonder how my quest had deteriorated to such squalid conditions.

I guess things really started going downhill after I realized that Cody had stolen my pigeons. He stopped calling, and then I heard through the grapevine that he'd given the pigeons to some other guy and gone back to chicken farming. With the pigeons gone, I didn't see any good reason to stick around Missoula for the rest of the winter. Diana had gone down to Dallas,

Texas, to teach a semester of English composition at a community college. Her absence added to my restlessness, so I moved out of my shithole apartment and put all my possessions, including my freezer full of accumulating ingredients, into the care of a friend who promised to keep an eye on it. Once I moved out of my place, I was going around from one friend's house to another. With my stuff in storage, my possessions were trimmed down to two duffel bags, a box of frozen elk meat, and two bird feeders. I wanted to hang the feeders up in order to lure in some birds, but I wasn't staying in any one place long enough to attract a bird's attention.

Then, out of the blue, a house opened up in Thermopolis. Diana's and my friend Anna Baker had bought the house a couple of years earlier. After living there for a spell, she moved out with the intention of renting the place. But none of the people who moved in ever paid the rent. The last guy to live in the house racked up a bunch of bills, then took the doors off the cupboards and stacked them in the bedroom before leaving. Eventually Anna gave up on the idea of making money off her house. She said that Diana and I could have the place for two hundred bucks a month.

Diana and I agreed to meet in Thermopolis as soon as her job ended. She'd come up from the south, I'd head down from the north; we'd meet in the middle. I packed my duffel bags, the bird feeders, some fishing equipment, cooking stuff, my box of elk meat, and a .22 rifle into my '87 Subaru. I tied my canoe to the roof and headed east until I crossed the Continental Divide, then turned south toward Yellowstone National Park. As I drove, a major cold snap was blowing into the northern Rockies.

Diana spent the first night of her trip at a friend's house in Aspen, Colorado. The next morning she continued driving northward in her Subaru wagon. After passing through Craig, Colorado, she slid on some ice and rolled end over end, bumper to bumper, down a steep ditch. Almost everything she owned had been packed into the now-totaled car. The force of the crash busted the car's windows out. As it rolled down the embankment, it sprayed her belongings into the snow like a dog shaking off water.

Meanwhile, I'd arrived at Anna's house in Thermopolis and had tried unsuccessfully to turn the heater on. I called Diana's cell to tell her I had arrived safely and was greeted by the voice of an emergency medical technician who was riding with Diana in an ambulance. The ambulance was headed for Craig, Colorado.

I was in such a panic to get to Craig, I forgot to unpack my car. All I thought to do was take the canoe off the roof and drag it through the snow and behind Anna's fence. I made the eight-hour drive and got to the hospital at about ten p.m. Diana's hand was semiparalyzed, her arm was in a sling, and the skin on her face and arms looked like someone had gouged out chunks of flesh with a melon ball spoon. I checked her out of the hospital and into a motel.

When we finally got to Thermopolis, the outside air temperature was minus thirty degrees Fahrenheit. The town sits along the Bighorn River, in the central part of the state. It gets its name from a spring of seismically heated water that leaks out of the Owl Creek Mountains. The hot water and the cold air combine and cast the entire town in a thick, spooky, sulfur-smelling haze.

All the pipes in Anna's house were frozen solid, and the gas lines had for some reason been ripped out. The electric baseboard heaters did not work properly. The waterbed mattress in the bedroom was frozen solid. After unloading our stuff, I went back outside and the car wouldn't start. Our supplies were down to the frozen bottle of Pepsi. Diana was in so much pain that she was writhing in her sleeping bag. I dug through my luggage and found the two bird feeders. I thought that getting some songbirds in the yard would cheer Diana up. I did not bother mentioning my intent to trap the birds and eventually eat them.

That I was trying to capture little birds while suffering from cold and destitution doesn't really jibe with Western civilization's general history of eating little birds. In ancient Roman times, eating little birds was symbolic of wealth and opulence. At celebrations, Romans would eat larks' tongues marinated in red wine. During the reign of Nero, in the first century AD, a writer named Petronius Arbiter wrote a satire of contemporary Roman culture called the *Satyricon.* In the book, the narrator is invited to a feast at the home of a man named Trimalchio, a former slave who inherited his master's land and then made a fortune exporting wine. Trimalchio is the Roman equivalent of nouveau riche. He's a horrible show-off. While most people at the time sprinkle their kitchen floors with sawdust, Trimalchio uses saffron petals. As entertainment, Trimalchio dresses himself in a burial robe, douses himself with embalming perfume, and pretends to be dead as his guests lavish him with praise and his slaves wail with grief over his "passing."

As an appetizer, Trimalchio serves each guest the egg of a peahen. The narrator opens his egg and is surprised to find a chick inside. Believing that his egg was mistakenly fertilized, he considers returning it. But he soon realizes that the "chick" is actually "a very fat figpecker," a small bird that frequents orchards. The next course is a wild sow. "Around it hung little suckling pigs made from pastry, signifying that this was a brood-sow with her pigs at suck." A slave, a "bearded giant" wearing leg bands and a hunting cape, approaches to carve the hog. "Drawing his hunting-knife, he plunged it fiercely into the boar's side, and some thrushes flew out of the gash. Fowlers, ready with their rods, caught them in a moment, as they fluttered around the room and Trimalchio ordered one to each guest, remarking, 'Notice what fine acorns this forest-bred boar fed on . . .'"

The idea that eating little birds was a pastime for the wealthy and vain did not end with the Roman Empire. In 1570 Pope Pius V, an inquisitor who banned bullfighting because it was cruel, held a banquet featuring spit-roasted songbirds with their tongues sliced over them, and spit-roasted skylarks with lemon sauce.

The world's first celebrity chef, a Renaissance-era man known as Maestro Martino, describes a recipe called flying pie in his cookbook, *Epilario*. To make flying pie, the cook produces a pie crust filled with plain flour. After the crust is cooked, a hole is cut in the middle and the flour is dumped out. Then, Martino instructs, "prepare another small pie filled with good stuff that has been well cooked and seasoned and that has been made as big as that hole in the large mold." The larger, hollow pie crust is crammed full of live little birds, and the hole is plugged with the smaller pie. At serving time, the plug is removed and the birds fly out. "This is done to entertain and amuse your company," writes Martino. "And in order that they do not remain disappointed by this, cut the small pie up and serve."

*Epilario* was the first cookbook published in Italian. Martino's predecessors wrote cookbooks in Latin. *Epilario* was translated into English and published as *The Italian Feast* in Great Britain in 1598. Flying pie was a big hit with the Elizabethans. A recipe not unlike Maestro Martino's was immortalized in the nursery rhyme "Sing a Song of Sixpence," a protest song that targets the aristocracy.

*Sing a song of sixpence, a pocket full of rye,*
*Four and twenty blackbirds baked in a pie.*

In the nursery rhyme, the pie, "a dainty dish," is baked for a king. After dinner, the king goes off to count his money, as kings are prone to do. The queen, in typical queen form, retreats to her parlor to eat honey. The poor old maid, who is out hanging laundry, suffers the backlash of the royal couple's frivolous culinary transgressions: "Down came a blackbird and pecked off her nose!"

If the author of "Sing a Song of Sixpence" could've seen me freezing my ass off in Thermopolis, he'd probably be happy that things had finally come full circle and that now the potential eater of little birds has to suffer as much as the serving classes. As I waited for some birds to show up, I tried to improve Diana's and my living conditions. I got a space heater, thawed the water lines out, and fixed some of the ruptured pipes. I got the frozen waterbed mattress thawed enough to partially drain it and squeeze it through the door and into the yard, where it promptly refroze. A plumber installed an electric hot water heater to replace the gas one.

The first bird showed up just as the house was getting comfortable. It was a black-capped chickadee, a small, melodious, and almost tame species of bird that I'm rather fond of. The chickadee—I assume it was the same one—came every day, always alone. He hung out at the feeders for four or five hours a day. He much preferred the bird feeder with suet over the feeder that had seeds in it. I was glad to be of service to the chickadee, though his species didn't fit into the narrow confines of what I was legally allowed to catch.

Back when Escoffier wrote *Le Guide Culinaire*, just one hundred years ago, he was flummoxed by the available variety of little birds in the markets of Europe. In the Feathered Game section of *Le Guide*, Escoffier acknowledges that there are way too many edible birds to give a treatise on each variety. "If it was necessary to list each and every edible wild bird the list would be far too long so only those in general use are given." He then breaks the "general use" birds into ten categories:

1) The various species of Pheasant; grey, red, rock, and American Partridge.
2) Hazel Grouse, Capercaillie, Sand Grouse, Grouse, Pintailed Grouse, Bustards.
3) The various species of wild duck; Teals, Pintails.
4) Snipe and Woodcock.
5) Various species of Plover; Lapwings, Sandpipers, Water Rails, Moorhens, Scoters.
6) Quails, Corncrakes.
7) Thrushes and Blackbirds.
8) Larks.
9) Warblers, Jacksnipes.
10) Buntings.

If you have a valid hunting license and you're competent with a shotgun, you can still legally procure categories 1–4 and portions of 5 and 6, most of which are large birds generally regarded as game. What it's like to dine on categories 7, 8, 9, and 10, commonly known as songbirds, is a knowledge relegated largely to the inhabitants of France's graveyards.

Long after flying pie faded from popularity with the Elizabethans, the French maintained a passion for consuming dainty birds. Louis XVIII, the king of France from 1814 to 1824, used to prepare for himself a dish made of buntings cooked inside a partridge stomach lined with goose liver and truffles. The author of *The Three Musketeers* and *The Count of Monte Cristo*, Alexandre Dumas, loved little birds. Nearing death, he wrote, "I intend that my last work shall be a cookbook composed of memories and desires; a book whose learning and wit will not frighten the practical cook and will perhaps merit reading by serious men and not-so-serious women whose fingers will not be too wearied in turning the pages." The book was published posthumously, in 1873, and included a recipe called "Larks in a Casserole." The larks are buried up to their necks with stuffing and bacon, then baked. Escoffier's career happened to just catch the tail end of Europe's passion for consuming little birds. The thrushes, buntings, warblers, larks, and blackbirds served in Escoffier's restaurants were sometimes caught live and fattened on millet for six weeks before slaughtering. Others were shot during fall migrations, when the birds tended to be naturally fat from a summer's feeding. In Escoffier's day, hunting parties would go after anything that moved. In 1885 Escoffier published a magazine piece in *L'Art Culinaire* about a hunting trip he had made to a buddy's great-uncle's farm in the Basse-Alpes of France. When it looked as though they might have to go home empty-handed, he and his friends shot up a whole flock of larks. That night, the smell of cooking larks "totally aroused their gastronomic awareness."

In the fourth edition of *Le Guide*, issued in 1921, Escoffier qualifies his mention of the dotterel, a blackbird-sized, tundra-dwelling bird of northern Europe, writing that "unfortunately, it has become very rare." The dotterel's flesh is suitable for pâtés but its nearly tame behavior is unsuitable for survival in the face of unrestricted hunting pressure. Other favorites of Escoffier, such as blackbirds, thrushes, buntings, and larks, were rapidly disappearing from the countryside as well as from the marketplace by the 1920s. Eventually, conservation laws blocked the taking and sale of songbirds in both the United States and Europe. From then on, the enjoyment of eating little birds was a thing of the past.

But it didn't need to be. Enter the English sparrow. Those are the little brown birds with black markings that you see flitting around beneath your car in the grocery store parking lot. The bird was brought to America to control insect pests in croplands, but after a few decades the English sparrow had exploded to such numbers that they were destroying more crops than the insects were. The English sparrow is now the most populous bird on the planet, and it enjoys a wider home range than any other bird species. Its nesting habits threaten to drive native cavity-nesting birds in America, such as the eastern bluebird, into extinction. Now, the English sparrow (as well as the European starling, whose history in America is basically the same) is completely unprotected. In fact, many conservation organizations and various state and federal agencies have a spoken though impossible goal of extirpating the pesky, bitesized little birds from the continent.

While I did not personally know anyone who ever actually ate a sparrow, eating a few seemed like a great way to kill two birds with one stone, so to speak. I'd be replicating a forgotten and odd facet of Escoffier's cuisine, while simultaneously being a good steward of the land. Plus, if these things tasted good and my friends liked them and started trapping them, just think of the impacts we could have! So I waited by the kitchen window. About a week of insanely low temperatures had passed before the first English sparrow showed up. It was a male. He ate a few thistle seeds that had fallen from the feeder and then flew off. A few days later he showed up again and ate fallen seeds. His visits became more regular, and soon he was there every day, eating whatever seeds had fallen from the sack. One day about ten sparrows showed up. They quickly discovered the mysterious source of the seeds, as well as the suet. The sparrows became permanent residents of the lilacs.

The sparrow colony in the bushes grew by the day, as more and more sparrows showed up and decided to live there. It was hard to count them because they were always flitting about, but I'm guessing there were about forty. I was very amused by the birds and had a hard time concentrating on much else. To stare at the sack of thistle from the kitchen window, with the sparrows hanging around it, I had to aim my face directly into the window of a neighbor, an old hermit of a guy who always snarled at me when I waved. He had to think I was some kind of weirdo. We had several uncomfortable moments when our gazes met. I'd skulk away, then I'd be right back at the window a few minutes later.

When I was ready to make my move with the sparrows, I took a paring knife and cut little triangular slits in an empty one-quart yogurt container, filled the container with mixed birdseed, and hung the container from the lilacs. The birds attacked the mixed seed instantly. Once they were used to the yogurt container, I moved it to the ground. They followed it down and kept right on eating.

With the sparrows enjoying the seed on the ground, I set about designing a sparrow trap. I constructed a classic string-and-prop trap, a design long favored by kids with poor imaginations. A string-and-prop trap is made from a box, propped up on one side by a stick. A string is tied to the stick; when the prey steps beneath the box to get the bait, the operator tugs the string, tripping the prop out and letting the box fall over the prey.

I went outside the window and placed the yogurt container inside a box and propped it up with a piece of wood. I tied a length of nylon cord to the stick and fed it through the kitchen window. As an afterthought, I sprinkled a little seed outside the trap, to get the sparrows interested in the box.

A string-and-prop trap has two significant problems. One of the problems is that they do actually work sometimes, which totally fucks with your mind. When I was a little kid, I managed to trap a pet chipmunk with a string-and-prop trap, so I continued to believe that the trap design was semireliable. The second problem with the trap is that you have to watch it like a hawk, because if you're not there to pull the string, you're never going to catch shit. Having a trap set makes it nearly impossible to get anything done. Whenever I'd go to take a leak, I'd get halfway through emptying my bladder and get this awful sense that, in my absence, sparrows were flooding into the trap. But any illusions I had about a quick success were squashed by the sparrows' chilly acceptance of the box. Rather than go in there and gorge themselves, the birds would search and search around the box for any last little crumb of a seed they might have missed during past meals.

Even when a couple of birds did take to eating in the box, they would exercise such politeness that no two birds would rush in together. One would go in and eat, and the others would wait patiently outside the box. When the bird on the inside had gotten his fill, another would go in and eat. I didn't want to spring the trap for just one bird. That would put the alarm up and then the birds would surely snub the box.

During my long vigils at the window, I was constantly reminding myself of that old proverb, "A bird in the hand is better than two in the bush." Rather than abandon the string-and-prop effort, I attempted a rather shrewd maneuver. I waited until one bird was inside. Then I focused my attention on another bird, who was waiting in line. He'd shift around a bit, scratching and pecking in the snow near the opening. I waited until just the right moment, when he was just beneath the lip of the box, and pulled the string. The box swung down, catching the bird on the tail. He jumped forward, right into the falling trap with his buddy who was obliviously pecking seed in the box. I slid a piece of cardboard under the box and carried the box into the house. I lifted it just enough to get the birds in my hand. I pinched their necks between my thumb and forefinger. The birds were dead within five seconds. I dropped the birds into a Ziploc bag, sucked the air from the bag to give it a vacuum seal, and popped it into my freezer.

From then on, the other sparrows wanted nothing to do with the box. They'd pick around it and stand on top of it, but they would not go inside. I waited a few days, but the birds remained stubborn. Two sparrows make for pretty slim pickings, even for just one person to eat. As I waited around for the other birds to grow comfortable again with the trap, I decided to try another pursuit.

One of the more notable things about Thermopolis is that the place is overrun with cottontail rabbits. I'd always see them hanging out in the yard and hiding beneath the waterbed mattress. The thing is, you can't shoot within city limits. So I started making some plans to go hunting outside of town, near the head of the Wind River Canyon. Moisan and my brother Matt came down to hunt with me.

The cottontail rabbits near Boysen Reservoir like to hang out near exposed outcroppings of sandstone, especially outcroppings with a nearby thicket of red willow, which they like to eat. When the sun is setting, the rabbits come out of their burrows beneath the sandstone to bask against the sun-heated rocks. The rabbits' main concern seems to be the threat of avian predators; they lie tight against the rocks, with a shielding ledge of sandstone over their heads. So long as they have protection between themselves and the sky, they relax. To a rough-legged hawk, say, who's flying four hundred feet above the earth, one of these sandstone outcroppings might look deserted of game. But to a dude with a pair of binoculars and a .22 rifle, who's lying quietly on the ground, the rock outcroppings look like rabbit hotels with a customer on every balcony.

We got twenty rabbits. We decided against hunting again the next day because we had all we needed. Instead, we skinned rabbits. Escoffier believed that only young rabbits were suitable for cuisine. "When the wild rabbit is old, it is tough, and can only be used for stock or forcemeats." He suggests two ways to determine the age of a wild rabbit. One is to palpate a lentil-shaped bone in the leg joint. When the rabbit is young, the bone is loose. When old, the bone fuses to the other bones of the joint. The other way is to "grasp one ear close to its tip with both hands, and pull in opposite directions; if the ear tears, the beast is young." My hunting partners and I attempted both of these methods but found each to yield inconclusive results. Our rabbits had frozen overnight, and we had skinned them before they were completely thawed. We agreed that we should try again some time with unfrozen critters. We did a careful, thorough job with the meat. We picked off any stray hairs on the flesh, trimmed away any blood clots, cut out any busted bones. Sometimes a piece of a bullet will pull a little tuft of hair down into a rabbit's meat. To get the hairs out, we twirled toothpicks in the holes. The hairs wrapped around the toothpicks, and then we could easily pull the tuft out.

When the meat was all clean, we froze a bunch of it for the

Escoffier feast. With the rest, we made a simple, homemade concoction we invented called special Chinese sweet-and-sour cottontail, and ate it for our supper.

With the rabbit hunting taken care of, I went back to the lonely vigil at the window. I tried hard, but I could never convince Diana that watching sparrows was very interesting. She was working as an online English tutor and was content to spend all her time at her computer. I kept waiting and waiting for the sparrows to go back into the trap, but trapping conditions only worsened.

Diana and I had agreed to leave Thermopolis in the spring, and now that time was coming. The waterbed mattress thawed out. The snow in the yard began to melt too. Bare spots of ground appeared, then grew by the day and joined forces with other bare spots. The ice that had accumulated on the roof eventually melted as well. Much of the runoff leaked through to the bedroom ceiling. The leaking water would form goiter-like pockets beneath the paint, and the goiters would hang there until I lanced them with a fillet knife. Eventually the bare spots in the yard surrounded and conquered the last remnants of snow that were hiding in the shade beneath the lilacs. The sparrows that had been living in the lilacs altogether lost interest in the bird feeders and moved out.

And then we moved out too. We celebrated our last night in Thermopolis by going out to dinner. The vegetarian options available to Diana were mushroom soup and a mushroom sandwich. When Diana eats too many mushrooms and drinks too many drinks, the drinks and the mushrooms get into a fight inside her stomach. That doesn't stop her, though. She ordered the wild mushroom soup and the portobello sandwich, drank a few vodka sodas, then suffered a twelve-hour paroxysm of vomiting while I slept, ate breakfast, and packed our stuff into the car. Finally I packed Diana into the car as well and drove north out of Wyoming. My elk meat was gone, and all I had to show for my five months in Thermopolis were some rabbits and two measly sparrows. This Escoffier feast was going to be the drag of the century if my luck didn't improve. But I did have one trick up my sleeve. In my notebook was a name of a guy I found on the Internet as I researched sparrows and sparrow trapping. The man's name was Floyd Van Ert.

# CHAPTER SIX

# Setting This World on Fire

FLOYD VAN ERT TRAPS ENGLISH SPARROWS AS A SERVICE TO THE United States of America. He is seventy-one years old, slightly rotund, and he dresses comfortably—usually in shorts, heavy work shoes, and a baseball cap. He lives near Carson, Iowa, about twenty miles east of Omaha, Nebraska. Floyd does not like the word *kill* applied to his work. When pressed, he will admit to *disposing of* English sparrows, but he much prefers to describe his work as the *control of* English sparrows. Floyd devotes most of his waking hours to the designing, testing, manufacturing, and selling of sparrow traps. Since he retired from his own commercial glass shop and took to building traps in 1995, he's sold about eight thousand devices of his own design. His designs include the Universal Sparrow Trap, the PVC Sparrow Trap, and—his personal pride and joy—the Urban/Country Sparrow Nest Box Trap.

By his own admission, Floyd doesn't even earn minimum wage for his efforts as a trap designer. As he's quick to point out, he does what he does for altruistic reasons; he does not desire financial reward. He's prone to giving traps away, often sells traps at a loss, and freely invites people to steal his trap designs from his Web site (www.vanerttraps.com). If a person was looking to pirate a sparrow trap design, that person could do worse than stealing one from Floyd Van Ert. On his ten-acre spread and testing grounds along the West Nishna Bounty River, Floyd has trapped over four thousand sparrows in the last five years. His traps work. Period.

If Floyd's a hard man with English sparrows, that's only because he's a soft man with the eastern bluebird, a beautiful and semirare indigenous bird that suffers mightily at the beak of the English sparrow. The bluebird needs holes where it can lay its eggs, preferably in old trees and stumps and farmyard fence posts, and the introduced birds often occupy all the available holes.

When Floyd first set out to help save the bluebird, he went into the workshop behind his house and built bluebird nesting boxes with bluebird-sized holes in the doors. He hung the boxes on trees and fence posts, then watched helplessly as most of the boxes were overrun by English sparrows. The few bluebirds he attracted were evicted by sparrows, which tossed the bluebird nests out of the boxes and cracked open the bluebird eggs. When the sparrows found bluebird hatchlings inside the boxes, they pecked the baby birds to death.

The terrible ferocity of the English sparrow makes Floyd unapologetic about his work. If anyone ever did question Floyd's morals as a sparrow trapper, Floyd would hand that person his sparrow-trapper résumé; he keeps a stack of these photocopies in his shop. When I went to Iowa, seeking Floyd's advice on how to better catch sparrows, he gave me my own copy. His résumé includes a list of environmental organizations that he belongs to: Iowa Bluebird Conservationists; Bluebirds Across Nebraska; American Bird Conservation Association; North America Bluebird Society. When Floyd showed me this list, he said, "People ask me, 'Well, why haven't you gotten hate mail, for as much as you're known all over the United States for trapping sparrows?' Well, I've never got a hate mail."

To explain why, he tapped the résumé. And then he turned his finger and pointed it at me. "And I never talk about killing," he said. "I might talk a little bit about *disposing*. But *killing*'s a big word."

Although Floyd Van Ert kills enough sparrows to open an all-you-can-eat buffet, he's never eaten one of the birds. In fact, I was the first guy he'd ever heard of who wanted to trap sparrows in order to eat them. Before I visited him, I requested that he start saving sparrows for me, to supplement whatever we happened to catch together. He let me know that he was not excited about saving the birds. "I'd rather flick a sparrow into the bushes than to wrap it up and put it into my freezer next to my food," he told me. But he had been true to his word and saved me a medley of twenty-seven sparrows and starlings. With that many birds, I didn't even need to learn how to catch my own.

If Floyd was mad at me about making him save sparrows, he got over it rather quickly when he started showing me around his place. He likes giving tours. Before we set out to explore his property, Floyd pulled his socks up to his knees in order to protect his legs from the tall vegetation. He started his tour just outside the front door of the house. He explained that he does not actually own this land or the house; it belongs to his second wife, Marty, who's quite a bit younger than Floyd. Marty was at work on the day we toured the property, but Floyd mentioned her often. He said he can't get over how much he loves her. He put it this way: "I've got a six-CD Bose stereo in my car, and when she's in there I don't even turn it on. We just like to talk." He thinks that their relationship derives strength from the fact that they each maintain their independence. Every month Marty gives Floyd a bill for what he owes in room and board at her house.

Marty is a bluebirder, which is what bluebird enthusiasts call themselves. She introduced Floyd to bird conservation. One of their first projects together was to restore her property, which was inundated with nonnative plants and grasses. Floyd persecuted the nonnative plants as vigorously as he persecutes nonnative birds. "I've got it all back to native plants and grasses now," he said. "This is all natural. Native grasses. Native wildflowers. It takes years to get it going and established. You really gotta care for it, but once you do it's beautiful. It's been fun too. My wife and I spent twelve hundred dollars on seed alone. This land is now registered with the National Wildlife Federation as an official backyard wildlife habitat. That makes us proud. We've counted over one hundred species of birds on this land. Marty's got a list inside, if you need to see it."

We walked down a slight hill to the foot of a long meadow that stretched along the river. Floyd said that I should have seen the meadow yesterday. Apparently, he had to mow the whole thing down because the wild lettuce was getting out of hand and threatening to choke out the other plants.

"This was a heck of a year for wild lettuce. It's an annual, and you've got to get rid of it. Otherwise it will go to seed. It started to set blossoms, so I mowed it all down with my tractor. I was mowing flowers down this tall alongside it." He held his hand up to his chest. "I about cried," he said, his voice cracking. He looked away for a moment.

The next stop on the tour was a bluebird trail that courses through the property. Floyd's bluebird trail comprises a series of wooden nesting boxes, about the size of shoe boxes. During the bluebird nesting season, Floyd tends the boxes every day.

He walks from one to the next, along his trail. Bluebirders often boast that bluebird trails are what saved the bluebird from extinction. That's not an outlandish claim. A hunter and naturalist named Dr. T. E. Musselman invented the idea of bluebird trails in Illinois back in the 1930s, just as the birds were starting to disappear. By the 1940s bluebirds had vanished from much of their traditional range. Dr. Lawrence Zeleny, who founded the North American Bluebird Society, popularized Musselman's bluebird trail idea with his 1976 book, *The Bluebird: How You Can Help Its Fight for Survival*. In the twenty years following the book's publication, bluebirds made a radical recovery. The recovery is considered by many to be the greatest grassroots conservation effort in American history.

When Floyd approaches one of his nest boxes, he talks loudly so that the parents will hear him, get scared, and fly off. The birds are only seven inches long, but they show up brightly, like tossed Frisbees, as they fly above the grass. Once the adults take off, Floyd opens the front of the box and makes sure that everything is going okay on the inside. He says that putting up a bluebird box and not monitoring it is worse than not putting up a bluebird box at all.

Floyd opened one of his boxes and was pleased to see five beautiful bluebird eggs arranged in the nest. He said, "She raised six babies out of here the first hatch. Now she'll raise five. I've had over sixty bluebird babies come off my land so far this year. If I didn't monitor it, that number might be zero. If I didn't trap sparrows, I might not have one nest."

If Floyd opens one of his boxes and finds a sparrow nest, he scatters it and busts the eggs. Then he places one of his traps in the box to catch the culprits. He mainly wants to get the adult male sparrows, which do the brunt of the bluebird killing. "An old male sparrow, he even looks mean," said Floyd. "And he's smart."

I wanted Floyd to give me a rundown on how to use his sparrow traps effectively, but first he wanted to go down and get a burger and a pop from Dairy Queen. I drove. On the way back to his house, he tried to convince me to help him write a book about trapping sparrows in cities. Earlier he had told me that bluebirds don't like cities, and that city people don't care about saving bluebirds.

I said, "If there are no bluebirds in the cities, and city people don't care about bluebirds, then why do city people need to know how to get rid of the sparrows?"

"Because they bitch all the time. I read 'em on the Web. They hate sparrows in a city just as bad as a bluebirder does. They hate 'em. But those people don't do anything about it."

I wanted to pursue this conversation with Floyd, but he suddenly got very excited as we passed the bank. He demanded that I turn into the bank's parking lot. He guided me around to the back of the building, where there was a telephone pole with a bluebird box nailed to it. The box was Floyd's. The hole in the box, where the bird would supposedly enter, was blocked by a metal flap with an orange, round sticker on it. This orange sticker is what Floyd had spotted from the window of the car.

"This is fun," he said. "I love this." He got out of the car and pointed to the sticker. "See, this tells me the trap's been set off, or tripped. Then I go over here and open this door." He cracked open a small sliding door on the side of the trap. "I open it up about that far," he said. "And pretty soon we see the beak."

The beak belonged to a European starling. Floyd hates starlings almost as much as he hates English sparrows, and he hates them for the same reasons. He's developing a line of traps for starlings. This trap with the starling was a prototype for a new design. Floyd said he was still working out the bugs in the system.

The starling wanted out in a big way. Floyd grabbed the bird's long, yellowish beak through the small door. He held it, then opened up the front of the house and grabbed the bird by the body. He reset the trap and climbed into the car, cradling the bird in his lap. He said he couldn't believe that anyone would eat one of these dirty things. We crossed the West Nishna Bounty River and drove up a hill and pulled into Floyd's yard. When he climbed out of the car, he realized that the bird had died in transit. "He had a heart attack," Floyd said. "Here's another bird for you to eat." We walked into the house to listen to his phone messages. A woman from the bank was on there, telling Floyd that his starling trap was tripped.

When I told Floyd that I had been trying to catch sparrows with a stick-and-prop trap over the winter, he just rolled his eyes. Floyd builds his traps from scratch, right from stock pieces of metal. He builds some of his own manufacturing equipment. He buys some of his equipment on eBay. He polishes the metal corners of his traps with a machine normally used to polish window glass. Once an engineer phoned Floyd to ask how he got such a nice polish on the corners of his metal. "He could hardly believe that's how I did it," Floyd told me.

Out in his workshop, Floyd showed me how the Universal Sparrow Trap works. He mounts the trap on the inside of a sparrow-infested bluebird box. When the sparrow comes in, it hits the trap's trigger and the metal flap swings up, lightning fast, and blocks the hole so the sparrow can't get out. Floyd held up a little block of wood that he wanted me to inspect. He uses the block to test the trigger tension on his traps.

"See how dirty this is?" he asked. "I've dropped this thousands of times. This weighs two-thirds of a sparrow's weight. A sparrow weighs twenty-eight grams. When a sparrow drops down from the hole, it has built up velocity too. So it weighs more than twenty-eight grams really. If I drop this block of wood and it trips the trap, then I know a sparrow is gonna get caught."

Floyd's traps are so reliable, he hardly needs to advertise. "A lot of my sales are word of mouth," he said. "That's what got my name started. Other guys who sell traps are just envious. They see me and they say, 'How do you do it? You're setting this world on fire.' I say, 'I ain't doing anything. I'm just making a trap.'"

As Floyd explained the supremacy of his traps, he got excited and his voice rose. He could tell that I liked hearing about it, so he pulled out a few of his competitors' traps. He keeps them around as a form of amusement. Floyd held up one trap that he considers particularly loathsome. To layman eyes, it was very similar to Floyd's trap, though it lacked the durable yet delicate flourishes of workmanship.

"An old male sparrow is too smart for this trap. It's worthless, because as soon as you put it in there, the sparrow won't go in." Floyd demonstrated how to install the trap in a bluebird box. He pointed to the hole. The trap had altered the hole's appearance. "A sparrow will see that little *bitty* tiny cavity that wasn't in the hole before. It sucks. You could put a different *screw* on the outside of the box and an old sparrow wouldn't go in. I just hate this trap. The guy that built this is out of Ohio, and he thinks he's got something. I know this guy personally. I asked him, 'How many of these traps do you sell?' He said, 'Oh, couple hundred a year. Why, Floyd? How many of your traps do you sell?' I just laughed. I didn't tell him how many I sell.

"Look," he went on. "The North America Bluebird Society had a bunch of different traps for sale on their Web site two years ago. And then the lady called me up and said, 'We're taking them all off. Except yours.' She said, 'You've got a trap. Those other ones are junk.' And they put mine on the Web and they sell them for eleven dollars. And I sell to them for six fifty. Everybody gets them for the same price. And I pay the freight."

Though he's sold traps to research scientists and municipalities, Floyd's primary customers are bluebirders. "Bluebirders are older people," he said. "If it weren't for old people, bluebirds would have disappeared. That's who I sell my traps to. I just send them out, before I get paid. No credit cards or nothing. But I always get paid. I'm working with a different class of people. They're bluebirders and they're honest people."

An MBA would cringe at Floyd's business model. There is no difference between his retail sales plan and his wholesale plan. There's a guy in Tennessee who sells Floyd's Universal Sparrow Trap inside one of Floyd's boxes for forty-nine dollars. Floyd sells the same setup for twenty-one dollars. And the Tennessee guy doesn't even buy the products straight from Floyd. He gets them from some other retailer. Floyd doesn't even know who.

"Why don't you call that Tennessee guy up?" I asked. "You could sell the traps to him at a higher price than you usually charge but at a lower price than he's currently paying. And why don't you patent your designs?"

"Because I don't care. He's buying 'em from someone who bought 'em from me. It's not like he's stealing 'em. If I sell a Universal trap to you for six fifty, and you turn around and sell it to Joe Blow for ten fifty, I'm not going to call Joe Blow and steal your customer. It's wrong. You've got to be happy at some point.

"For me, I'm happy to make a good trap. I've got a handle on this trap market. My traps, they just trap sparrows like crazy. If I kept my feedback, you wouldn't have time to read it all. I have the best trap on the market. I know that I do. Everybody tells me that. And I don't do it for money. I do it for recognition."

# CHAPTER SEVEN

# In the San Juans

ABOUT A WEEK AFTER I GOT HOME FROM IOWA WITH MY BOX OF sparrows, I was drifting around in a canoe off San Juan Island, about a hundred and fifty miles north of Seattle. I was out in front of a house where two of my buddies from college, Mark and Pooder, live. I was trying to catch a ling cod, a long slender fish known for its firm, white, sweet-tasting flesh. Escoffier used Atlantic cod for all sorts of dishes, and I was betting that a Pacific ling cod is just about the same thing. I wasn't having any luck, and I was thinking about trying a different spot. And that's when the killer whales showed up.

All of a sudden, I heard a gargled blast of water and air, like someone clearing a snorkel after surfacing from a dive. But this noise was more like someone clearing a snorkel through a loudspeaker. I whipped my head around and saw an impossibly large mound of what looked like black and white rubber rolling out of the waves and disappearing again. The rubber mound was so close, I could have hit it with a bow and arrow. I thought, Oh my God, a whale's going to kill me.

I started frantically reeling up my bait. The killer whale rose again, blowing a blast of mist maybe twelve feet in the air. As its back cleared the water, its long dorsal fin quivered in the air like a car's radio antenna when you bend it back and let it go. The fin was almost as tall as me. As the fin disappeared underwater again, three other whales rose out of the waves behind it. The lead whale would miss my canoe, but I wasn't so sure about the other three.

My first impulse, before fleeing, was to look up toward the lighthouse on Lime Kiln Point. Mark and Pooder live in the lighthouse keepers' quarters. I wanted to make sure they weren't watching, because they'd be embarrassed as hell if they saw how afraid I was. They've each worked as sea-kayaking guides in the waters around San Juan Island, and they love to talk about the gentle, harmless nature of killer whales. Except Mark and Pooder don't call them killer whales. They use the more politically correct and socially acceptable term *orca*, which is actually a generic Latin word for whale that probably stems from the Greek word for vessel. Mark and Pooder defend their use of the word by saying that there has never been a documented killer whale attack against a human and that the whales suffer bad PR because of their name. The thing is, killer whales didn't get their name for attacking humans. The name is actually a corruption of an older title: whale killer. Orcas, or whatever you want to call them, are the only cetaceans known to eat other warm-blooded mammals. As I sat in the canoe, I couldn't help but think that, from beneath, I probably look a hell of a lot like a baby whale resting on the surface. So I decided to get the hell out of there.

I paddled the canoe toward shore and pulled into a deep cove beneath the lighthouse. I felt safer in there, so I lowered my ling cod bait—a dead herring—back down to the bottom. The next time I looked up from my fishing rod to check on the location of the killer whales, I realized that one of the damned things was now closer to shore than I was. The whale was practically scratching its sides on the rocks to the north of my canoe. It blew from its blowhole and smacked its tail on the water's surface. I reeled my line back up and paddled over to a little indent in the cliff beneath the lighthouse. There I dragged the canoe onto the rocky shores of San Juan Island.

HUNDREDS OF TOURISTS COME TO SAN JUAN ISLAND EVERY summer with hopes of having the sort of up-close experience with a killer whale that I'd just fled, but I had not come for whales. I had come for cod, a fish that Escoffier prepared any number of ways, including broiled, boiled, grilled, fried, and salted. Also I was there to redeem myself. Years before, my buddy Drost and I had come to San Juan Island because we wanted to take his little brown rowboat to a small, outlying island and live off the land like Robinson Crusoe for a long weekend. Our adventure was bookended by bad luck. A bee stung my right eyelid when the trip began, and another bee stung my left ankle when the trip ended. In between these stingings, a procession of disasters played out, uninterrupted. We never caught a thing, not even a clam.

When Drost and I left the island, we vowed to never return. But once I decided to get a ling cod for my Escoffier feast, I developed an almost MacArthuresque desire to return to the island and vindicate myself in the very waters where I had once been shamed. For my expedition companions on my return trip, I selected Diana and her New Yorker friend Becca, whom Diana met in Israel years ago. Becca is very exotic-looking. Her ancestors are from Eastern Europe, but she looks almost Egyptian. She has eyebrows similar to the hieroglyphic figures on Egyptian tombs, but she doesn't pluck them to look that way. Becca flew into Seattle, and Diana and I made the trip from Montana to pick her up.

The next morning, we got up bright and early and drove north toward Anacortes, the departure point for car ferries heading out to San Juan Island. Once our ferry pulled away from the dock, we got out of our car and walked up to the deck. Rain was coming down in a slow, steady shower. We stood on the deck in our raincoats, drinking coffee.

There are between 172 and 700 islands in the San Juan Archipelago, depending on how you define an island. Some of the islands could also be called rocks. The islands and/or rocks in the archipelago are the tops of old mountains, gouged and scraped by passing glaciers over the millennia. As the ferry traveled through the archipelago, Becca and Diana commented on the beautiful shapes of the islands we saw, the curvaceous cliffs and deeply scratched rocks and thick growths of cedar.

The ferry ride took seventy minutes. We landed at Friday Harbor, which is like the capital of San Juan Island. It was the spring season, so the streets were fairly empty of tourists. We looked around a bit, and I bought my fishing license and some fishing tackle. I made some inquiries around town about renting a skiff for fishing, but the boat rental places were not opened yet for the summer. I hadn't anticipated this particular setback. How could an island's boat rental shops be closed? It seemed as though my efforts to catch a ling cod were thwarted from the beginning. We got into our car and drove off toward Lime Kiln Point.

Lime Kiln Point got its name from some old lime quarries that operated on the island for sixty-odd years. The quarries finally petered out in 1920. The kilns on the point were used to fire the limestone into usable lime, a constituent of cement. The Coast Guard built the lighthouse in 1919 and also constructed two large, colonial-style houses for the lighthouse keepers to live in. Once electricity came to the island in 1960, resident lighthouse keepers weren't so important. The Coast Guard eventually handed the land over to the state of Washington, which turned it into Lime Kiln Point State Park in 1984. Fourteen years later, my buddies Mark and Pooder stumbled into two of the choicest jobs on earth, and one of the greatest houses.

At night Mark and Pooder can lie in bed and hear passing gray whales clear their blowholes into the ocean air. They can look up from flipping a burger on the porch and see pods of feeding porpoises. Needless to say, Mark and Pooder don't have much trouble getting women. But they're insulted when I suggest a correlation between their prowess with women and their living situation. I guess I can't prove the correlation, but I do know that if Mark and Pooder lived in a cornfield in Iowa, I sure as hell wouldn't visit them.

Luckily, or maybe not, Mark and Pooder had access to an old aluminum canoe. For a fellow like myself, who wanted a solid boat to tame the treacherous saltwater environs surrounding San Juan Island, a canoe was less than ideal. Mark and Pooder made it pretty damn clear that I shouldn't risk taking the canoe onto the ocean.

We walked out onto their porch and stared at Haro Strait, which flowed past their house. Miles away, across the strait, we could see Canada's Vancouver Island. Drift logs and uprooted kelp whisked past in the current. The strait was flooding with an incoming tide. The shoreline was pockmarked with coves and bays, some no bigger than your average supermarket. These inlets were separated by points of land, or peninsulas, jutting into the sea. The swift current in the strait formed swirling eddies inside the coves. A small buoy was anchored in the cove below the lighthouse; it was pitched over at a sharp angle in the current of an eddy.

"That water is forty-eight degrees. You know how fast you'd die if you flipped over in that water?" asked Mark.

"How fast?" I asked.

"Fast."

Mark has spent years guiding in the San Juan Islands, taking tourists out in sea kayaks to camp on remote beaches. He has a calm, measured demeanor and wears a ponytail that gives him an outdoorsy yet academic look, which lends his warnings greater credibility.

Pooder tried to warn me away too, but he had to admit that he'd taken the canoe out fishing a few times himself.

"It's a matter of timing," said Pooder. He put his hands into the pockets of his greasy work pants. "You've got to watch the tides, and be careful. Water levels can rise twelve feet here on a high tide. A big tide like that creates a lot of current. What I'm saying is, if you're not careful, you'll get pulled way the hell out." He shrugged. "It's your call, man. I just want you to know what you're getting into."

In the morning, just as it was getting light, I took a look at the water out in front of Mark and Pooder's house. The small buoy floating in the cove was standing upright; the tide was slack. I woke up Becca and Diana. The three of us were sleeping on child-sized mattresses butted up together in a guest room. Becca opted to keep sleeping, but Diana got dressed and came outside with me. The air was cool and wet. We lowered the canoe off the rocks and climbed in.

Pooder doubted that I would catch a ling cod in the cove. Ling cod tend to hang out in superdeep water, he said, but I wasn't willing to go way out and risk getting caught in a current. With a heavy weight on my line, I lowered a ten-inch-long herring down to the bottom. The water was several hundred feet deep. I'm used to fishing in lakes and rivers, where the water's maybe ten or twenty feet deep. In such shallow water, I think that the fish and I are in close proximity, the primary difference being that the fish are underwater and I'm above water. But now that I was fishing in water that was one hundred yards deep, the fish seemed so far away that I couldn't picture my actions having any effect on them. It seemed impossible to hook into something so far away. So I was more than surprised when I felt a fish sock my bait.

At this point in our relationship, Diana had developed a very slight interest in fishing, but she had by no means decided to become a full-on fisherman. I could never assume that she wanted to fish; instead, I would offer fishing to her the way you might offer a drink to a visitor at your home. After the fish took my bait, I looked at her and held the rod toward her. "You wanna take it?" She thought about it for a moment, then took the rod and started cranking on the reel.

"It just feels like a weight," she said. "I can't feel it swimming around at all." She stopped reeling. Faintly, the rod bounced. There was a fish down there, somewhere. She reeled some more. In about five minutes, she reeled up a rockfish. I didn't know it was a rockfish, but I looked it up in a guide book that I'd brought along. The fish was reddish, about as long as a big shoe, with a fat, toothy head. It had needles on its dorsal fin that you could probably sew clothes with. It weighed maybe three pounds. We got the fish up in the boat and into the cooler. I rebaited the line and lowered it back down. Within minutes, I pulled up a small green ling. A green ling is similar to a ling cod in name, though not appearance. Still, I felt like we were getting close to catching what we were after. I lowered a fresh piece of bait down to the bottom, but then I noticed that the buoy was cocked on its side and water was flowing around it the way a river passes a rock. The tide was on the move. Quickly, we paddled for shore. We carried our fish back up to the house and cleaned them, then climbed back into our little beds.

Later in the morning, after we ate breakfast and Mark and Pooder went off to work, I made a few local phone calls to inquire about clam-digging spots. As long as we were on the island, I thought that I might get lucky and collect some other good ingredients in addition to the cod. Pooder said that suitable clam-digging beaches on San Juan Island are scarce, though, because there simply aren't many beaches to begin with. Most of the island's shoreline is formed by tall, vertical cliffs.

I called a sporting goods store in the town of Friday Harbor, but the clerk was being tight-lipped; he apparently didn't want to give shellfish-collecting information to some clueless tourist on the phone. I attempted to dial another sporting goods store but screwed up the number and, through a weird twist of fate, got hold of a chef at a restaurant in Friday Harbor instead. When I started asking about shellfish, he thought I was inquiring about that night's menu. Once I apologized for calling the wrong number, I asked the chef my question anyway, just for the hell of it. He said that the only clam-digging spot that he knew on the island was near a place called British Camp. I looked through the Washington Department of Fish and Game's shellfish regulations. Rather than listing the beaches where a person can go clam digging, the book listed the beaches where a person *can't* go clam digging. The beach at British Camp was on the no-no list, but the listing stated that the closure extended only to the dinghy dock. I didn't know what the hell that meant, but we decided to go there and take a look.

One of San Juan Island's nicest features is that every road

eventually leads to every place, or at least it seems to. No matter where you're going—to get some ice cream, to dig clams, to shoot pool at a bar—you can just start driving and you'll eventually get there. This was a mystery of the local infrastructure for which I was never able to provide a clear explanation. To find British Camp, I took a left or a right turn out of Mark and Pooder's driveway—it didn't really matter—and after ten minutes we saw the sign for British Camp Park.

The parking lot was surrounded by cedars and firs. The forest was interspersed with madrona trees. The trees had glossy, leathery leaves and reddish bark that seemed to be peeling away in places, as if the trees were diseased, which they definitely were not. The branches of the madronas spread out in broad, strong, beautiful arcs; I've never seen a tree more suitable to a tree fort than a big madrona.

Next to the parking lot was a map delineating the routes of various footpaths. The map did not mention a dinghy dock or a clam-digging spot. From the parking lot, we walked down a hill on a trail and came to an open grassy meadow the size of a couple of football fields. The meadow ended at a small harbor, which looked as placid as a backyard pond. There was an old white building in the meadow, with a U.S. Park Service sign out front. Although the sign said that the visitor center was not yet open for the summer season, I saw that the door was ajar. Inside, a gray-haired woman in a green fleece jacket was vacuuming the curtains.

"I'm sorry," she said. "We're not open."

I told her that I was wondering about the dinghy dock that separated the open clam-digging beach from the prohibited clam-digging beach. She didn't know what I was talking about. "This is my first summer as a volunteer," she said. "The only dock I know of is that one." She pulled the curtain she was vacuuming aside and pointed out the window to a small wooden structure floating in the bay.

We walked through the grass to the dinghy dock. Diana guilt-tripped me into relinquishing my rubber boots to Becca. I walked into the water on the other side of the dock, barefoot. The water was cold. I winced as crushed shells and sharp rocks cut into my feet. After a few unpleasant steps, I looked down and saw a mussel clinging to a rock. The mussel was the size and shape of a Brazil nut. This was the first mussel I'd ever noticed that wasn't for sale. Surely I'd seen countless mussels on docks and pylons before, but I'd never mentally registered one's presence until that moment, because I'd never been looking to eat one before. When I plucked it from the rock, it made a slight crackling noise like a weed being pulled out of the dirt. The crackling noise came from the mussel's connective threads, or byssus, which held it to the rock.

I consulted the regulations and found a description of the blue mussel, a circumpolar species that occupies both of the U.S. coasts and the shores of Western Europe. My shellfish license allowed me ten pounds of these babies a day—much more than I would need to prepare several of Escoffier's mussel dishes. I looked around and plucked another mussel from a different rock. We hadn't toted anything along to put our shellfish in, so I set the mussels on the beach and walked all the way back to the car. I got a two-liter pop bottle out of the trunk and used my Leatherman to cut off the top, then ran back to the dinghy dock to collect my catch. Diana and Becca were wading around in the water, looking for more mussels.

We had access to such a nice shellfish beach thanks to a dude named Lyman Cutler. Cutler killed a pig on San Juan Island back in 1859 because it kept getting into his potato patch. Cutler was an American, but the pig was British, owned by the

Hudson Bay Company. The 1846 Oregon Treaty had established a border between the U.S. and Canadian mainland at the forty-ninth parallel, but the agreement was vague about the cluster of islands between Canada's Vancouver Island and the territory of Washington. American and British citizens both lived on San Juan Island, tolerating one another's presence, until Cutler happened to avenge the destruction of his potato patch. The British came to arrest Cutler, but the Americans refused the British claim of jurisdiction. Each country backed up its argument with a battleship. The British garrisoned a small army at what would become our clam-digging spot. The Americans set up camp at the other end of the island. The confrontation became known as the War of the Pig, even though no shots were ever fired. The standoff lasted until 1872. It was resolved when an impartial mediator, Kaiser Wilhelm I, who was the king of Prussia and the emperor of Germany, sided with the Americans. The British left, and the Americans eventually turned the vacated British camp into a national park.

Kaiser Wilhelm I was responsible for another, to my mind, important event. During the Franco-Prussian War, Kaiser Wilhelm I led the army that held Auguste Escoffier as a POW. Years after that experience, Escoffier cooked for the kaiser's grandson, Kaiser Wilhelm II, on the maiden voyage of a luxury liner that was crossing the Atlantic. Wilhelm II was nervous that Escoffier might take revenge on him, but Escoffier assured the kaiser that he "wasn't on board to poison him." This gesture of Escoffier's demonstrates his ardent professionalism. Later Wilhelm II helped lead Germany into World War I, where Escoffier lost a son. After his son's death, it is rumored that Escoffier expressed regret about not killing the kaiser when he had the chance. Whatever the kaiser's sins against Escoffier, if it were not for Wilhelm I, I wouldn't have a beach on which to collect Escoffier's ingredients. Still, I wondered about my loyalties.

Mussels and clams are both bivalves, meaning they have two shells. Despite that similarity, the two shellfish have different habits. Mussels live out in the open, directly exposed to the water. I could walk around and pluck mussels quite freely. Clams, on the other hand, use an appendage called a foot to dig themselves way down into the mud, which makes them nearly impossible to find. As I surveyed the beach, I knew that I could be looking at thousands of clams. Or none at all.

The three of us poked around on the beach while we waited for the tide to go out. As it did, it exposed fresh mud. I noticed that spurts of water were shooting out of small orifices in the mud, like blasts from a squirt gun. Some of the orifices were as big around as a finger, while others were as small as pinholes. I jabbed my index finger into one of the larger holes. About an inch beneath the mud's surface, my fingertip met a slimy and very alive object that retreated from my touch. I shoved my finger in farther and caught up with the slimy object. It retreated deeper still into its lair. The object I'd touched was obviously a clam's siphon, which it uses to get oxygen and food. The hole left in the mud by the siphon led down to the clam in the same way that an electrical cord leads to an appliance.

I started digging down with one hand, following the siphon's hole until I was up to my elbow in muddy water, holding the top of a clam's shell, which was a handful in and of itself. I invited Becca to follow my hand down to the clam, to see what it felt like. She took hold of the clam and tugged and tugged, but it wouldn't come up. She got her other hand in there and really started working at it.

As the clam began coming loose, you could hear faint gurgling noises as water filled the vacant pocket. Becca hoisted a ball of mud, then rinsed it off. The horse clam was the size of her hand, minus her fingers. In response to getting hoisted out of its hole, the creature had drawn its foot and its siphon into its shell and clamped shut like a vacuum-sealed jar.

The success of our clam extraction inspired Diana to start digging at another orifice in the mud. Becca resumed digging too. At that moment I was probably the only guy in the world who was digging shellfish, which are not kosher, with two Jewish girls.

Diana's relationship with shellfish up to this point had been somewhat dynamic. Up until her third year in college, Diana counted shellfish among her list of top ten favorite foods. She had no problem slithering back a few raw oysters, and she'd happily munch on buffet-style peel-and-eat shrimp. Then she went to live in Israel for five months, and she gave up eating shellfish.

Jewish dietary law, called kashrut, prohibits the eating of fish that do not have fins and scales. For instance, shark, eel, clams, and oysters are *treyf,* or unfit for consumption. The Hebrew word *treyf* means "torn," probably in reference to animals that have been killed or mortally wounded by beasts. The dangers of eating infected or sick animals may have been a basis for Jewish dietary law. Kosher slaughterers, or *shochets,* consider all wounded animals to be *treyf.* They inspect the lungs of slaughtered animals for signs of diseases, past or present. If an animal has a lesion on its lung, it is *treyf.* The lungs should be unblemished and smooth. The Hebrew word for smooth is *glatt.* Nowadays, *glatt* refers to a very strict interpretation of kashrut. Juvenile sturgeon and swordfish have scales but lose them as they mature. If you're *glatt,* you don't eat swordfish and sturgeon. If you adhere to a less strict interpretation, you might say swordfish and sturgeon are okay.

Diana, traveling all over Israel, only once saw shellfish on a menu. She was in the northern city of Tiberias, on the shore of the Sea of Galilee. She ordered and ate the shrimp, then felt guilty, so she decided to stop eating shellfish. By the time she moved back to the United States, she had lost her craving for seafood altogether. As long as she wasn't eating her favorite form of meat, she decided not to eat any meat at all, *treyf* or otherwise.

So ostensibly Diana was just digging clams for the hell of it. She had no intention of eating them. I felt sad for her, bent over and breaking her fingernails all to pieces for something she didn't even want. I admired her open-mindedness and fortitude, though I felt a little manipulative because I was always getting her into these situations in order to turn her into an enthusiastic meat eater that I could span the years of my life with.

However, Escoffier himself was not above manipulating his guests. He went to great lengths to change the cautious eating habits of his clientele, especially of his female clientele. He and Ritz were annoyed that the refined Victorian women thought it was imprudent to be seen dining in public establishments. The partners overhauled their dining rooms to appeal to the tastes of upper-crust women. Using Ritz's wife as a model, they tinkered with lighting and lamp shades to find the most flattering combinations for the "delicate complexions" of ladies. They designed entrances that did not draw overt attention to guests and offered discreet corner seating. They decorated with a feminine touch, with lots of flowers.

And Escoffier tampered with their food. One of his lifelong clients was the leading French actress of his day, Sarah Bernhardt. Like many upper-class women, Bernhardt considered garlic taboo, because of the way the herb creates bad breath. On her birthdays, Escoffier would go to Bernhardt's hotel room and make her a simple meal of scrambled eggs. Some of Escoffier's biographers suggest that Escoffier pleased Bernhardt in ways beyond the culinary, as well. However, Escoffier was married to the same woman for most of his life and tried to maintain the appearance of fidelity. Either way, Bernhardt declared Escoffier's eggs to be the best in the world. Because he couldn't reveal to her that he was using garlic, he lied and said that the eggs got their taste from a special silver pan.

Another trick of his was to name dishes after fashionable women. Supposedly it was to pay homage to the women, but it had an effect not unlike hiring a pop star to pose in a certain brand of shoes. He named Melba toast and peach Melba after the Australian singer Nellie Melba. For Sarah Bernhardt, he created soufflé Sarah Bernhardt. For the Prince of Wales's wife, he made peach Alexandra. He made a rice pudding for Napoleon III's wife, Eugenie.

Rather than slipping a clam into Diana's tofu, or changing the lighting in my apartment, or naming a variation of an elk burger after her, I thought that exposure to fresh air and natural environments and outdoor labor would bring her around to being an omnivore. She certainly enjoys the outdoors; after all, she was out in the water digging for clams with a smile on her face. It seemed like the logical next step for her to eat one. Watching her dig, I thought of that old saying about how you can lead a horse to water but you can't make it drink. But, I thought, if you lead the horse to water a hundred times, and all the other horses are drinking, at some point it's bound to get curious. Escoffier may not have practiced this particular approach with the women in his life, but he certainly would have understood my motivations.

Scratching deep into the mud after horse clams, we kept turning up much smaller clams with textured, more solid shells. These were butter and manila clams. Butter and manila clams have to be an inch and a half in diameter to be of legal size. Most of the clams we found were big enough to keep. We carefully returned those that weren't to the mud.

The daily limit for clams was forty per person, no more than seven of which could be horse clams. It didn't take long to fill the two-liter container, at which point I started filling my little backpack. Once the pack was filled, we decided that we had all we would need. And my hands had taken as much abuse as they could. We all had shell fragments jabbed under our nails, which were bruised, and myriad little wounds on our fingers that looked and felt like paper cuts.

That night I prepped the clams and mussels for a trip back to Montana. Pooder took a few handfuls of the mussels and prepared one of Escoffier's mussel recipes for an appetizer. He cooked the mussels with onion, parsley, white wine, butter, and ground pepper, then thickened the cooking liquid over high heat and gave it a shot of lemon.

"Oh my God, Diana, you'd love these," Becca said.

Diana was drinking a beer and playing darts with Mark, but I could tell she was dying of curiosity. She came in for a closer look at the mussels and regarded them with interest. She asked if the mussels were cooked all the way through. They were. She opened a shell with her fingernail, which still showed the black grit and scratches from our expedition. She popped a mussel down, then had another. Then she ate a couple more. I didn't want to make her feel self-conscious about her conversion, so I tried to act laid-back and indifferent, the way people who don't do drugs behave around people who do. But just under the surface, I was jumping up and down with joy. Escoffier was helping me out.

The day after our clam-digging expedition, I went out beneath the lighthouse again and tried to catch a ling cod. That was the day I got run off by the killer whales. When I came up to the house, I could tell that Pooder was starting to pity me. He knew that I'd keep fishing until I either drowned or got what I was after. To save me from myself, he took a look at his tide charts and told me that the following evening would be a good time to give it another try. And he'd come along with me.

"We can ride the incoming tide northward a few miles," he said. "That's a good spot. It's deep. We'll fish through the slack tide, then ride back south on the outgoing tide. We'll get one."

In the early afternoon, we lowered the canoe off the rocks. The current was moving fast; it created a back eddy inside the cove. Once we paddled outside the cove, the current picked us up and we started hauling ass toward the north. Pooder set his line and started jigging.

"Try to feel the bottom with the weight," he said. "Lift it up, set it down, lift it up, set it down. Adjust your bait as we roll over the depth changes, so it doesn't drag along the bottom."

The canoe shot past the small cove and we skirted beneath a sheer cliff. We passed a couple of harbor seals on a rock. A flock of pigeon guillemots was feeding along the edge of a kelp bed. When the birds came up from a dive, they'd flick their heads with a gentle twitch to get the water off.

"I caught an octopus out here," Pooder said. "Accidentally. It wrapped itself almost completely around the canoe when I brought it up. Just grabbed on to the canoe. I could see arms over each side. It was, like, six feet long. Easily. It was changing into these crazy colors. And its mouth was full of scallops. It let all the scallops go when I pulled the hook out, then it dove straight down. All those scallops it dropped drifted back down behind it. It was crazy."

As Pooder and I drifted along, we caught small rockfish and

green ling. We kept a couple, but threw most of them back. We were after ling cod and tried to keep our eyes on the prize. We lost hooks and weights and loads of bait on the rocks. The lighthouse became a distant speck, way up the shore. The wind had switched and the waves were picking up considerably. They were getting so big and choppy that they'd now and then slap water over the gunwale. The current was way too strong to paddle against. I started to get nervous, and I kept anxiously checking our progress against the shore.

"If we had to, we could ride this current down about four miles and pull the boat out there," said Pooder. "There's a break in the cliffs with a little beach there. We'd have to walk back to the house. But I'm also worried that the current would change before we got to the beach, and then we'd be even more fucked."

We were discussing our options when Pooder's rod got slammed by a nice fish. We were zipping along at a good clip. We forgot about our predicament as the fish rose and dived, rose and dived. Pooder didn't try to force it, he just took his time. Once the fish was tired out, we lifted it into the boat with a net. It was a ling cod. I was so excited that I wanted to stand up and jump around; the only thing keeping me in my seat was the thought of rolling the canoe over and losing our fish. The ling cod was a mottled orange color. Because we couldn't get up and celebrate, we sat there and admired the fish. We were perfectly happy, and there really wasn't much to say. Finally Pooder broke the silence. "They've got big heads, don't they?"

He was right. The fish's head was grossly disproportionate to its body; it looked like it could turn around and swallow itself. Where we were fishing, a ling cod has to be between twenty-six and forty-four inches in length to be a legal keeper. Ours fit comfortably, at twenty-nine inches.

When a big wave slapped the boat, I was abruptly reminded of how scared I had been before the fish hit. The waves clearly were not letting up, and the wind was gathering strength. "Maybe we should get up against the cliffs," I said. "The friction there might slow the current down." We pulled in, but we could only get so close without getting smacked into the rock wall by a wave. The incoming waves bounced off the cliff at an angle. The ricocheted waves would hit other incoming waves and make a slapping noise and shoot sheets of water into the air. A thick foam was building up against the rocks.

Despite the confusion of waves, the current was slightly diminished near the cliff. We found that we could make some up-current progress by paddling our asses off. We took a few waves over the bow, but not enough to swamp the boat. We struggled around a point of land and caught an eddy inside a small cove. The eddy carried us a quarter mile back toward the lighthouse.

At the south end of the cove, we had to break out of the eddy and struggle against the current to round another peninsula. We then rode another eddy through another cove. We did this two more times. It took an hour, but we were making progress. After resting in a cove, we got all set to enter the current again. We pulled out.

But there was no current. The tide was slackening, just like Pooder had said it would. It had grown dark. We could see the beam from the lighthouse. Pooder and I paddled along, easily now, careful to keep the waves at a manageable angle to the canoe. When we got to the lighthouse, we had to do a kamikaze-style landing on the rocks. When a big wave washed in, we rode it in and slammed the bow of the canoe into a break in the rocks. I hopped out; Pooder and the canoe slid back out on the receding wave. He spun the boat around and rode the next wave in, backward. I grabbed the canoe as Pooder hopped onto the rock. We gathered up our gear and walked to the house. I burst through the door, hoisting the fish. Mark gave us a round of applause. We were alive, and we had a ling cod.

# CHAPTER EIGHT

# Hansel and Gretel

ANYONE WHO DOUBTS THAT PIGEONS ARE THE LEAST EXPLOITED food source in the country just needs to take a look around. Whenever you go to a bar, there's a pigeon cooing in the alley. Walk out of any airport and the first animal you're likely to see is a pigeon. Drive down the road and pigeons are flying overhead and walking down the sidewalks. If you step out of your apartment and step into some whitish goo, you guessed it—pigeons. As I tried to collect Escoffier's ingredients, the pervasiveness of the pigeon became like an ongoing insult about my failure to raise a real, genuine, flightless squab. After all, each and every pigeon that you see came up from a squab. To me, the skies and streets of America's cities seemed like a pageant of missed opportunities.

After much hemming and hawing, I had settled on Thanksgiving weekend as the official date of my Escoffier feast. It was still the spring—I had months to go—but I was feeling uptight and nervous about getting everything in order. Experience had shown me that producing squabs is a dicey enterprise, and I was hoping to get the whole affair over with before the fall hunting season. I'd be practically living in the mountains come September, and that's the one place where you don't run into pigeons.

As I walked around—down a sidewalk in a town, say—I'd often stop to observe the comings and goings of pigeons. If I was watching some pigeons, I'd usually look around to see if anyone else was watching them too. No one ever was. It was strange to think that I was the only person on a given street at a given time who was thinking about pigeons. If someone said that he thought about chickens a lot, you'd just think he liked chicken. But Americans draw the line with pigeons. In general, people just don't like them.

The unpopularity of the common pigeon is puzzling, especially when you consider that Americans once had such a keen taste for the passenger pigeon, which isn't so different. When Europeans arrived in what is now the United States, the passenger pigeon was the most prolific bird living here. Passenger pigeons occurred in such enormous numbers that early explorers had a hard time describing the flocks. Anytime you see the passenger pigeon mentioned in print, you're almost guaranteed to read a reference to how the passing flocks were thick enough to block out the sun's light for hours or even days on end. Twenty-five to forty percent of all avian life in this country was in the form of the passenger pigeon. Estimates peg their population at three to five billion.

The passenger pigeon's fate was sealed by the double-barreled problem of vulnerable nesting behavior and human greed. The birds nested and flocked in great colonies, sometimes swooping down en masse on farmers' fields to eat all of the crops. In turn, farmers netted the birds by the hundreds and fattened hogs with the carcasses. Professional market hunters also killed passenger pigeons. In 1878 the last great nesting flock was sighted near Petoskey, Michigan, not far from where I grew up. Witnesses have claimed that market hunters killed about seven million birds from that flock. From 1909 to 1912, the American Ornithologists' Union offered $1,500 to anyone who could find a nesting pair of passenger pigeons, but no one ever collected a cent of that money. The last living passenger pigeon, Martha, died at one p.m. on September 1, 1914, at the Cincinnati Zoological Garden.

Before they were wiped out, passenger pigeons were popular table fare with both the wealthy and poor classes. They were sent from hunting grounds to markets on the East Coast in refrigerated railcars. Many went to Delmonico's Restaurant, in New York City. Opened by a family of Swiss immigrants in 1827, Delmonico's was the first American restaurant not affiliated with an inn or tavern. Its menu was published in French and English. A lot of famous dishes originated at Delmonico's: eggs Benedict, lobster Newburg, Delmonico steak.

In its heyday, Delmonico's was the American capital of wild game eating. Under the command of the famous French chef Charles Ranhofer, the restaurant set the standard for American-style haute cuisine. It enjoyed an international reputation, and the menu included an array of distinctly American dishes, such as black bear and whitetail deer and jambalaya.

The restaurant enjoyed a ninety-three-year run of business, enduring address changes and many internecine battles within its family of owners. What it could not endure, however, were the changes occurring outside its doors. Prohibition, enacted in 1919, was a deadly blow: without legal access to alcohol for cooking, many popular wild game dishes had to be eliminated from Delmonico's menu. The other problem was the wildlife depletion of the late nineteenth and early twentieth centuries, which can be attributed to unregulated hunting and fishing and a woefully inadequate understanding of wildlife population dynamics. Many of the restaurant's early specialties became endangered rarities: diamondback terrapin, canvasback duck, striped bass, Atlantic cod. And, of course, the passenger pigeon. By the time Delmonico's closed its doors for good, on May 1, 1923, a proliferation of state and federal laws had banned the sale of wild animals and birds. Never again would a comparable wild game restaurant exist in the United States.

And never again would pigeons be a very popular food item, no matter the species. One might guess that Americans were so upset about the extinction of the passenger pigeon that they would no longer tolerate any form of pigeon slaughtering, but that's not the case. In recent decades, most major municipalities tried to wipe out the street pigeon with poison-laced food. Pigeons shit on monuments and cars and buildings and they carry all those skin mites and a handful of diseases. So pigeons are stuck in a weird limbo. They were brought here as food, to be cared for. Then they escaped and were turned loose, and now they've overstayed their welcome to the point where some people want to kill them in the least humane way possible, with poison. If pigeons can think, they've got to have one overriding thought on their minds: What the hell do these people want from us?

I MADE NEW PLANS TO RAISE AND FATTEN SOME SQUABS IN MILES City, Montana, 488 miles east of Missoula. My brother Matt had received his doctorate from Montana State University, in Bozeman, and taken a job as an ecologist with the U.S. Agricultural Research Service, a division of the USDA. He bought a small greenish-colored house with a big garage and a place for a garden. Diana and I moved all of our stuff there as well. Besides the rent-free living, Miles City seemed like a great place to continue my food search. It sits at the confluence of the Tongue and Yellowstone Rivers, on the Great Plains. Remote expanses of sandstone badlands stretch away from the rivers, which are lined with cottonwood groves and long, thin irrigated grain fields. Ranches, some occupied and others abandoned, are scattered across the landscape. The yards of the homes look like fertile oases, marked by shade trees of Russian olive and windrows of Lombardy poplar. In and around Miles City are herds of deer and antelope, and sage hens, grouse, wild turkeys, and pheasant. Masses of waterfowl come through in the fall and winter.

And there are loads of pigeons. One of the first things I did in Miles City was cruise around on Diana's bicycle to locate some flocks of birds. You can chase pigeons in the middle of the day in Miles City without worrying about upsetting anyone, because the citizens of Miles City are generally opposed to the existence of pigeons. In Missoula, residents might suffer the mild inconvenience of having to clean pigeon shit from their windshields, but in Miles City, a pigeon might shit in a grain silo and contaminate a hundred thousand dollars' worth of wheat. Hence, a pigeon hunter around Miles City is a do-gooder for the common man. I looked at an old railroad bridge spanning the Tongue River. A plethora of pigeons lived in the steel framework that rose in a high arc over the bridge. When trains came, the pigeons would flap around and buzz circles until the railcars passed. Between trains, I walked the rails out to the middle of the bridge and climbed up into the framework. As soon as I got up there, I heard a train coming and had to climb back down, then run along the tracks to get out of its way. I rode to an abandoned train depot and found where someone had poisoned a bunch of pigeons. The birds were lying around on the gravel beneath the buildings' busted-out windows. In town, I discovered more plausible hunting grounds. I found a pair of birds living behind the air-conditioning unit in the back alley of a place called the Cowboy Cobbler. The nest was slightly higher than I could reach. I rode back home to report my find to Matt. He and I drove to a store to purchase two fishing nets, which I taped to a pair of long wooden handrails that Matt had removed from a stairwell in his house.

Once it got dark, we drove down to the Cowboy Cobbler with an extension ladder and a box. At the count of three, we thrust the nets up to the two openings behind the air-conditioning unit and a pigeon flew smack into my net. Just as I moved my net to secure the one bird, another flew out and escaped into the night. We tucked the captured bird into the cage and set up the ladder. Matt ascended and then yelled down to me that something was moving in the nest. He reached into the nest, then pulled his hand back and squealed.

Matt's a big, strong guy, over six feet tall, almost two hundred pounds; he could whip Danny and me together in a fight, easily. It was unsettling to see such a physically imposing guy acting like a candy-ass about grabbing a hatchling. "Don't be such a candy-ass," I told him.

"Hey," he said, "you should respect my honesty. It's not like I'm trying to hide the fact that I'm afraid. Should I act like I'm not afraid in order to look cool?"

"No, I guess not," I said.

We switched places.

The two pigeons in the nest were fragile and gray and curled up into little muffin-sized balls. Their oversized beaks were soft and rubbery. Their bones felt like dried straw. Their wings were long and clumsy and had minds of their own, opening and closing and bending in a way that seemed neither voluntary nor beneficial. The birds' eyes were opened wide, but they didn't know enough to be afraid of us. I had one in each hand, and they made faint squeaking noises.

I moved toward the truck to reunite the birds with their caged parent. In their normal habitat, both male and female pigeons care for their young. In captivity, with plenty of available food and water, one parent can handle the rearing alone. I opened the door of the box to insert the two birds. The parent pigeon stormed the opening and blasted right through my hands. It hit my chest dead on, then fumbled in its flight. Matt made a swipe at it with his net but came up empty-handed. The pigeon disappeared.

"Holy shit," Matt said. "That pigeon just got away."

I was just standing there, slightly stunned, like some kind of idiot, holding the two baby pigeons. "Holy shit" was all I could think to say.

"Should we put them back in the nest?" Matt asked.

"I don't know," I said. "I really had my heart set on these squab, you know."

"But you'll have to feed them by hand. Try to imagine just how much of a pain in the ass that would be."

Thus far, I thought, my life had been organized in such a way as to avoid commitment and responsibility. I had no pets. I was unmarried and childless. I was not a home owner. I had no investments to look after. Clearly I had plenty of time to devote to feeding and caring for baby pigeons. But taking on that responsibility would corrupt my otherwise freewheeling lifestyle. I'd be like a farmer, tied to the farm.

On the other hand, I thought, what sort of wild game Escoffier blowout would I have if I didn't collect any squab? I'd plotted and sweated over baby pigeons, and now here I was with two fistfuls of them. What more could I ask for? I told myself to stop being a crybaby and to stick those birds in the box.

When we caught the two birds, Diana and Jen were having drinks down the road at the Montana Bar. We walked down there and told them the news. "They're really cute," I said. "You might as well not even look at them, though, because you'll just get attached, and you know what's going to happen to them in the end. Consider this a fair warning."

I went back to Matt's and started studying up on squab care. Thanks to a subculture of humans known as "pigeon fanciers," the Internet contains a bit of information about raising and caring for baby pigeons. Pigeon fanciers come in a variety of forms. Homing pigeon enthusiasts have Web sites devoted to racing competitions and discussions of which breeds of pigeons are fastest. Other sites have a more urban, park-bench motif, with chat rooms for people who like to stare at the pigeons nesting on their apartment windowsills. Some pigeon fancier Web sites explain how to raise pigeons just for the hell of it.

However, I did not find any Web sites for pigeon fanciers who want to eat squab. As I struggled with raising my two squab, I found myself returning time and time again to Pigeons.com, a Web site devoting much of its space to the civil rights of street pigeons. One article on Pigeons.com described "the plight of the feral pigeon." The article downplayed the health risks posed by street pigeons. There was an emergency posting on Pigeons.com for a petition drive to save street pigeons from "cruel and needless slaughter" by poisoning. The petition was addressed to the "U.S. Food and Drug Administration; U.S. Fish and Wildlife Service; Other Authorities and Bodies for which the following may be directly relevant."

The petition was the result of an incident that took place at an apartment complex in Miami, Florida. The managers of the complex hired pest controllers to kill the resident pigeons, probably with a poison called Avitrol. A local pigeon fancier tried to save two of the poisoned birds. She rushed one bird to the vet, but it died before the vet could get an activated charcoal solution down its gullet. When the rescuer got home, the other pigeon was dead. The rescuer described the death throes of one pigeon: "The look in her eyes is the most heartbreaking look I ever saw. God help us all, this world is just getting too bad."

I signed the petition.

Pigeons.com also has a photo gallery called The Loft, filled with pictures of baby pigeons. I found a photographic essay portraying the day-by-day development of a pigeon named Sara. Sara was born on May 12 and was the size of an egg. It's nearly impossible to determine a baby pigeon's sex by looking at it. Beside the first photo, Sara's owner writes, "We hope for a girl. I feed Sara every 2 hours a mix of baby bird formula and water. Oh Dear!"

The caption for Day 20 reads: "Looks like those feathers will need to fill in a little more before lift-off." In the photo, Sara stands on the palm of someone's hand, stretching. My two new pigeons looked just like the twenty-day-old Sara. I also learned from Pigeons.com that baby pigeons will begin feeding themselves at the age of thirty days. So, I guessed, my two new pigeons were about ten days away from being able to take care of themselves. The problem was, Diana, Matt, and I had to leave town for a couple of days, and my only recourse was to let Jen take care of the birds in my absence.

Jen is thirty-six years old. She tends to wear clothes made out of velvet. Her voice has velvety textures, as well; it is the voice of someone who would own cats, which, in fact, Jen does. Two of them. (She did own three, but she lost Goo in a custody battle with her ex-husband.) Because Jen loves cats so much, and because cats love to kill birds, I made the erroneous assumption (more like a hope) that Jen would not have a big soft spot for birds. Right away, though, Jen started asking if it was really necessary to butcher the squabs.

I tried to answer without answering. "Perhaps," I said, "but I'm not totally positive."

Diana attempted to warn Jen off. "Don't let Steve bullshit you," she said. "He's going to kill those birds no matter what. He's just using you so you'll feed them."

Diana was right; I was using Jen. But Jen didn't heed Diana's warning.

"What should we call them?" asked Jen.

"Nothing," I said quickly. "They're not pets. The important thing is to make sure the birds survive infancy. That's it, for now." But ultimately, Diana began calling the pigeons Hansel and Gretel, because she felt their plight bore a resemblance to the characters from the old fairy tale. I went down to the pet aisle in the grocery store and stocked up. I bought a bag of mixed birdseed and a sack of millet seed. I bought two eyedroppers, baby bird formula, a nutritional supplement for birds, and a bird drinking fountain. When we got home, I ground some birdseed in the coffee grinder and mixed it with formula. Jen made a daily routine of feeding the birds with the eyedropper and playing with them in the yard.

In my absence, the birds matured rapidly. Their beaks grew firm and sharp; their feathers filled out and took on shades of blue and black and white. When Matt and I got back to Miles City, we constructed a very nice pigeon coop against the garage. We dug holes for corner posts and cemented the posts in place. We screened the walls with chicken wire, hung two doors with homemade hinges, and shingled the roof. We furnished the inside with feeders and perches and nesting boxes. A pigeon couldn't have asked for a nicer home.

Once Hansel and Gretel were completely weaned and able to hop around from place to place, I fitted them each with a white ankle band and moved them into the coop. Since the birds had become self-sufficient, I assumed that Jen would lose interest in them. As an added assurance, Matt and I caught a few adult pigeons and put them into the coop; we hoped that Jen's love of Hansel and Gretel would be diluted by the other birds, and our plans for slaughter could proceed with minimal fuss. Things would not be so easy.

## CHAPTER NINE

# The Sacred Trinity

ONE DAY I WAS DIGGING THROUGH THE FREEZER FOR SOMETHING to eat when I came across a two-pound margarine container filled with something that wasn't margarine. I scraped the frost from the lid, revealing some writing from a purple marker. The penmanship was my brother's, but I couldn't make out what it said. I opened the tub and was surprised to find about forty frozen goose livers. Moisan and my brothers and I had shotgunned a bunch of Canada geese the year before, during the winter waterfowl migration along the Yellowstone River. We had eaten all the geese but had saved the livers for pickling. Pickled livers are a pretty good snack when you're sitting around drinking beer. Apparently I'd forgotten about the livers and no one had ever gotten around to putting them into a pickling brine.

Finding those goose livers was a potential but incomplete solution to a problem I'd been anticipating. Throughout *Le Guide Culinaire*, Escoffier mentions three ingredients almost relentlessly: foie gras, Perigord truffles, and beluga caviar. I'd come to think of the ingredients as the sacred trinity of haute cuisine. Escoffier used these three items so enthusiastically, and so often, that I was beginning to doubt whether a successful Escoffier meal could occur without them. But at the same time, I couldn't think of a reasonable way to obtain them.

While Christianity's Trinity—the Father, the Son, and the Holy Ghost—is said to enjoy an eternal, omnipresent existence, the sacred trinity of classic French cuisine is constantly plagued by diminishing supplies, exorbitant prices, and legal and ethical barriers.

Caviar, according to Escoffier, is "without doubt the finest of all hors-d'oeuvres." But when Escoffier said "caviar," he wasn't generalizing about just any ol' fish eggs. He used the beluga sturgeon of the Caspian and Black Seas. Now, the U.S. Fish and Wildlife Service lists the beluga sturgeon as threatened. The fish's population spiraled downhill after the collapse of the Soviet Union, in 1991; the fledgling breakaway nations did not have adequate resources to regulate the harvest, and poaching of the fish became a free-for-all. In the following years, the import caviar industry in the United States was rocked by smuggling busts, and the U.S. government has threatened to completely ban the importation of beluga caviar if the import industry doesn't clean up its act.

Perigord truffles do not face extinction, but no one's accusing them of overpopulation either. An underground fungus, truffles grow on or near the roots of certain trees and are harvested by an ancient method involving specially trained pigs and dogs. Obviously, I wasn't going to stumble into any truffles inside a frosty margarine container in my freezer. Among connoisseurs, truffles are rumored to be an aphrodisiac: they bring to mind the rounded, knobby shape of a man's scrotum, and they have an organic, earthy odor that allegedly resembles the smell of a brothel bed. The thing about truffles is, if you use them, you're not supposed to skimp. To fully appreciate all the effects of the truffle, gourmands insist, you must eat them in prodigious quantities. Colette, a French novelist of Escoffier's day who published some fifty novels exploring various aspects of female sexuality, felt about truffles the way some people feel about cocaine: if you're going to do it, you need to have enough to make it worthwhile. "If I can't have too many truffles," Colette said, "I'll do without truffles."

Nearly half the dishes I wanted to make called for truffles in some form, either as an essence or a garnish or a primary ingredient. There are about seventy varieties of truffles in the world, with thirty-two varieties in Europe, but many are considered unfit for consumption. Escoffier was adamant about his preference for the black truffles of the Perigord region of southwest France, which come in winter and summer varieties. The winter Perigord is the king of truffles, by far the most flavorful, but it's a rarity. The fungi have experienced declines in population due to deforestation, land development, the aerial spraying of pesticides on orchards and vineyards, and overharvesting. A pound of fresh winter Perigord truffles costs a couple of thousand dollars. So, I wasn't going to be buying "too many" of those.

And, lastly, the goose livers. Foie gras (pronounced *fwah-grah*) translates literally from French as "fat liver." Escoffier used foie gras in everything from pâtés to soufflés to mousses to hors d'oeuvres to main courses. The fattened livers come from domestic ducks and geese, both of which are perfectly abundant; if foie gras goes extinct—and it might, at least in America—it will be because of politics, not ecology.

Animal rights activists have a gripe with the methods of foie gras production. The birds' livers are fattened through methodical, forced overfeeding. Producers stick a tube down the throat of the fowl and pour in about a pound of corn a day. The birds are restrained from exercising, and the extra food is stored as fat in the liver. As the feeding regimen goes on, usually for about a month, the liver swells to about ten times normal size—to maybe three pounds for a goose. The transformation of the liver is almost metaphysical. In the first century AD, the Roman poet Marcus Valerius Martialis wrote a short, revealing epigram about his impressions of eating foie gras.

> When you see how the liver has swollen larger than the whole goose itself, you cry in surprise, "Hello, where have you come from?"

Animal rights activists have picked some impossible fights over the years. For example, People for the Ethical Treatment of Animals (PETA), the most outspoken animal rights group, has called for such measures as the termination of fishing and pet ownership; they say that even a cure for AIDS would not justify medical experimentation on animals. But in the foie gras battle, animal rights activists have an advantage: it's hard to argue that the sponsorship of a painful, deadly disease in livestock is not an abomination of animal husbandry. Here in the United States, there are only two foie gras producers: Sonoma Foie Gras in California's Central Valley, and Hudson Valley Foie Gras in Ferndale, New York.

At the time I was digging through the freezer and discovering my leftover, unfattened goose livers, Arnold Schwarzenegger, the governor of California, was considering a bill that would impose a statewide ban on foie gras production. He would later sign the bill into law, effective July 1, 2012.

After passage of the California bill, lawmakers in New York began pursuing similar legislation for their own state. In a global sense, foie gras isn't on the edge of extinction. France, Hungary, and Israel are the world's top three foie gras producers, so the United States is obviously not an imperative component of the industry. However, it seems that in the United States, eating fattened livers is becoming about as popular as eating fattened puppies.

Finding a tub of wild goose livers in my freezer didn't mean a domestic goose would be spared the pain of having corn shoved down its throat; I hadn't planned on using any portion of the trinity anyway, because I didn't think I could produce it on my own. However, finding the goose livers that were meant for the pickling brine made me wonder what real foie gras was all about. If people have been making it and poets have been discussing it for thousands of years, there must be something special about it.

My chance to try real foie gras came in San Jose, California. Diana had been awarded a creative writing fellowship at San Jose State University. In accordance with the terms of the fellowship, she was supposed to be "in residence" for the entire academic year. We went over there to scope the place out ahead of Diana's move. The city's streets were lined with palm trees. Discarded shopping carts abounded; one occupied most every corner. Our motel's parking lot was surrounded by a high fence and a gate. After checking in, we went for a walk to get something to eat. On East San Fernando Street, I stopped to read a menu that was pasted to the window of a restaurant called Stratta. The menu listed a foie gras appetizer with pickled bing cherries and a honey-sherry demiglace for $13.50.

Since the restaurant was expensive, we decided to go in just so I could have the foie gras, and then go somewhere else for dinner.

Inside, I asked the owner where he purchased his foie gras.

He said it was from the place called Sonoma Foie Gras, in the Central Valley. The waiter brought it to the table in a large, shallow bowl. The slice of foie gras was lying in the sauce, next to a couple of croutons. I dug in. It was the richest, fattiest, most obscenely delicious thing I'd ever tasted. What cheesecake is to dessert, foie gras is to meat. I could no longer hope that my regular ol' goose livers from Montana were even in the same category as these fattened and abused, soon-to-be-outlawed livers from California.

I thought about my upcoming feast, about how its authenticity would suffer without some real foie gras. What would Escoffier do? He'd buy the real foie gras. And he wouldn't give a shit who thought it was cruel. But I was willing to defy Escoffier on this one. I had wanted to try foie gras, but now that I had, I was no longer interested in it. I couldn't fully enjoy it, delicious as it was, because I knew I was eating a delicacy that had been produced through force-feeding. It was a double dose of gluttony: fatty and inhumane.

I felt like I learned a valuable lesson from the experience: while procuring my own food is enjoyable and healthy, there are some great tastes that just can't be replicated in the wild. But maybe there's a good reason for that: nature doesn't have much use for a duck that can't migrate a thousand miles, let alone a duck that's so fat it can't walk. When I kill a healthy wild duck that's cruising over a marsh, I get to sit down to a meal that offers more than just taste; that meal symbolizes the functioning apparatuses of the natural world. And that tastes pretty damned good to me.

When I decided to make some foie gras dishes with my regular goose livers, I started feeling like I'd broken up the trinity. I once heard someone compare the Holy Trinity to the shell, the yolk, and the white of an egg—separate but one. By making goose liver, I'd left the yolk and the white to themselves. I started devising plans to get them all back together at my feast.

Rather than contribute to the woes of the beluga sturgeon, I knew right off what I'd do for fish eggs. The summer before, I had spent a day with Ben and Joe Peterson, two fifth-generation commercial fishermen who live in Michigan's U.P. and fish the waters of northern Lake Michigan. Through their company, Fairport Fisheries, they market Great Lakes whitefish all over the country and have recently been processing the eggs as well. Just a few years ago, there was no market for whitefish caviar; the Peterson brothers threw the eggs to seagulls. But as the more traditional sources of caviar from Asiatic sturgeon vanished, consumers became more willing to experiment with alternatives. A market developed for whitefish caviar, also called American golden caviar, in part because the fishery is well regulated and sustainable. A European distributor agreed to purchase all of the caviar that Fairport Fisheries could get. Ben and Joe, who had never eaten whitefish caviar until they started selling it, agreed that it was pretty good. When I went fishing with them, they said I'd probably like it too. Now I was ready to take them up on their offer. Next to procuring my own whitefish caviar, getting some from the Peterson brothers was the best I could hope for. I'd been on their boat and watched them haul nets, and I'd cleaned fish in their shop, so I felt intimate with their operation.

The Petersons get up awfully early. Because of the time difference, I had to set my alarm for two a.m. one morning in order to call them at their dock before they left for a day's fishing. They promised to send me two pounds of *malossol*, or lightly salted whitefish caviar. "Tell me when you're ready for it," said Ben Peterson, "and I'll put it in the mail."

Getting an alternate variety of truffles wouldn't be as easy or as cheap as getting the caviar, so I reckoned that I might substitute morels in many of the dishes. My brother Matt was sitting on a surplus of dried morels, one of the most coveted fungi in the United States. Granted, morels are not known as aphrodisiacs, and they look more like human brains than human scrotums, but they do share some charms with the black truffle. Morels have a deep, earthy odor and a somewhat rubbery texture. In the arid West, they tend to sprout in the wake of forest fires that burn through stands of Douglas fir and lodgepole pine. In the spring that followed the great forest fires of 2001 (the fires dominated the national news for an entire summer), Matt camped up in the Bitterroot Mountains in western Montana and collected over a hundred pounds of morels. His mushroom-hunting expedition ended when a late snowstorm rolled through and buried his treasure. He came down from the mountains and dried his mushrooms on window screens, which compounds the potency of their odor. When you open a bag of dried morels, the smell fills the room.

Unfortunately, one of the things I most dearly wanted to make was *carpe à la ancienne,* and I knew morels wouldn't cut it for that dish. As Escoffier writes in *Le Guide, carpe à la ancienne* "borders on the realms of fantasy as far as the preparation of food is concerned." To build the dish, *Le Guide* says to remove the head and tail of a carp, then mix the flesh with butter to form a cream. After molding the cream back into the shape of the carp, you reattach its head and tail and garnish it with fish quenelles, poached oysters, button mushrooms, and *espagnole* sauce made with fish fumet. And truffles. Wearing that kind of getup, a carp would make the elegant and beloved rainbow trout of the Rocky Mountains look like a snaggle-toothed street beggar. But besides the truffles in the garnish, the whole damned five-pound carp is supposed to be covered in mock scales made from thinly sliced truffles. I did some quick calculations in my head, and determined that using Escoffier's preferred truffles would cost me about three hundred bucks in fake scales alone. That's a pile of money, especially since I was planning upwards of fifty or so dishes altogether.

Now, it's important to understand here that carp are the ugliest, lowliest, most despicable, cursed fish on our planet, or so I was raised to believe. Escoffier's description of a carp dish as bordering on "fantasy" puzzled me endlessly. To me, it seemed like pure fantasy to suggest that someone would eat one of the bastards. Carp prefer warm, stagnant water, and seem to have a special affinity for sewage-polluted cesspools. When I was growing up, eating carp was symbolic of human poverty, on a par with the sorts of horrible tragedies that befall the characters in Classical Greek theater. In the nineteenth century, the carp was introduced into the Great Lakes by fish culturists as a potential source of human food, but it never caught on as anything but a public nuisance. The fish proliferated over the years, unchecked by harvest, and wrought ecological havoc on the scale of Pandora's box. They killed off various aquatic plants and destroyed the spawning grounds of native fishes. Ecologists would like to see the extermination of the fish in the Great Lakes. Fisheries biologists sometimes kill off whole lakes' worth of carp with a fish poison called rotenone, accepting the loss of other fishes as "collateral damage." Bow hunters are welcomed by the state to shoot carp, which they often do, leaving the fish to rot.

So, naturally, I was anxious to try *carpe à la ancienne*. The dish seemed to perfectly embody what I loved about Escoffier's style of cookery. I marveled at the contradiction of a nasty ol' carp dressed up with such a beautiful name and elegant description. But cooking a carp seemed like a difficult feat. If I was going to properly resurrect the horrible carp and make it palatable, I couldn't risk screwing it up by having inadequate ingredients.

To start out, I went through a lot of trouble to get the perfect carp. I didn't want one of the nasty, warm-water carp you see in mucky swamps, so I tried to get one from the Great Lakes, where the bottom is sandy and the water is cool and fresh. First, Drost and I tried to shoot one with a bow and arrow in Grand Traverse Bay, but all we managed to do was nearly rip the motor off his skiff when we smacked the prop into a washing machine–sized rock. After that, some buddies and I went carp hunting in Lake Michigan with skin-diving equipment and spearguns. I hunted out along the Muskegon Pier in fifty-five-degree water, following a long line of rocks that forms a breakwater for a shipping channel. The tops of the rocks held sunbathers and vacationers; the bottoms of the rocks rested on the floor of the lake, forming small caves and crevices that housed a variety of fish.

I spotted a carp hovering near the bottom. I dove down, coming in from behind it. I pulled back the rubber tubing and launched my spear into the fish's side. The fish took off with the dart. I didn't have time to get another breath before chasing after it. I caught up with it and grabbed the dart like it was the fish's handle. I then got my index finger up into the carp's gill plate, so deep that my fingertip came out of its mouth. Its mouth was shaped just like a toilet plunger, and felt like one.

I rose up to the surface and made a loud gasping noise. Then I made some coughing noises and a retching noise because I'd gotten a bunch of goddamn water down my windpipe. My ears sounded like I had a seashell against them, because I hadn't adjusted to the pressure changes as I dove. I was hundreds of yards out from the shore, but only twenty feet from the breakwater. Exhausted, I swam over and tried to climb out. The waves were banging me against the rocks and the rocks were slimy as hell. I floundered and fought, with the carp bucking around on the end of my finger. I drew a small crowd. After battling the carp for a couple of minutes, I beached myself on a rock like a walrus and dragged the carp up after me. I nodded at the sunbathers and vacationers who were perched on the rocks. Then a wave plucked me from the rock and slid me back into the water. I crawled out again. Looking as nonchalant as possible, I walked along the phalanx of gawking beach-goers spread up and down the pier. Many of them shared with me how repugnant they thought carp were. One guy asked me if I like carp. I didn't want to admit that I didn't know, but I also didn't want to look like some idiot who can't tell a carp from an edible species of fish. I should have acted in control. I should have said that I was going to make Auguste Escoffier's *carpe à l'ancienne,* with poached quenelles and oysters and a truffle dressing. Instead, I said, "Hell, yeah!" and walked away.

# CHAPTER TEN

# Putting Up

THE HALIBUT ON THE END OF DANNY'S LINE FIRST APPEARED AS a distant white flash deep beneath the *Dilligas,* an aluminum landing craft that looks like the assault boat in the movie *Apocalypse Now.* The fish was moving so fast through the water that it vanished beneath the hull as quickly as a spring-loaded window shade that's been pulled down and released. I'd been leaning out over the gunwale, watching carefully for the emergence of the halibut. In the days I spent up in Saltry Cove, Alaska, fishing with my brother Danny and his buddy Ron Leighton, I'd taken a great interest in the visual trickery of things rising from the depths of the ocean. Whether we were cranking up a shrimp trap or a fish on a line, I enjoyed the moment when the ascending object first came into view beneath the boat. It happened in a surprising, beautiful way, and I would catch myself holding my breath as I waited for that initial glimpse.

The halibut reappeared, bursting into total clarity just a couple of feet below the surface of the water. The fish had been somewhere under the boat, and it rubbed against the hull as it emerged. I jumped back, startled. The fish was as long as

I am. It had a mottled gray upper side, tipped by two large eyes. The fish sounded, flashed its white, eyeless bottom side way down in the water, then vanished. Danny cranked on the rod, and the halibut rose again. Its head broke the water's surface, surely for the first time in its life. "It's not hooked good," said Ron Leighton. He was holding a six-foot stainless-steel harpoon. The detachable head of the spear was connected to fifteen feet of cable, which lay coiled on the deck. The cable was tied to a mooring cleat. Danny strained the rod to hold the fish's head at the water's surface. Ron leaned over and sunk the harpoon through the fish's gill plates as nonchalantly as you'd pierce a piece of lettuce from a salad bowl. As the harpoon sunk in, the fishing hook popped right out of the fish's mouth and flung up at us like it was fired from a slingshot. The fish dove, freed from the hook but carrying the harpoon head. It made a fifteen-foot free dive, gaining considerable speed. When the fish hit the end of its cable leash, the boat jolted like we had hit a log. *Ka-thump!* The vibration sent ripples fanning out from the *Dilligas*.

Ron turned around and leaned the harpoon shaft against the gunwale. He raised his eyebrows at me, as if to say, "That halibut ain't going nowhere now."

Ron Leighton is a Tsimshian Indian. He resembles, in shape and strength, the pylons that support his house over the tidal waters of Saltry Cove, Alaska, about thirty-five air miles west of Ketchikan. He was born in 1948. His hair is white and slightly wavy. His mustache is neither trim nor out of control. On his left wrist is a tattoo of a stylized wolf head—the symbol for his clan. He wears canvas pants and heavy cotton shirts. He changes his shirt every two days, but he changes his pants on a slightly more flexible schedule. He carries a penlight in his shirt pocket. His suspenders are S&M

grade—black and thick and trimmed with leather. He wears key-chain flashlights on the right and left straps of his suspenders, hanging from swiveling metal rings. The flashlight on his starboard side casts a green light. His port-side flashlight is red. "You see," he once said to me, "I'm wired just like a boat."

With the halibut tethered off, Ron strolled purposefully back to the wheelhouse and emerged with a .410 Snake Charmer shotgun. He stopped to have a sip of his beer. We'd been out on the *Dilligas* for several hours. So far, everything had played out in precise concinnity, and Ron Leighton wasn't about to get all excited just because we had a big fish thumping around beneath the boat.

Earlier in the morning, we had pulled up about a hundred pounds of shrimp in Ron's traps. To visualize one hundred pounds of shrimp, imagine a large washing machine full of them. Once the traps were checked, we motored out to a marker buoy that Ron had anchored in a large bay. The buoy marked a place where he often finds halibut. We went through the whole tub of shrimp, popping off the heads. We iced the tails and packed the heads into two burlap sacks, along with a couple of volleyball-sized rocks. We tied the sacks shut with nylon cord, leaving enough extra cord to tie a loop at the head of the sack, like a handle. After lowering the door of the landing craft, we dragged the sacks to the front of the boat and slipped the anchor line through the loop. I pushed the sack overboard with my foot and the three of us watched it slide out of sight. We were in 360 feet of water. Ron said, "Crabs'll rip that burlap right open, once it hits bottom."

With the chum doing its work, we set our lines and waited for halibut. Our hooks were baited with salmon bellies and octopus tentacles. After a while, one of the rods jumped a few times, like how a branch dances when a squirrel is running along it. I leapt toward the rod.

Ron said, "Don't touch it. Let him take it good. You don't want to set the hook until he's pulling out line."

The rod bucked again, like it might get tugged into the water, but no line pulled out.

"Now?" I said.

"No."

"What do you think is going on down there?" I asked.

"I think there's a fish down there fucking with your bait, is what's going on," Ron answered.

Wham, the fish fucked with the bait again. This time, though, it got a good bite of the hook and began stripping out line. My brother Danny grabbed the rod. Danny's a couple of years older than me, in his early thirties. He looks sort of like a rough-hewn marathon runner. He cuts his own hair, short and trim, and he's usually sporting a five-o'clock shadow. He was wearing a pair of blue swimming trunks and rubber knee boots. The fish moved away from Danny in slow starts and abrupt stops, like a garbage truck making its rounds from house to house. Danny would gain a little line on the fish and the fish would gain it all back. After twenty minutes, the fish started to come in. Not like it was losing the battle, but more like it had just decided to locate the source of this annoyance. Eventually I saw the quick flash of white zipping beneath the hull.

When Ron came forward with the .410 shotgun, he told me to put on a pair of gloves and pull the cable up. I lifted the fish toward the surface. It swam in large circles, like an airplane's holding pattern. When the fish flattened out on top of the water for a moment, Ron put a slug into its brain. I dragged the fish around to the lowered door of the landing craft, and Danny and I heaved the body aboard with a gaff. Ron Leighton lifted the fish's gill plate. The plate was as big around as a human head. He took a long knife and severed the gills. A stream of blood flowed across the deck of the *Dilligas* and coagulated in the sun. The fish's flops grew weak and stopped altogether.

IF YOU LIKE SEAFOOD—BE IT SALMON OR SHRIMP OR CRAB OR halibut or sea cucumbers or scallops or mussels or clams— then you're probably going to wish you were friends with Ron Leighton. I became friends with Ron Leighton through a pint-sized jar of his smoked octopus. A few years ago, Danny came down from Alaska to visit me in Montana. He had the jar of octopus in his duffel bag. Danny's an ecologist at the University of Alaska, and just before he came to Montana, he had traveled by floatplane to Prince of Wales Island, to sample water quality and levels of biodiversity in the small, unnamed stream that drains into Saltry Cove. Ron Leighton took a great interest in Danny's work, because the stream is where he and his wife, Joan, get their drinking water. The U.S. Forest Service was planning to log off the forest above Ron's house. While Danny worked at Saltry Cove, filling vials and taking measurements, he stayed in Ron and Joan's guest cabin. Ron is a subsistence hunter and fisherman, meaning that the bulk of his food comes from the wild. In the evenings, Danny would tag along with Ron to check shrimp traps. A shrimp trap can hold hundreds of shrimp; octopuses sometimes squeeze in as well to gorge on the catch. When Danny left Saltry Cove, Ron Leighton tucked a couple of jars of smoked octopus into his bag as a souvenir.

The arms of the octopus had been diced, the way a grownup might cut up hot dogs for a kid. The slices ranged in diameter from a fifty-cent piece to a dime. Ron brined the pieces in sugar and salt, smoked them over alder, and pressure-canned them in glass jars. The result: one of the best things I've ever eaten. The octopus was firm and rubbery to the touch but melted away under the pressure of teeth. The flavor was mild and smoky. The taste of the octopus itself was so faint I had to chase after it, but I managed to catch it with every piece. I've long counted shrimp as my favorite food, and it was a pleasure to learn that such a delicious treat as smoked octopus was a side benefit to being a shrimp trapper.

Once I started going full-bore on collecting the stuff from *Le Guide Culinaire,* I often thought of Ron Leighton and his smoked octopus. It occurred to me that he might be a good man to visit. I asked Danny to arrange a trip. He said that he'd see what he could do. Once late June rolled around, Diana flew out to the East Coast to visit her grandma and I made my way up to Alaska to meet Ron Leighton.

Prince of Wales Island, where Ron and Joan live, is the second-largest island in the United States. It is 2,231 square miles, about half the size of Hawaii Island. The island sits near the southern end of the Alexander Archipelago, the string of 1,100 islands that forms the Alaska Panhandle. In 1879 the naturalist John Muir traveled through the archipelago by steamship and wrote that the islands are so numerous "that they seem to have been sown broadcast." The Panhandle is characterized by rain forest, rocky islands, and narrow ocean passes. Alaskans refer to the area generally as Southeast. Like much of Alaska, the hinterlands of Southeast are a bitch to get to. I had a layover in Seattle, then flew up to the town of Ketchikan, on Revillagigedo Island. Ketchikan is a Tlingit word that probably means something like "spread wings of an eagle." The town itself spreads along the shore in a long thin band, squashed between the water and the mountains. The population is about fifteen thousand. Economic boom and bust cycles in lumbering, mining, and fishing roll through the town like weather patterns.

Danny flew from Anchorage to meet me. To get from the Ketchikan airport to downtown, Danny and I had to catch a small ferry. From the ferry landing, we took a cab to the float-plane docks at the northern end of town. We purchased some produce and beer as a gift for the Leightons, then chartered a small floatplane to fly us westward, toward Saltry Cove. The plane flew at one thousand feet in a cloudless sky. Looking down, I could see water and small islands. The wet, barkless drift logs floating in the water reflected the sun as brightly as automobile windshields. After cutting a wide half circle, the plane dropped down below the tops of the hills and entered the mouth of Saltry Cove. We touched down in choppy water, then taxied to a floating dock that was about the size of a high school classroom. I could see Ron and Joan's house at the end of the bay. It stood about ten feet over the water at high tide. Joan had stepped outside. She was waving. Two enormously fat chocolate labs danced around her feet, panting and wheezing and snorting and barking. I watched Ron walk across the rocks on his beach and climb into a small skiff. When he motored up to the plane's mooring dock, I shook his hand and told him how much I enjoyed his smoked octopus.

Until I met the Leightons, I had been a little apprehensive about my visit. Joan and Ron live in the wilderness; they have to constantly work their asses off to ensure a steady supply of food, water, and heat, and I could just imagine what they would think of me: here comes this guy from the lower forty-eight who wants to fly 1,300 direct miles by jet and floatplane to trap a few pounds of shrimp and crab for some highfalutin

French dinner he's planning. On the contrary, though, Ron and Joan Leighton were stoked about having visitors who were interested in their lifestyle. The way they saw it, I guess, I was a hunter-gatherer and they were hunter-gatherers, and we might as well hang out and get to know each other.

When Danny and I climbed up to the house from the beach, Joan gave Danny a big hug. "If you're Dan's brother, you get one too," she said. Joan was born in 1931, in Oakland, California, seventeen years before her husband. She has a strong hug, and bright, beautiful silver hair. Her T-shirt had a wolf airbrushed on the front. Her eyes are sharp; they are the eyes of someone who concentrates on what she's doing. When she walks, she gives each step a careful consideration before taking it, probably because of the circumstances of her "yard," which is an elevated wooden platform with no rails and two frantic canines hopping about.

Joan gave Danny and me a brief tour of what would be our home base for the next few days. The Leighton homestead consists of a house and seven outbuildings, spread along a series of gangplanks and platforms built over the high tide mark. Behind the buildings, a steep rocky slope rises from sea level to a thousand or so feet. To live in the wilderness with full, modern comforts requires mechanical skill and a willingness to build things. When Ron and Joan bought their place on Saltry Cove, the homestead was nothing but a small cabin.

They added on to the cabin, building both out and up. Walking north from the house along the elevated platforms, we traveled either through or past the rest of the structures: a reserve tank house, for water storage in case the stream froze or ran dry; a storage shed full of meat-processing equipment and a chest freezer; a woodshed with nine cords of split and stacked driftwood; another storage shed with fishing equipment and a freezer full of bait; a powerhouse with a hydroelectric generator wheel, piping and duct work, a diesel generator, two banks of 24V batteries, and an electric transformer and inverter; a work shed stuffed to the gills with tools and maintenance equipment; a greenhouse full of various root crops and vegetables; and, finally, a guest cabin.

The equipment and materials at the Leightons' home didn't just show up on a truck one day. Ron builds with driftwood, especially yellow cedar. Whatever materials didn't wash up on the beach had to be purchased from the village of Kasaan and brought in on the boat. Pronounced *kuh-SAHN,* the village is a ten-mile trip by water from Saltry Cove. Kasaan serves as the Leightons' port of call and shipping address. The village population is forty-three. Roughly one-half of the residents are Native Alaskans, mostly Haida. Before Ron and Joan moved to Saltry Cove, in 1995, Joan ran a community health clinic in Kasaan. She moonlighted as the mayor of the village, an elected position.

Every week Ron takes the *Dilligas* to Kasaan to pick up mail and supplies. He used to serve as the president of Kasaan's tribal council. Now he often brings fish and game to the village in order to help feed the elders. The trip takes him about thirty-five minutes, depending on the weather. Storms are common. Sometimes the trip has to be postponed indefinitely. Thus Joan doesn't take gifts from the mainland for granted. She was excited that Danny and I brought out some fresh produce. We were in the kitchen, where Joan was preparing dinner. Ron wasn't planning any excursions that evening, so he went outside to pound nails into a scaffold that he was building so he could paint the house. "We don't have a lot of control over the quality of our produce," Joan told us. "I grow whatever I can, of course or I can order it and pay to have it flown out here from Ketchikan, which is expensive. You're essentially paying for it twice. Usually we make do with whatever's available in Kasaan."

If Joan feels that she lacks control of her produce on Saltry Cove, she makes up for it by exercising maximum control of her fish and game. Instead of a conventional kitchen where store-bought food is prepared and eaten, the Leightons' kitchen was more like the processing room at a meat and fish wholesaler. They had deep, industrial sinks, canning equipment, grinders, large tubs, a vacuum sealer, scores of knives and sharpening steels, and heavy chopping blocks.

Joan was peeling a pound of shrimp tails and carefully wrapping them in thin strips of smoked bacon. "You'll see that we do a lot of different things with shrimp," she said. "I hope you like them." With the wrapped pieces laid out, she began peeling another pound for addition in a tomato sauce that was simmering on the stove.

Next Joan sliced open a vacuum-sealed freezer bag and slid a halibut steak onto a platter. The piece of fish weighed several pounds. The flesh was white, nearly translucent. "Halibut's a forgiving fish," Joan said. "You can't mess it up. We froze this a month ago, but it will keep in the freezer for six months and you wouldn't know the difference. I bread it with this Japanese stuff—I think it's puffed rice that's been crushed down—and I just bake it. Four hundred degrees. Once it's baked, we'll take the leftovers and mash it with onions and dressing for sandwiches. Ron takes them on the boat. Halibut's also good smoked. You wouldn't guess that, would you? Ron brines it and smokes it. Almost like smoked salmon, but not so strong. We'll even lay thin slices of halibut out in the sun and dry it just like that. Right out on the deck. It's good."

"Where'd you catch that fish?" I asked.

"Just outside the cove."

Joan slid the fish into her oven, stirred the tomato sauce. She poured Danny and me a glass of white wine from a box of Franzia. She gave us some dried seaweed to munch while we waited for dinner.

IN THE MORNING, WITH OUR HALIBUT SANDWICHES PACKED INTO a cooler, we drove the small skiff to the floating dock and boarded the *Dilligas*. The *Dilligas* is perhaps the ugliest boat I've ever been on. The boat is not intended for comfort. It's twenty-three feet long, built entirely of welded aluminum. The *Dilligas* does not have one delicate line, embellishment, or decorative touch. There are no seats or cushions. The wheelhouse is a three-sided aluminum box with Plexiglas windows. Ron designed the boat and hired a guy in Ketchikan to put it together. All the welds are as thick as a thumb. *Dilligas* is an acronym: Do I Look Like I Give A Shit.

The day before Danny and I showed up, Ron had set ten shrimp traps in a nearby cove where he usually gets good catches of spot shrimp. Heading out to pull those traps, we motored out of Saltry Cove. From behind the Plexiglas, Ron surveyed floating logs with his binoculars. When a particular log catches his eye, he ties it off to the *Dilligas* and tows it home. Floating timber is not the only thing that catches Ron's eye. We saw a sow black bear. She had a young cub no bigger than her own head. We stopped to study an outcropping of white quartz that Ron was very curious about. The quartz was impregnated with many metal flakes, so that it looked like a gigantic set of human molars with substantial dental work. Ron pointed out a pod of porpoises crossing the mouth of a strait. He showed us a string of eight landslides that had eroded a hillside in the aftermath of a large logging operation. "Look at that bullshit," Ron said. We stopped for several minutes and stared at the destruction.

As we traveled, I quickly became lost. We rounded point of land after point of land. Prince of Wales Island is only half the size of Hawaii, but it has four times as much coastline. Deep bays and inlets nearly cut the island in half in many places. It was difficult for me to discern which land belonged to Prince of Wales and which land was part of another, smaller landmass. We pulled into a long inlet that seemed to end at the base of a single timbered mountain. As we neared, the mountain split into two and a channel opened. We entered a waterfilled canyon, then emerged on another body of open water. We followed the shoreline, made a sharp left, and entered another narrow bay. This one was different, though, because it was dotted with ten orange buoys.

Ron throttled the motor back. He yelled at me to catch the first buoy with a gaff. He kept the buoy off to the port side, and I reached out to snag it. Ron came up and slung the buoy line over an electric pulley hanging from the wheelhouse. He threw the switch.

"Coil that line *neatly* in the tub," yelled Ron. He pointed at a large garbage can beneath the pulley. Getting the line to coil in the bottom of the tub was like trying to keep a litter of kittens all in one place for a photo. The line came and came, until the tub was nearly full.

Ron looked at my work. "That's a bowl of spaghetti, not coils."

"How deep is it here?" I asked. My arms were getting tired.

"Sixty fathoms."

"What's a fathom?"

"A fathom is six feet."

"That's a lot of line."

"That's why you're supposed to coil it *neatly* in the tub."

As I made a mess of the line, I took a few glances over the side of the boat. The line descended and faded from view. After several more minutes I looked again, and a shrimp trap was taking form far beneath the boat. I coiled a few more wraps and took another look. The trap emerged as a mesh disk, as wide and deep as a tractor-trailer tire. The disk rose toward me through the water; in the bottom, a swirling mass of reddish objects spun and dodged, like a psychedelic kaleidoscope. As it burst from the water, Ron threw the switch and swung the trap into the boat. The trap held an orgy of shrimp. The orgy was four or five inches deep. The shrimp, all flipping and flapping and drenched with water, made a noise like a car driving on a wet road.

Ron opened the door and Danny helped him tip the catch into another tub. The shrimp poured out, along with a length of salmon spine, including the tail fan—the remainder of the bait. The bone had been cleaned by the shrimp to museum-quality specifications. Danny fastened a fresh, two-pound piece of salmon inside the trap with an overgrown safety pin and hurdled the trap overboard. One down, nine to go.

I sorted through the shrimp in the tub. The spot shrimp were huge. Cradled in my hand, as much of a shrimp would hang over the sides of my palm as would fit into it. Each had a large pair of spots on the upper tail. Ron told me and Danny that, in a few months, toward October, these spot shrimp would be laden with eggs. "The eggs are real good," he said. "They develop under the tail; you can suck them right off the tail. They're like bubbles. They pop in your mouth. But I don't like to catch too many like that. I don't like killing all those eggs, you know. Those are the new shrimp."

Apparently, a piece of dead salmon lying on the bottom of the ocean at sixty fathoms was appealing to many things besides shrimp. There was a little fish in the trap. Danny identified it as some sort of sculpin. Ron said to flip it overboard. There were two different types of crab. One was a small blue crab that looked edible. Overboard. The other crab looked like a spider. Overboard. A sea star had climbed inside the trap to eat the shrimp. The sea star must have thought it landed in paradise. It had shrimp antennae sticking out of its mouth. Overboard. I found a small scallop. "Holy shit," I said. "A scallop." Its shell was two inches across. I had the beginnings of Escoffier's scallops parisienne. I showed it to Ron. "Is this considered a bay scallop or a sea scallop?" I asked.

"If a gull is flying over the sea, what is it?" he replied.

"A seagull, I guess."

"So if a gull is flying over a bay, what is that?" I started to answer, then just smiled like an idiot.

Ron looked at the scallop. "We get scallops around here bigger than your hand," he said. "Throw that poor little thing overboard."

I found a handful of coonstripe shrimp. They were smallish and delicate, just two inches long.

"Joan feeds those to the cat," said Ron. "Save those."

RON'S MATERNAL GRANDMOTHER, A TSIMSHIAN NAMED EMMA, traveled and fished the waters of Southeast Alaska by dugout canoe. Emma was born south of Ketchikan, in the Canadian waters of British Columbia. When the United States purchased Alaska from Russia, she traveled north with a small party in order to live in U.S. territory. Her people established a village called New Metlakatla, on Revillagigedo Island.

Except for his service in Vietnam, as a helicopter crew chief through 1966 and 1967, Ron has spent his life on the same islands and waters as his grandmother. Ron was born in Ketchikan. His father, an Irish-American police officer, died when Ron was just a kid. Looking back, Ron thinks his dad must have died from undiagnosed colon cancer. His mother painted totem poles to help support her family. As a kid, Ron pitched in by cutting cheek muscles from the heads of halibut carcasses discarded by a waterfront cannery. The cheeks are a local delicacy; he sold them to restaurants for forty-nine cents a pound. One day he caught a gigantic halibut off the cannery's own dock. A cannery worker used a forklift to haul the fish in. Ron sold the halibut to the cannery. He was eight years old. At fourteen, he started working on an uncle's commercial salmon-fishing boat.

In Ron's mind, he is bound by ancestry to protect the land and water where he lives. Like his father, he worked for the Ketchikan police. He left the force in 1987. In 1988 he started a group called SEACOPS (Southeast Alaska Coalition Opposed to the Pirating of Salmon). SEACOPS had a gripe with Asian fishing vessels, which were abusing international water boundaries to target juvenile fish that would otherwise mature and return to American and Canadian waters. Ron traveled back and forth to Washington, D.C., ten times, and made his case to anyone who would listen. Listeners included the State Department, members of the Senate and Congress, and even the Soviet ambassador to Washington.

Ron would come back from Washington with blisters on his feet from walking from one office to another. SEACOPS finally had their grievances addressed when Congress stiffened trade embargoes on offending nations, forcing a reduction in the use of high seas drift nets. Ron attributes his successes in Washington to the fact that he wore his wool halibut-fishing shirt. "They see suits all day long down there," he explained. "My clothes got their attention."

Ron's deep regard for the landscape is also reflected in the careful, considerate way that he handles his food. Ron has a cool term for the process of preserving meat and fish. If an item isn't to be eaten fresh, it gets "put up." The Alaska Department of Environmental Conservation once asked Ron to design and conduct a course for the citizens of Ketchikan on the proper methods of putting up fish and game. I imagine Ron's course was a tremendous success. His interest in putting up salmon easily exceeds a banker's interest in putting up money. If you mention your mom's tomato garden to Ron, he'll ask how she puts up her surplus crop. If you mention antelope hunting, he'll want to know if you have to put up antelope differently than you put up deer.

To put up seaweed, Ron places the plants on racks and dries them in the open air. Venison gets put up in vacuum-sealed bags. He dries or cans whatever venison he doesn't freeze. He does his canning with glass jars. He prefers Kerr brand jars over Ball, but he likes the seals and lids produced by Ball better than those produced by Kerr.

Most of the halibut gets put up frozen in vacuum-sealed bags. He puts up shrimp in heavy-duty Ziploc freezer bags, because the sharp spines on a shrimp's tail can puncture vacuum-sealed bags. Octopus gets smoked, then put up in pint-sized glass jars. He puts up salmon, both smoked and fresh, in vacuum-sealed jars. He even puts up salmon spines. He places the bones in jars, stacked upright like Vlasic pickle spears. He pressure-cooks the spines for so long that the bones turn soft and digestible. One night over dinner, Joan showed me a cabinet full of salmon spines and said of them, "It's good calcium."

Ron puts up his Dungeness crabs in the freezer after cooking them halfway through. One day he took Danny and me out in the *Dilligas* to catch a few crabs. At the back of a bay, Ron showed us where a freshwater stream dumps its load into the ocean. "This stream gets good salmon runs," he said. "All those salmon die after they spawn, and the carcasses wash down, and the crabs come in here and pig out on carcasses. Big, big shrimp too. Sometimes they're right in the shallows with the crabs. Four, five fathoms. I get shrimp here up to nine inches long, not counting the antennae. Ten of those tails to the pound." He gestures off to the distance. "A shrimp that big makes those shrimp we were catching look like babies. Who knows where those shrimp are now, but the crabs stay in here year round."

Outside the stream mouth, in twenty fathoms of water, we set four crab traps. The traps were round, three feet in diameter, and had two funnel-shaped openings. Crabs climb into the trap to snack on salmon, but they can't find the opening to get back out. The next morning we pulled the traps and had thirty-two Dungeness crabs, and they were big ones. They weighed a couple of pounds apiece.

Ron set up a large propane burner with a five-gallon kettle of water on the deck of the house. He added salt to the water until it was as salty as soup broth. Dungeness crabs are known for delicate, sweet-tasting flesh. "If the water's not salty enough," said Ron, "you lose that sweetness. I don't understand why."

The water came to a rolling boil. Ron placed six crabs in the kettle basket and lowered them in. He checked his watch. "You should cook these crabs for twenty minutes," he said, "*if* you're going to eat them fresh. If you want to put them up *whole*, like how we're doing so you can bring them home, you cook them for ten minutes now. Then we bag them and freeze them. You thaw them in cold water and cook them another ten minutes before eating them. And remember to salt the water good the second time too, or you'll lose that sweetness."

HALIBUT FISHING DOES NOT END WITH THE HALIBUT'S GETTING lugged up to the boat. After Ron sliced open the gills on Danny's big halibut, we waited for as much of the blood to drain as possible. Ron washed the gaff and the harpoon head with salt water. "Getting that blood out of the fish keeps the meat whitish and clean, not red and splotchy like you sometimes see it," he said.

Once the fish was good and bled out, Ron blocked up a sheet of plywood on the deck of the *Dilligas*. We lifted the fish up to this workbench and gently set it down.

"Don't bend the fish and mess with it too much when it's going through rigor mortis. Let it set up naturally, or you'll break down the fibers and make the flesh mushy," Ron said. "I was down in Pikes Market, in Seattle, watching those idiots throw fish around to impress tourists. What idiots. That's the worst thing you can do with a fish. If the fish wants to curl, let it curl. It don't need to be flat."

Ron showed me how to remove the halibut's fillets in four large pieces, each about as big around as a person's lower leg and twice as long. It was beautiful meat. We skinned the pieces and cut them down further. The flesh filled two five-gallon pails. We poured ice over the top. "Now put that meat in the shade," said Ron.

I cut open the halibut's stomach to see what it had been eating. It was stuffed nearly full with our shrimp heads, along with a couple of crabs. "See that," said Ron. "Everybody's down there eating each other."

Before too long I caught a small shark and cranked it up to the boat. Ron said that kind of shark isn't too good to eat. "It's got the same stuff in it that's in your piss. Urea, I think is what it's called."

"You don't have to eat it," I said. "I'll eat it."

"Go ahead then, you can keep it. But you better climb into the water with it, because you're not bringing that smelly son of a bitch up on my boat."

We popped the hook and the shark darted back toward where it came from. As it disappeared, Ron suggested that we head in. With a good load of shrimp and halibut on board, he didn't want to sit in the hot sun and risk spoiling our food.

Joan was hanging out at the house when we got home that day. She doesn't spend too much time out in the boat. Instead, she takes her time away from Ron to work on her paintings and drawings. She does landscapes and portraits. She often works with sepia, or octopus ink, taken directly from Ron's catch. She learned to draw from a Jesuit priest who volunteered at a hospital in Ketchikan where Joan used to work. The priest encouraged her to take a few community college art courses. She began showing her work at various Alaskan galleries back in the mid-1970s, when she was still a nurse.

Joan moved to Alaska in 1957. She discovered the state through her work as a flight attendant for Western Airlines, back in the fifties. She flew routes up and down the Pacific Coast. "They didn't have stewards back then," she said. "Just stewardesses. To keep the job, you couldn't be married, your hair couldn't touch your collar, you had to wear a panty girdle, you had to be thin. You couldn't accept tips, unless the tip was over fifty dollars. That qualified as a gift, and you could keep it. I was very naïve." She gave me a knowing look. "I was afraid to sleep alone in the hotel rooms."

When she settled in Ketchikan, she trained for work as a nurse. She learned to put in stitches by sewing up cuts on a severed and shaved pig's foot. In 1959, when Joan was twenty-eight, an eleven-year-old boy came into her hospital with a spike through his foot. The boy had been helping his uncle rebuild a house when he took a bad step. After the boy was fixed up, he went home and told his mom that he was going to some-day marry the nurse. The boy's name was Ron Leighton.

Ron and Joan didn't marry until 1973, after they had each had children with other, ill-fitting partners. They each maintained custody of their own children, and they raised their kids together. After Ron's retirement from police work and commercial fishing, they turned to the subsistence lifestyle. Their love has seen them through countless pounds of shrimp, crab, and halibut.

Joan was filling a large steel sink with water before we even had our day's catch of shrimp and halibut up to the house. Ron wanted to handle the shrimp first. The halibut would be easy, because the meat was ready to be sealed and frozen. The shrimp needed a good washing in fresh water, to clean up the residue from when we popped their heads.

Ron washed the shrimp by holding them beneath the stream of water. He handled them delicately, as if he were playing with the contents of a friend's aquarium. "Your catch is valuable," he told me. "Treat it with respect." He filled Ziploc bags with the tails, two pounds per, now and then picking out a coon-stripe shrimp for the cat. Ron's water comes right out of the stream behind his house, but it's perfectly safe to drink. The water is piped through a simple charcoal filter that strains out harmful microbes.

Ron doesn't take the water for granted. His battle with the Forest Service began in 1997, when they initially proposed letting out logging contracts in the national forest land above his house. Ron believes that logging activities would surely compromise both the stream and Saltry Cove, and he's damn sure right. Sedimentation would cloud the water and potentially destroy fish habitat downstream. Traces of petroleum products, including hydraulic fluid and chain oil, would contaminate the water. Ron suffers from an acute allergy to petroleum products. He once went into anaphylactic shock because he drank from a can of beer that had been exposed to diesel fumes.

One day Ron took me uphill to inspect his water source. He showed me where his pipes intercept a percentage of the passing stream, probably less than one-hundredth of the total volume. We looked at the stumps of gigantic yellow cedars that Indians had felled for canoe building long ago. The cuts were made with crude axes, literally thousands and thousands of strokes. We checked out an old kitchen midden, where some long-ago resident had piled shellfish remains into a stack the size of several hay bales. The midden was mostly grown over in trees.

A representative from the Forest Service, perhaps out of frustration, once suggested to Ron that, should the water in the creek turn bad, he could have water shipped in from Ketchikan. "That's not the point," Ron said. So far, Ron's strategy in protecting his watershed has been to act like a total pain in the Forest Service's ass. He writes letters to various government agencies, makes phone calls, challenges assumptions. Once, when Ron felt as though the Forest Service had threatened him, he reported his concerns to the FBI. He also got his hands on an abominable snowman suit. He wants to put the suit on and streak through the woods the next time the Forest Service comes snooping around. "If that doesn't scare them," Ron joked, "they'll have to deal with this being an endangered species' habitat."

As Ron and Joan's battle with the Forest Service wore on,

the *Anchorage Daily News* ran a story about the proposed cut. Greenpeace, the radical environmental group, promptly offered to anchor a boat in Saltry Cove as a gesture of solidarity. Joan's instinct was to decline the offer. She and Ron were suspicious. Why would a bunch of vegetarian tree huggers want to help him maintain his hunting and fishing grounds? wondered Ron. It didn't make sense.

I tried to explain to Ron why a group like Greenpeace would care. I tried to explain that even the most ardent tree hugger understands that habitat protection is more important than saving individual fish. But I couldn't convince him. He doesn't see his crusade to save Saltry Cove as being of global or even national significance. Instead, he sees it strictly in terms of his own food—for instance, whether his water is suitable for putting up shrimp.

When I left Saltry Cove, Ron and Joan invited me and Danny to return the next summer. Ron promised to show us how to smoke octopus. He knew of a reef where we could collect them off the rocks at low tide. Our floatplane took off in a smooth, upward arc, then circled Saltry Cove. I looked down at Ron and Joan's house. The forest rose up behind it. I locked the image in my mind, especially the way the stream flowed like a deep secret beneath the canopy of trees. When I go back, I thought, it may not be that way anymore.

# CHAPTER ELEVEN

# The Deaths of H&G

BEFORE I GOT TANGLED UP IN THE BUSINESS OF RAISING A SQUAB, I always thought I could become a farmer if hunting became illegal. It seemed like the two pursuits were close cousins; in essence, both pursuits boil down to the job of producing food. But I realize now that I'm not cut out for farming and, in fact, farming and hunting are opposites. That idea, that hunting and farming are irreconcilable, is at least as old as the Bible. There's a story in Genesis about two brothers—Jacob, a farmer, and Esau, a hunter. Esau was the firstborn, and their father, Isaac, loved him the most. When Isaac was nearing death, he sent Esau out with his bow and arrows to kill some venison, which was Isaac's favorite food. Esau must have had slow hunting that day, because by the time he returned, Jacob had killed a domestic goat, disguised himself as Esau and the animal as wild, and stolen their father's blessing.

My problem with farming doesn't stem from a historical or even biblical sense of distrust about civilization and agrarian society. My problem with farming is much more simple than that. It has to do with death. If something dies while you're hunting, it's a good sign. But if something dies while you're farming, it's bad.

These thoughts occurred to me when I was up in Alaska, making arrangements to have my seafood shipped home. My cell phone rang. It was Matt. I thought he must be calling because one of the pigeons had eggs.

"Hey, Matt. What's up?"

"I've got bad news," he replied. "Hansel and Gretel are dead."

"What the hell happened?" I said.

Matt said it was a long story, but he'd give me the shorthand version. Since I'd been away, Matt and Jen had implemented a few managerial changes on the pigeon coop. For one, Matt had closed off the divider in the center of the coop, forming two distinct aviaries. Hansel and Gretel, who Matt considered to be pets rather than food, were given free range of one side. All the other pigeons lived on the opposite side. Matt had cut a small door near the roof on H&G's side and fastened it in place with metal hinges. He had gotten into the habit of leaving the door open. Hansel and Gretel would wake up in the morning and take a fly around town, then maybe go for another cruise in the afternoon. Identifying the two pigeons by their white ankle bands, Matt would often see them hanging out on nearby buildings.

The pigeons were always back home by nightfall, Matt said, but Jen had feared for their safety. She had suggested that Matt shut the coop up at night so nothing could get in. Matt thought this was silly. "After all," he said, "one of the benefits of living in town is that you don't need to worry about weasels killing off your pigeons."

Matt continued to allow H&G their freedom, which ultimately led to their demise. The morning of the day he called me, Matt had gone outside to check on the birds.

"Must have been a cat," he said. "It climbed the chicken wire and got in through the flight door. H&G were lying on the ground, graveyard dead. Jen's really upset."

"Like, crying?"

"Big time."

"Jesus, Matt, why didn't you do like she said and just keep the damn door shut?"

Matt was growing exasperated. "We would have forgotten to shut it eventually *anyway*," he said.

As we talked, it occurred to me that the cat might have actually done me a good turn. Hansel and Gretel had gone from pet pigeons to fresh pigeon meat.

"Did the cat chew 'em all up?" I asked.

Matt couldn't see where I was taking this. "It snacked on one of them a little," he said, "but the other one looked untouched except for being dead."

"Cool. Do me a favor. Pluck and gut them both, and make sure you save the giblets. We don't want them to have died in vain, you know?"

Matt was silent.

I repeated myself. "You know?"

"It's too late for that," he said.

Trying to minimize Jen's trauma, Matt had wrapped H&G in newsprint and tossed them in the garbage so she wouldn't see them. Then, before he even called me, he and Jen had left town for a camping trip on the Missouri River, to see if they could catch a paddlefish.

I thought of Matt's neighbors, Wes and Agnes. Wes is well into his eighties, but he's spry and he owns a slaughterhouse in Miles City. It didn't seem like he'd be too bashful about digging through the trash and getting the birds out to pluck them.

"Maybe you should call Wes and ask him to get those pigeons out of the trash."

"Steve," he said, "that's just not something that's going to happen. I'll talk to you later."

After Hansel and Gretel died at the teeth of a cat, Jen wanted to replace them with two new hatchlings. By the time I got back to Miles City, Matt and Jen had already gone down to a pigeon hangout behind a secondhand furniture store on Main Street and nabbed two nestlings. Jen named them Hansel and Gretel II.

"These pigeons are *really* cute," said Jen. She was holding them both in a towel that was folded in her hands. They weren't even weaned yet. As Jen fed the birds, she cuddled them and whispered songs to them and tried out different cute names on them. The birds chirped and flapped excitedly in Jen's presence. It was obvious that I'd never be allowed to eat them. At least not while Jen was alive.

I spent the next three days hunting pigeons, in an effort to get my own squab count up to one. I finally caught one, weaned it myself, and put a red band on its ankle. I told Jen that whenever she sees it, she should repeat the mantra: "Red equals Dead."

ONCE H&G II WERE ABLE TO FLY AROUND, MATT INTEGRATED them into the coop and started training them as homing pigeons. In the mornings he'd take them out for a cruise around town and then toss them out the window. Because he didn't want cats to have access to the other birds, he'd leave the door closed while H&G II were out and about. When the birds came back to the yard, they'd have to wait around on the neighbors' rooftops until someone let them back into the coop.

If I were Matt's neighbor, I never would have bitched about the pigeons' being on my roof, because to bitch about such a thing is so terribly conventional and suburban. Apparently, though, some of the neighbors weren't concerned about being predictable in this way, and they started to raise a fuss among themselves. Matt's neighbor Wes, the guy with the slaughter-house, caught wind of the complaints. He personally didn't give a shit about the pigeons, but he warned Matt that someone might complain to the cops about our pigeon coop, because it's illegal to have livestock within city limits. We thanked Wes for the tip. Thanks to the complaints, Matt discontinued the flight training. The coop now had six occupants, including H&G II. Only one bird, Red, was a certified squab. I couldn't believe it. All those months of work, and all I had was one squab! The feast was coming soon; it was only five months away.

I did notice, however, that a pair of the adult birds had claimed one of the two nesting platforms and begun building a nest out of feathers and juniper twigs. I pinned all my hopes on these two birds. If they had babies, Jen wouldn't need to touch them; the parents would raise the birds themselves, and no human-to-pigeon emotional bonds would form. I banded the two breeders with yellow leg bands.

An epoch of extreme territoriality settled upon the coop. A mateless adult laid claim to the remaining nesting platform. Red, who was big for his age, battled vehemently for domi-nance of the coop's lower level. He usually had someone else's feathers stuck to his beak. I worried that I might have to build a separate coop for Red, because he was being such a bastard to his coopmates. He wouldn't let H&G II roost on any of the perches, so they had to spend the night down in the much less cozy feeding area. I thought they must be terrified down there at night, eye level with any cat that happened to peer through the wire screen.

Matt disagreed. He said, "The sum total of all those pigeons' fears about the outside world is less than their fear of confronting Red. So they can't be that scared."

One day Matt went out to feed the pigeons and failed to lock the door when he was done. Apparently the door swung open in the wind, because all the pigeons except Red took off. When Matt and I went out to survey our losses, Red was sitting there, all alone, on his perch.

Matt said, "It's almost sad. That bird is completely institutionalized."

Jen was worried sick about Hansel and Gretel II, but I was delighted. "Those pigeons never loved you, Jen," I told her. "If they come back, we'll eat 'em."

"No," she said. "If they come back, I'll forgive them."

Sure enough, they did come back. Jen was elated and convinced that her bond with Hansel and Gretel II was as strong as ever. Within two days all the other pigeons had returned except for one of the two yellow-banded birds that had been building the nest. Any hopes of the returned breeder's getting hooked up with a new mate were crushed when Red made a power play and kicked the mateless bird out of the nesting box. A pigeon takes about six months to reach sexual maturity, and Red wasn't that old. I actually had a prepubescent bird dominating one of the nesting boxes. I watched for a few days, hoping that the remaining yellow-banded bird would find a new mate and retake the nesting box. Instead, it moved to a lower perch and assumed a monastic existence.

I freaked out on Matt. "Matt! Now I don't even have the one pair of breeders. How could you leave the door open?" I made a decision: "I'm sick of acting like we're operating some kind of damned pigeon refuge. H&G II just got placed on the menu. And the menu's written in stone. There's nothing anybody can do about it."

"H&G II ain't yours to put on the menu. They're Jen's. She found them. She raised them. If you want to act like you own everything in that coop, then get the coop off my fuckin' property."

He had a good point. I'd have to get some new birds.

A couple of weeks later, we rigged up the nets and went down to the same secondhand furniture store where Matt and Jen had caught H&G II. On the alley side of the store, there was an overhanging roof, like a carport. Up in the joists, there was a long ledge where pigeons could get out of the weather and build nests.

Matt and I stood outside the carport, formulating our plan.

"Once you duck under there, have your net ready," said Matt. "They'll come busting out, from right over the doorway."

We ducked under the carport and whipped our nets up. Instead of hitting squabs, our nets smacked right into a freshly installed screen. Apparently, the proprietor of the store had gotten sick of the birds and fenced off the roost with chicken wire. There was only one little portion of a ledge left, as though he had run out of chicken wire before he finished the job. I set up the ladder and climbed up for a look.

"Holy shit," I yelled down. "There's a pigeon up here. He's just sitting there." I nabbed it with my bare hand, then aimed my flashlight at it. It was wearing a yellow band! I couldn't believe it. "Matt, it's the other breeder!" I handed it down to Matt and he put it into the pet transport box.

When we got home, we expected a reunion scene to rival the end of *The Graduate,* when Dustin Hoffman and Katharine Ross get back together on the bus. Instead, the yellow-banded birds acted like they'd never seen each other before in their lives. They moved to separate perches and wouldn't give each other the time of day.

# CHAPTER TWELVE

# The Boars of Bear Valley

ONE TIME, A FEW YEARS BACK, I WAS ALMOST KILLED BY A DEAD pig that fell from the sky. This was in the Philippines. I was there with a group of Americans who wanted to be the first people to descend a remote river in the central highlands of Luzon Island. In order to float the river, we had to secure trespass permission from the Kalinga, a tribe of former headhunters who seldom allow interlopers on their land. As we rafted through a deep gorge, I noticed a Kalinga man step out of the jungle on a high cliff above our heads. He was wearing a loincloth and a U.S. military fatigue shirt. His backpack was an empty laundry detergent bottle. The shoulder straps were made from twine. He walked out over the river on a rickety rope bridge, carrying a dead wild pig and a rifle. He lifted the pig up over his head and hurled it down at us. The carcass spun a few rotations as it fell through the air. I jumped to one side of the raft, and the carcass slapped into my abandoned position with a slippery thud, then splashed into the river. I hauled the carcass up to the raft's pontoon, thinking it was some sort of welcoming gift. It was obviously not a gift, though; the pig smelled rotten. After I pushed it away, my hands were covered in clumps of wet, black hair. The carcass drifted along with us through some rapids, then got hung up in a back eddy. I turned around and watched it disappear around a bend in the river.

I saw a lot of weird shit on that trip to the Philippines, but my favorite experience was the one with the wild pig. The image of that pig, twirling through the air, was branded into my memory. Of course it had been rotten and shedding, but the idea of getting my hands on a good one began to consume me.

When I came home, I talked about my encounter with the wild pig quite a bit. In the United States, encounters with wild pigs are a rarity. Montana has every native big game animal in the lower forty-eight, but wild pigs aren't native. In the United States, as in the Philippines, wild hogs are the descendants of runaway farm animals that went feral. Scattered populations of wild pigs are located in the South and in California. I asked around to various friends about specific wild pig whereabouts, but without much luck. The only tip I got came from my friend Anna Baker, the girl who owns the home in Thermopolis, Wyoming. Anna's thirty-four. She's gorgeous and also a lot taller and more elegant-looking than most of my other friends. As much as I love Anna and enjoy hanging out with her, I did not pursue her tip.

Here's why: it is not always easy to get specific, practical pieces of information out of Anna. She's lived for spells in Poland, Algeria, and Morocco. She has worked as a massage therapist in California, trained for fiber optics work in Montana, taught English to police officers in Budapest, worked at a boys' disciplinary school in Wyoming, worked as a nanny in Turkey, and played the accordion for donations on Eastern European trains. She's lived all over the United States. She once walked across the entire country, coast to coast. She has dated a cotton farmer, a Bedouin, and a poetry student. Anna has done all this in thirty-four years. It's been such a frantic, hell-bent trip that she hasn't had time to mentally process all the mundane details that would allow her to convey practical information about her life to other people.

For instance, I once asked Anna how she got into the business of playing an accordion on Eastern European trains. Her answer involved a short treatise on train schedules and then segued into a narrative about the time she blacked out while drinking with two witches in Poland and then woke up in Russia.

When Diana and I hang out with Anna, I always get in trouble with Diana because I try to impose my need for logic on Anna. When Anna mentioned the witches on the train, I couldn't let it go.

"What do you mean, witches?" I asked. "Like, they actually thought they were witches? You don't think that, do you? And what's that have to do with the accordion?"

Later Diana told me that if I wanted to hang out with Anna, I'd have to shut up and let her tell her stories without interruption. "Stop asking people to explain themselves all the time. Especially our friends."

I agreed to bite my tongue. Then I'm talking to Anna at a party and out she comes with the news that her parents' cattle ranch in Northern California has wild pigs cruising around on it. I didn't even know that Anna's parents had a ranch. A dozen questions immediately popped into my mind. First off, I wanted to determine whether there actually *were* wild pigs on the ranch. If there were, I wanted to determine whether the population was stable enough to support limited hunting. If it was, I wanted to determine whether her parents would allow hunting. If they would, I wanted to determine where, exactly, the ranch was located, and whether the pigs tended to feed most actively in the morning or the evening. Getting all those answers just seemed like way too much work, and Diana would probably kill me if I tried. Besides, by that point Anna was telling us about how the women in Turkish baths often pinched her belly to see if she'd make a good wife for their sons.

Then, a year or so later, *Le Guide Culinaire* fell into my hands. Imagine a pig falling from the sky. If all the parts of it that Escoffier used were subtracted from the animal in midair, there wouldn't be anything left to hit the ground. *Le Guide* describes uses for the tail, bladder, intestines, kidneys, liver, lungs, heart, brains, ears, tongue, fat, and feet, not to mention all the meat. He recommends, but does not describe, a use for the whole head. He offers many uses for a pig's caul, which is the thin membrane that lines the abdominal cavity and the organs within the cavity. The book renewed my interest in getting a wild pig, and I knew what I would have to do. I called Anna, who had since moved to Oxford, Mississippi, to attend graduate school.

"Anna," I said, "I've been wondering about those wild pigs on your folks' ranch that you mentioned a while back."

In response, Anna told me a story about some firemen who once traded her dad a water pump for hunting permission. "My dad wanted a pump so he could try to save the house in the event of wildfire. My mom worries about wildfires. She always thinks she smells them. My sisters call her the fire ranger. But, you know, those were turkeys."

"What were?" I asked.

"The firemen traded the pump for *turkey* hunting permission. You'd have to ask my dad about pigs. I don't know what he'd say."

Once I secured permission, both Anna and Diana decided to

come out to California with me. Neither of them was remotely interested in actually shooting a pig, but they were excited to hang out together and go wine tasting while I ran around in the hills. As I packed for my wild pig hunt, I had a vague notion that I'd be chasing grape-stuffed hogs through the posh and temperate vineyards of Napa Valley. Anna had said that her parents live in Napa Valley, but she was generalizing. Her parents do in fact have a ranch in Napa Valley. It's not far from their veterinarian clinic, in Saint Helena. There is also a Baker ranch in Bear Valley, up in the mountains about three hours northwest of Napa. Another Baker ranch sits near the town of Willow, even further north. On a day-by-day basis, Anna's parents live wherever the most pressing needs arise. As for the wild pigs, they tend to hang around the ranch at Bear Valley.

Bear Valley is the opposite of Napa Valley. Napa is cool and temperate and green; Bear Valley is hotter than balls and baked brown. When Anna and I stepped out of the car to unlock the gate at the Bear Valley ranch, the heat was unbelievable. It was so hot that I actually laughed. I laughed like you would if someone knocked on your door and asked for a thousand dollars. It was an incredulous, insulted laugh. Diana sat in the back of the car and changed into shorts and a tank top. Anna was wearing blue sweatpants and Turkish jewelry and gigantic Chanel sunglasses. Her head was piled with masses of blond and brown hair, all pinned and tucked into a precarious formation atop her head. She took the pins out and replaced them with a straw cowboy hat.

We couldn't get the damn gate open. The combination had changed, or Anna was remembering it wrong, or something. We set off on foot to cover the mile and a half to the ranch house. We were headed north on a two-track. Grasshoppers jumped around in the hot, dry grass like popping popcorn.

When the grasshoppers landed, their bodies sent up little puffs of dust.

The road twisted through meadows and shady stands of pines. Below us, on the left, a valley stretched for three hundred yards, then rose up toward a ridge. The grass in the valley was all dead and brown, except for a greenish strip that marked the course of a small stream. On the right, the hill rose up toward a steep ridge capped by exposed rock and stunted brush. Three roadrunners zipped across the road, one after the other. We cut across a set of wild pig tracks in the sand. We saw where hogs had scratched up the ground beneath some trees. The road zigzagged a bit, and then we came to the ranch house. It was a low white building with several barns and sheds surrounding it. Beside the ranch house stood a corral full of cattle. The animals seemed confused, all of them bellowing and kicking around, like they'd just been rounded up. The thermometer in the shade on the porch said 107 degrees Fahrenheit.

Anna's mom and dad, Karen and Glenn, rode up on a couple of ATVs. They'd been out chasing cattle, checking the animals' health and administering vaccinations. Glenn's eyes looked watery and irritated from the dust. He was wearing denim overalls and his beard reached clear down to his throat. Anna's mom was as tall and trim as a college volleyball player. She had a bandana tied around her face in the classic gunfighter fashion.

Anna wrote down the proper combination for the gate's lock, and we took a four-wheeler back to get the car. While we were gone, Karen made a broccoli salad with raisins and put some burgers on the grill. The meat was from one of their cattle, right from that property. Glenn Baker took a seat at the head of the table and promptly dozed off. When he woke up, ten minutes later, he ate a couple of burgers and then gave a brief history of the wild hogs on his ranch. His story was a retrospective, beginning in San Diego.

"I was a beach punk," he said. "I wanted to work on the water when I was kid." He took a job fishing for albacore tuna on a commercial vessel. In 1966, when he was twenty, the boat he was working on sank thirty miles off the coast of northern Mexico. One of his friends died from exposure while they clung to a hatch cover in fifty-degree water.

"After that, I didn't want to work on the water anymore," said Glenn. He went to veterinarian school and then he and Karen opened their own clinic. They did a lot of work on large animals, which eventually got them tangled up in the business of raising cattle and sheep. When they bought the Bear Valley ranch, a small herd of potbellied pigs came with the place.

"They were only twenty pounds," added Karen. "Just little things. And tame. They just ran around the yard." Over the years, wild boars sneaked into the farmyard and had their way with the potbellied sows, and gradually corrupted the potbellied bloodline. "Now you can barely tell them apart," said Karen.

The legacy of the potbellied pigs on the Bakers' ranch is consistent with the mixed pedigree of California's wild pig population. European settlers introduced the state's first pigs by accident. Rather than fence a domestic pig and feed it, a farmer could let the animal range freely to fatten itself on acorns, grasses, roots, grubs, birds' eggs, birds, rodents, fruit, and whatever else. When the farmer wanted his pig, he'd head out with a rifle and bring home the bacon.

As time passed, many of these free-range pigs evaded the harvest and lived to go completely feral. Around 1925, Californian hunters introduced truly wild Eurasian pigs as well.

Eurasian pigs, often called Russian boars, are the not-so-distant ancestors of the common domestic pig. The Russian boars thrived in California and had a strong genetic influence on the feral pigs that were already cruising around in the hills.

Such a mixed ancestry means that California's wild pigs do not have consistent physical qualities. In general, a wild pig will *tend* to have certain characteristics: dark coloration; a long, straight tail; tall, erect ears; an elongated snout; pronounced tusks; long, agile legs. Usually, though, a hunter can rely on a fairly simple test: if a pig is not in a pen, it's probably a wild pig.

A wild pig hunter has no such luxury regarding easy identification on the Bakers' Bear Valley ranch. The farm pigs, which look like wild pigs, run freely about the place. And the wild pigs, which don't necessarily look entirely wild, are sometimes running around on the farm.

To further complicate things, the Bakers have a ranch hand who has adopted certain pigs as pets. The hand is an old hermit who walks with a cane and lives in a camper trailer. He sort of came with the property when they bought it. He feeds his pet pigs dog food and keeps padded beds outside the door of his trailer for the pigs to sleep on. He has pictures of his favorite pigs hanging on the fridge in the ranch house, like a reminder to hunters: Don't shoot these pigs.

I looked at the photos. "Anna," I said, "I'm a little worried about killing one of the farm pigs. Or worse, one of that dude's pets. I don't want to hunt a pig whose father used to play fetch here in the yard."

"You'll know the difference when you see one," she said. "The wild ones are really wild."

I said, "You keep saying that, but I don't know if I believe you."

"A wild pig can jump over a fence as swiftly and easily as a deer," she explained.

"What if there are no fences around? Or what if the pig just doesn't jump the fence while we're watching? You have to consider that . . ." I remembered my promise to Diana about arguing with Anna. "Never mind," I said. "You're right. I'll know a wild one when I see it."

Glenn takes a different approach to pig identification. He told me that the wild pigs are nomadic. In the summer they will travel long distances in search of water. He said they might move upwards of twenty-five miles a day. They tend to be most active in the early morning and the late evening, like deer. And they usually seem like they're traveling somewhere.

"They act wild," he said.

To be on the safe side, he suggested that I go bang on the door of the camper trailer and talk to the ranch hand about where the wild pigs have been hanging around. That didn't particularly appeal to me. Instead I decided it would be best to take a long walk, in order to get a feel for the land and maybe check out some wild pigs. I left my rifle behind. I waited until the sun dropped toward the horizon, not that the sun's disappearance helped much as far as the temperature went. The ranch still had a sub-Saharan feel to it.

Anna and Diana walked along with me, in order to get a bit of exercise. About a mile from the house, we saw eight pigs scattered up and down a timbered slope above the road. They were rooting around under some pines in a laid-back fashion, oblivious to the threat of predators.

"So you think those pigs are affiliated with the ranch house?" I asked Anna.

"Wild pigs would be running off by now," she said. "Those pigs are not wild. You'll see."

We walked a couple more miles. Diana was wearing flip-flops, so we were confined to the easy walking on the road. We eventually found a cattle trail and left the road. We followed the trail through a saddle in a low ridge line. The ranch buildings started to seem far off and unrelated to the land we were on. Whatever cattle we encountered trotted off, as though humans weren't an everyday part of life. There were lots of coyote tracks around. Coveys of quail crisscrossed the road, clucking as they dodged through the brush. The birds made a noise like a dripping faucet: *putt, putt, putt.*

Once we passed through the saddle, I could see a long stretch of hillside that was covered with a scattering of pines. The pines were sparse enough that you could see bare patches of ground between the trunks. I scanned the hillside with my binoculars. Once I lowered my binoculars, something caught my eye. I thought I saw a flash of black, at least a quarter of a mile away. I put my binoculars back to my eyes, and sure enough, a pig was zipping along through the trees. I could see it in choppy glimpses, like it was a dog running along behind a picket fence.

"A pig!" I shouted. "There goes a wild pig!"

We'd obviously spooked it. It was running directly away from us. As it ran, it looked back over its shoulder several times in our direction. It vanished over the next ridge without ever stopping.

BEFORE I WAS BORN, MY DAD TOOK MY MOM ALONG ON A BOW-hunting trip for the renowned razorback hogs of Arkansas. There, in a swampy thicket, a razorback chased my mom up a tree. She had to wait up there while my dad looked for a lost arrow that he'd shot at a different pig and missed. When he found his arrow, he shot the boar out from under her. As a kid, I considered my mother to be the last thing in the world that you'd find up a tree. That a wild pig managed to get her up one said a lot about those animals.

My dad had the pig's rump mounted in our bathroom. The mount had a curly corkscrew tail and a perfectly vivid bunghole. On the other side of the wall, outside the bathroom, he hung up the head of a different boar. The animal appeared to be stuck in the wall, like the head and feet of a magician's assistant inside the sawing-in-half box. Michigan doesn't have wild pigs, so this was the only one I knew as a child.

The first real live boar I met was in the mountains of Patagonia. The pig and I had only a brief encounter, during which my friend and I almost accidentally killed it: we were driving in the dark on a mountain road when we rounded a bend and the pig leapt in front of the truck. My friend slammed on the brakes and missed the pig by inches. The animal was as tall as the hood of the truck, yet it slipped into the brush and disappeared as stealthily as a gecko. The next wild pig I saw was in the Philippines. It was falling from the sky.

So my impression of wild pigs was that they were elusive, almost metaphysical creatures. This healthy-looking pig running across Bear Valley hardly contradicted my earlier experiences with the animals. As the pig vanished over the ridge, it seemed somehow wilder than a deer. That made sense, I thought, because a pig has more to lose than a deer. The pig's flight was fueled by normal animal fear, sure, but I saw in it something beyond that as well. A wild pig carries with it the horrors of its domesticated past. Wild pigs have history with man—fences and pens and slaughterhouses—so it made sense that they would run like hell from a man. This reasoning was pure anthropomorphism, of course—the kind of sloppy thinking that would make a biologist crazy. But it felt true and solid to me at the time. Anna agreed.

"I told you," she kept saying. "They're really wild."

The next morning I got up at daybreak and loaded some water and gear into my backpack. I dressed in my usual warm-weather hunting garb—cottony earth tones—but Diana and Anna looked like they were heading to an aerobics class. They each had sports bras and bright-colored sweatpants and flashy sneakers. The three of us piled onto a four-wheeler and rode a couple of miles down the road. We parked up near the saddle in the ridge where we had seen the animal the day before, then started walking. We'd cover a little ground, then I'd sit and glass hillsides while my companions applied sunscreen and talked about books and movies. Within twenty minutes I had yelled at Diana and Anna about five times to please talk quietly. Eventually they quieted down, if only because they got sick of my complaints, and started looking for boars.

We came across a watering hole with two llamas drinking from it.

"I didn't know you guys had llamas," I said.

"Those llamas hang out around here," said Anna. "I don't know where they came from."

Pig tracks dotted the edges of the watering hole. I glassed the surrounding hills for animals. We jumped up a large covey of quail. Half the birds flew away and half of them ran into a patch of thorny brush. We jumped up a jackrabbit. Its bounds were so long and lazy that it seemed to hover, midair, almost in a restful pose. We moved on and glassed some more hills. The valley spread out in a large bowl. Way off, cattle moved through the valley from south to north. I studied the hills above the valley. Anna said, "Isn't that one?" She pointed to the cattle.

"No, man. Those are your dad's cows."

She walked over to a barbed-wired fence and looked across the valley. "There's a boar."

"Anna," I said, "there's a bunch of cows over there. Cows. Those black specks are all cows."

"I'm not talking about those cows, Steve. Look!"

I raised my binoculars and looked through the herd of cows. Sure enough, I could see an animal's black back moving along through some tall grass. It disappeared and reappeared several times as it crossed little gullies and thickets of brush. It was alone and moving at a steady pace. Here and there it would stop and feed for a few seconds.

Anna and Diana agreed to wait while I stalked the pig. I climbed down into a dry creek channel and closed the distance a bit by keeping out of view. When I climbed out, the pig was a couple of hundred yards away and still moving. I climbed back down into a low place and moved parallel to its path, trying to get ahead of it. When I poked up for another look, I could see that I was out in front of it. The wind was blowing from it to me; it wouldn't get a whiff of me until it passed. The pig traveled in a zigzagging line. Whenever it found a patch of clover, it ate a few mouthfuls.

Among hunters, there is a general consensus that bigger is better with regards to prey. Given a choice between a ten-point buck and a younger deer with pencil-thin antlers, most every hunter is going to shoot the big one. I grew up with the understanding that targeting young animals is effete and un-American. From where I was lying, though, watching the pig through my rifle's scope, I could tell that the animal was small and I was glad; Escoffier had warned me away from big pigs.

"In France," he writes, "the young boar of up to the age of 6 months is referred to as a Marcassin and its flesh is highly esteemed, whereas the term Sanglier is reserved for the wild boar when it has become fully mature. In this case its flesh is little used in the kitchen except perhaps for the legs, which in any case should be subjected to the action of a very strong marinade before cooking."

If this animal wasn't a marcassin, it was damn close. It wasn't much bigger than a medium-sized pit bull. It passed by me, only sixty yards out. The pig's feet moved so fast that its legs were a blur; it looked like it was floating along. I was well hidden and the animal was oblivious to my presence. I had a heavy-hitting rifle, a .30-caliber, which makes a big hole when it hits. I didn't want to hit the animal in a place that had lots of good meat. Because the pig was so close, I did something that I normally wouldn't do. Usually I shoot for an animal's lungs or the front shoulder, but instead I held the crosshairs behind the head, at the base of the neck. The pig stopped at a patch of clover. I squeezed the trigger.

The pig went down right in its tracks. I walked up and saw that it was a young sow. Diana and Anna ran across the valley to see what had happened. As they approached, I could hear Anna saying, "I can't stop thinking of the way it pranced along on its dainty feet. It looked like a little ballerina, just prancing along."

Since Anna had never been hunting before, I was afraid she was traumatized. She ran up and inspected the pig's feet. She described the animal over and over again as lovely and dainty and ballerinalike. This is not how I like to discuss the animals that I'm going to eat. I was already feeling a little self-conscious about its being small, and she was making me feel downright insecure. The day was already over a hundred degrees, so I didn't want to waste a lot of time before field-dressing the carcass and getting it somewhere cool. But I also didn't want to appear callous by interrupting the eulogy. Once Anna and Diana were through with their inspections and commentaries, I broached the subject of what needed to happen next.

"Oh!" said Anna. "I'll help you gut it out!"

Diana wasn't terribly interested in the gutting project, so she lay down in the clover with a backpack for a pillow and stared at the sky. I positioned the pig on its back and Anna held the front legs. I was worried about getting the pig into a cooler, and I was so delirious from the heat, that I wasn't thinking too clearly when I gutted the pig. I was operating on autopilot as I made the initial incision. I nicked the bladder, ruining my chances to use it for poaching a duckling, and then zipped right through the peritoneum. I pulled the intestines and lungs out and laid them on the ground, where they became hopelessly dirty. As I worked along, I peeled a kidney off the inside of the back, and then it dawned on me that I was supposed to be saving as much of this stuff as possible. I slipped the kidneys, heart, and liver into the Ziploc bags that I'd brought along for that purpose. I tipped the carcass back over to drain the blood, then filled out and dated my kill permit.

We were back to the ranch house by midmorning. It was 107 degrees in the shade. There was a large freezer in the house where I could cool my meat down, but first I had to cut it into manageable pieces. Anna's mom pointed me in the direction of an old skinning gambrel and a block and tackle hanging from a tree out by the corrals.

With a skinning knife, I cut a slit behind the tendons on the hog's rear ankles and slipped the gambrel hooks through the holes. Once the animal was hoisted into the tree, I sawed the feet off at the ankles. In food terms, the feet are called trotters. I bagged the trotters up. As I was working, a gang of small, tame-looking piglets walked up, sniffing the air suspiciously. I felt embarrassed, as though I'd been caught doing something wrong. I tried to shoo them off, but they wouldn't budge.

As I was shooing them away, the ranch hand climbed out of his trailer. He had his cane, and he was coming toward me across the dusty yard. His cowboy hat was pulled down to his eyebrows. Without saying anything, he walked right up and gave the pig a careful inspection.

"Nope, I don't know that one," he said. "Where'd you get it?"

"Way down at the far end of the ranch. Past that watering hole with the llamas."

"Why'd you go way the hell down there? There were wild ones right here in the yard this morning." He took another look at the pig. "You shot it in the neck, huh? Betcha she didn't go far." Then he walked off, going back toward his trailer. He stepped over a sleeping pig at the foot of the steps and climbed back inside.

I made a cut down the inside of each leg to the gutting incision. The animal was still warm; the hide pulled off as easily as spandex. I skinned the head out and retained it and the ears. I left the tongue intact inside the head, because I wanted to save it. I trimmed off whatever fat there was and cut the ribs down into serving-sized pieces. I filleted the loins off the back. The tenderloins, on the inside of the rib cage, were no bigger than large cigars. I removed the shoulders. The bullet hadn't left much good neck meat, but I kept what I could and tossed the rest away. The piglets fought over the scraps. Ashes to ashes, dust to dust, pig to pig. The last thing I did was take off the hams at the ball joint. I wrapped all the cuts in butcher's paper and placed them in the freezer to cool off.

Later, as we made the long drive back down south toward

Napa, I could feel the temperature drop as steadily as if I were standing in the shower, letting the hot water run out. I wanted to tell Anna that I owed her an apology for doubting her claims about the pigs. I refrained, because an apology would have meant admitting to those doubts. Instead, I listened to Anna talk about the pig's final prance through the clover field. And we talked about witches and accordions. That led to a discussion of Blanche DuBois, which got Anna thinking about an upcoming party at a winery where she was being paid to dress up as a chicken and tell jokes. It was the same basic chatter that any couple of old pig hunters might engage in, but it helped to pass the time as we watched the arid hillsides out the window turn slowly into vineyards.

## CHAPTER THIRTEEN

# Nymphs at Dawn

I WAS STANDING UP TO MY WAIST IN THE SWAMPY MUCK OF LAKE Dubbonet, about ten miles outside of Traverse City, Michigan. The lake is, by anyone's definition, a swamp. I had an annoying little guppy or leech or something trapped between my left foot and the sole of the sandal. It was wedged in the pocket formed by my foot's arch, right where you'd tickle your girlfriend for maximum effect. No amount of wiggling my toes could get the bastard out of there, and the water was too deep to reach down and extract it by hand. Every time I tried to lift my afflicted foot to loosen my sandal, the increased weight on my other foot would cause it to punch through the lake's false bottom, which was composed of the interwoven roots of aquatic plants. Whenever my foot broke through, an eruption of methane gas bubbles and supercooled water would percolate past my scrotum as I plunged eighteen inches down to the real bottom. My dad always called this type of muck "loon shit."

Standing there, I couldn't help but think about how much less of a man I'd become since I was a kid. Sure, I had improved in some respects: I'm a much better shot with a rifle.

I'm more open to criticism. I'm more adept at following complicated instructions. I'm more likely to take the little piece for myself and let someone else have the big piece. But standing in Lake Dubbonet rendered all of that inconsequential; in terms of frog catching, I had become a total loser.

"Man, this sucks," I yelled to Drost, my supposed frogging partner. I wanted to make him feel guilty. He was standing in the woods on the shore of the swamp. He had on the same pair of camouflage cutoff shorts that I swear he's owned since we were kids, and they were perfectly dry. At that moment I resented him horribly.

Drost teaches high school biology in Traverse City, about 140 miles up the Lake Michigan shoreline from where we grew up. After finishing college in the U.P., he moved to Seattle for six years and struggled his ass off to make a living. Then he moved back to Michigan to take this job. Because he's a schoolteacher, Drost continues to have school-kid notions about how summer is supposed to be utterly relaxing. For his summer vacation footwear, he had opted for a pair of cushioned, rubbery slip-on sandals, forgoing the practical versatility of strap-ons, which I myself prefer. When we arrived at Lake Dubbonet and shone our flashlights into the water, it was obvious that the muck would strip those brand-new slippers right off his feet.

To be honest, though, there was little point in his wading into the swamp, because, sadly, we were unarmed. Our initial hunting scheme was to gig for frogs. Frog gigging involves a three-tined spear, called a gig, and a flashlight. Gigging was the tried-and-true method of our childhood and is still practiced by frogging enthusiasts from Massachusetts to California. Drost and I had built a gig and purchased an oversized flashlight, but when we stood under the floodlight in the store's parking lot to look at the frogging rules in the Michigan

Department of Natural Resources Fishing Guide, we made a heartbreaking discovery: "Frogs may be speared but NOT with the aid of an artificial light."

Since we'd brought the flashlight, I wanted to walk through the swamp anyway. If I found a frog, I'd think of some way to get it without using a spear. As I struggled in the muck, I cast the beam of my flashlight around. Looking for a frog in this impenetrable lime green vegetation was like looking for a hay-colored needle in a haystack. I could hear frogs croaking all over the place. Whenever I heard one close by, I'd excitedly try to sneak up on it. I'd slowly part the vegetation, and then the frog would shut up. It was like being at a concert that ends just when you're finally getting ready to dance. Eventually I did find a frog in the cattails, but it was tiny, with legs not much thicker than linguini. It sat there, as vulnerable as a lamb tied to a stake. I thought of thumping it with a stick, or trying to grab it, but I was paralyzed by indecision. Instead of taking action, I stood there and looked at it, thinking about how that frog would be deader than a doornail if I were still ten years old.

The frog's throat bulged in and out like a beating heart. I felt as repelled by the frog's stationary pose as I would by its jumping down my shorts. I guess it wasn't the frog's waiting around that bothered me; I was more disturbed by what it was waiting for—the chance to use its long, sticky tongue to zap flies out of midair. When we were kids, my brother Matt used to tie a bug-sized piece of red felt to the line on his fly rod. When he saw a frog, he'd make a cast and land the felt in front of the frog's nose. The frog would think the piece of felt was a bug and suck the felt so far back into its mouth that Matt could reel it in before it could spit the felt back out. That frog-catching method didn't bother me at all back then.

In fact, I thought it was as exciting as hell. But at some point over the years I had apparently lost my stomach for removing frogs from the end of a fly rod, or even touching them at all.

With the image of a long, nasty tongue playing through my mind, I turned my back on the dinky little frog in Lake Dubbonet and started walking the hell out of the swamp. By the time I climbed into the dry woods and found Drost, the guppy in my sandal had either atomized or escaped.

"What'd you see out there?" Drost asked.

"I saw that I'm not half the man I was twenty years ago."

I HAD MADE ARRANGEMENTS TO STAY IN TRAVERSE CITY because—besides the fact that one of my best friends lives there—the place is a virtual Escoffier smorgasbord. It sits on Grand Traverse Bay, on the eastern shore of Lake Michigan. The land surrounding the town is coursed through and through with rivers and streams and pocked with hundreds of lakes. Chefs will tell you to design your menus based on what products are in season, and a scavenger has to design his year's plans with the same thoughts in mind. I figured that spending the month of July in Traverse City would pretty much max me out on freshwater ingredients. I went to Traverse City thinking that I could get a lot of the stuff I usually fish for, such as walleye and smallmouth bass and northern pike and bluegills and perch, but also some oddball Escoffier stuff, like fish semen, crayfish, lampreys, and carp. In a brilliant stroke of luck, Diana landed a monthlong teaching job at Interlochen, an artsy summer camp for kids.

My brother Matt wanted to come to Michigan to "inherit" all the tools out of our dad's barn, so he agreed to drive us to Traverse City. We crossed eastern Montana and zipped through North Dakota and Minnesota, got lost for a while in northern Wisconsin, and then crossed into Michigan's U.P. just ahead of the sunrise. It was the first time I'd been back to my home state since my dad died. I hadn't slept all night, so old memories and regrets and depressive sentiments about mortality and the passage of time flooded my exhausted mind. What made things even worse was that I was going to spend part of the month hunting frogs. When my brothers and I wanted to do a favor for our dad, we'd get him a dozen frogs. He loved to fry the legs and eat them as an appetizer to fried fish. Matt and Diana and I were riding up front, watching the sun rise. A delicate fog was hovering over the cedar swamps. The northern tip of Lake Michigan lay flat and sleepy out the passenger window. We talked melancholically about frog hunting and being kids and how much everything has changed now that Dad . . .

And then Matt yelled, "Snapper!" and slammed on his brakes. All the luggage in the back of the truck come crashing against the topper window. Sure enough, a big snapping turtle was lying in the road. It was like my dad had sent the turtle out from the livery stables of the afterlife. Matt had a valid Michigan fishing license, so he hopped out and grabbed the turtle by the tail. We put the turtle into a large backpack and stashed it away beneath the cot. Suddenly being back home felt great. Michigan was our land of plenty, welcoming us with open cupboards. We crossed the Mackinac Bridge to the Lower Peninsula and motored on toward Traverse City. Later that night I was groping around in the muck of Lake Dubbonet, thinking about what a sissy I'd become.

I hated myself for thinking that frogs were revolting, though I certainly wasn't the first dude in the world to think it. Early American colonists believed that frogs were possessed by the souls of dead children; that killing a frog would invoke the dead child's bad luck; that if you killed a frog, you would stub your toe; that if a frog died, cows would either produce bloody milk or die; and on and on.

I wasn't worried about my toes or my luck or anyone's cows, but I sympathized with the underlying sentiment of those superstitions. The thought of killing a frog gave me an almost visceral sense of dread. At night I kept thinking of the last frog I'd handled, back in the eleventh grade. Mr. Rogers, my fifth-hour biology teacher, assigned an extra-large frog to me and my lab partner. It weighed about as much as a Cornish game hen. My first impulse was to ridicule those classmates of mine who groaned and complained about how "gross" their frogs were. I'd already garnered the school's annual Excellence in Biology Dissection Award, so I was feeling high and mighty. I bragged that I might just eat the frogs' legs after class. I bragged that I get frogs bigger than this in front of my house, and that I was dissecting frogs for fun back when most kids my age were sucking their thumbs. I blathered on and on until my lab partner made the incision to open the frog's stomach. Then I shut up. Inside, a mouse was curled into a ball like a partially digested human fetus. We both screamed. I stood up and paced around the classroom a few times before my heart resumed its normal rhythms.

What bothered me the most about my own frog aversion was that Escoffier was deeply annoyed by people who didn't like frogs. When he first came to work in London, he was dismayed that the British considered frogs to be disgusting. Not only that, but the British considered people who ate frogs to be disgusting as well. Escoffier observed, "The English sometimes amuse themselves with caricatures showing the typical Frenchman eating frogs. They even call us 'the frog-eaters.'" It irked him so bad that he decided to trick his London clientele into trying frog legs.

He made his move at a banquet attended by the Prince of Wales. Escoffier wrote, "At the time when I managed the restaurant of the Savoy, nobody would have dared to present a platter of frog legs at an English meal, and even less so at a gala banquet for 600 people comprising the elite of English society. For my frog legs to have the success they merited, it was necessary to rebaptize them!" He poached the frog legs and served them chilled, submerged in a paprika-colored jelly with a garnish of parsley meant to look like seaweed. He called the dish "nymphs at dawn." Apparently, the dish was meant to evoke the image of a nymph's dismembered appendages floating in a pond. It worked, and Escoffier had his success. The dish was a great hit.

While Diana and I were staying in Traverse City, I thought of just about a hundred excuses to put off frog gigging for one more day. One of my excuses had to do with Diana's newfound love for seafood. After eating the mussels out on San Juan Island, she'd taken quite a shine to eating fish. In fact, the more she ate, the more she craved. When Diana and Drost's wife, Rachel, got home from work at night, I would try to have dinner ready for them. I always wanted to make fish, because I was trying to develop Diana into a carnivore. That meant Drost and I had to do a lot of fishing. We'd take his skiff out in the morning and then come back to the house in the afternoon and clean our catch. Escoffier used close relatives of most of the freshwater fish we caught, so whatever we didn't eat I'd freeze for the upcoming feast.

Another way to avoid frog gigging was to sit around discussing what the perfect frog gigging spot might look like. One morning Drost and I were drinking coffee on his porch and discussing this topic. We agreed that the perfect spot would have dry banks, no poison ivy or other irritating plants, no bubbles of methane gas, and frogs that were out and about during the daylight hours. We'd already checked out a few places since Lake Dubbonet—some drainage ditches, a decorative landscaping pond at the hospital, the creek that flows through Drost's neighbor's yard. But each place lacked either frogs or the proper physical characteristics for comfortable gigging.

As we sat on the porch, Drost's friend, also named Matt, stopped by to say hi on his way home from walking his dog, Roscoe. I've found that avid dog walkers are often treasure troves of useful information regarding the whereabouts of wild animals, so I filled him in on our predicament with finding a suitable frog-gigging location. He said that he often chases his dog down into a small pond at a place called the Commons. For what it's worth, he said, he usually sees frogs in that pond.

Drost and I hopped on his two bikes and headed down to the Commons. Drost had bought his bikes for ten dollars apiece at an auction where cops sell stolen stuff that was recovered but never claimed. Neither bike was in top shape; one squeaked and the other clacked. Despite these noises, we could hear frogs loud and clear as we closed in on the Commons. The call of a green frog sounds like an amplified note from a loose banjo string—a bit different from the call of a bullfrog, which sounds like someone saying "jug-o-rum."

We looked down at the pond from the bike path. It was perfect for gigging. Nice firm banks. No poison ivy. No gaping muck pits or false bottoms or gurgling bubbles of methane gas.

"Hear that?" Drost asked. The frogs were making as much noise as frogs do at night, but in perfect daylight. "The last thing on their minds is a frog hunter."

"They're going nuts," I agreed.

The frogs were calling from a narrow ring of cattails that lined the pond. The pond was bounded by a highway and the heavily used bicycle path. Cyclists whizzed past. I felt swishes of air from passing vehicles. Drost seemed edgy. He nervously shuffled his cushy sandals and took his hands in and out of his pockets. He looked at the passing cars and frowned.

I knew he was feeling exposed. As a local high school biology teacher, Drost often finds himself in compromising situations. He's got long, greasy hair that hangs to his chin, and he generally looks likes he's up to no good. So he's the kind of teacher that students automatically like and parents automatically distrust. Sometimes he'll be in a downtown bar, having a beer and a cigarette with his wife, and he'll run into a student's parents; he can almost smell their disapproval.

He could just imagine what would happen if some student and her mom drove by the Commons while we were frog gigging: "Mom, Mom," Drost said, affecting a whiny high school voice, "why is the biology teacher walking around with a dead frog on a stick? How gross!"

"That's cool," I said. "I'm sure some other spot will present itself."

I was trying to be sensitive to Drost's concerns. He was being a great sport, but I could tell he was wearying under my constant, nagging pressures to go out scavenging. The Escoffier quest was having adverse affects on many aspects of his life, including his marriage. He and Rachel usually live a relaxed, easygoing life, and I was adding a lot of unnecessary tension to the family dynamic by making constant demands on his time. I tried to pay back their hospitality by pruning their shade trees, but when I finished, I got the impression that they'd liked the trees better before.

The last thing in the world I wanted to do was go frog gigging by myself, but things seemed to be heading in that direction. The only thing worse than the thought of solo frog gigging was the prospect of not gigging any frogs at all—failure in its purest form. I had considered taking Diana with me but concluded that it would probably be a diplomatic nightmare to expose her to the death of a frog; I worried that she would spiral back down into complete vegetarianism.

I still had a week to get some frogs, and I trusted that an opportunity would present itself if I was patient. Besides, with only one week to go, I still needed to accomplish another, perhaps more important goal. I needed some crayfish or, as some folks call them, crawdads. I was planning on making a crayfish mousse, a crayfish soup, and crayfish butter. Also, Escoffier garnished dishes with crayfish tails as freely as if he were tossing around parsley stalks. After adding up all of the uses for crayfish in *Le Guide,* I determined that crayfish were way more important to Escoffier than frog legs were.

I expected Drost to excuse himself from the crayfish-catching expedition. The best time of day for crayfish catching is right after dark, when they come out of hiding to feed. In northern Michigan in the summer, dark doesn't happen until ten thirty p.m. At that time the typical married man is finishing up dinner with his wife or popping in a DVD with his wife or heading out for a nightcap with his wife or rubbing his wife's feet. I didn't want to be any more of a burden on Drost's marriage than I'd already been.

But Drost wouldn't hear of missing out on the crayfish action. Since he'd moved to Traverse City, he had pioneered a new crayfish-catching technique that he was very proud of, and he wanted to demonstrate it to me. At night we rode the bikes to a downtown boardwalk along the Boardman River, where there were lots of pedestrians and restaurants and bars. We followed the boardwalk to Hannah Park, between the Cass Street and Union Street Bridges, right in front of the Fire Fly

Bar. The Boardman River is backed up by a dam, which forms a small pond. The boardwalk is well lit with street lamps, so you can look over the handrail and observe the multitudes of crayfish that crawl out of the rocks to scrounge around at night.

Drost opened his pack and pulled out his gear. He tied a small fish's head to a piece of fishing line and pinched a lead weight above the head.

"Pick whatever 'dad you want down there," he said.

There were hundreds of them, easily. "That one," I said, pointing to a big one with bluish green claws.

Drost dangled the fish's head over the rail of the boardwalk and let out line. The head sank slowly and came to rest right in front of the crayfish I'd selected. The crayfish grabbed the bait with both claws and Drost tugged it right up out of the water. "Is that the one?" he asked.

"That's him, all right."

He shook the fish head over the bucket and the crayfish plopped in. We had forty crayfish in no time, all big fatties. As we fished, pedestrians would come by and act like our crayfish were the coolest thing to ever happen. They'd get all excited. They would tell us how they always order crayfish in restaurants but never knew that crayfish lived around here. They'd tell us that they were going to catch some crayfish tomorrow night, come hell or high water.

When Drost and I got home with our catch, we put a pot of water on the stove to boil. Diana and Rachel joined us, and we had a late-night, candlelit crayfish dinner on the porch.

The next night we were forced to go out again, because I hadn't saved any of the 'dads for the Escoffier feast. We went back to the boardwalk and caught a bunch more. Strangely, none of the pedestrians from the night before showed up with their own gear; again, we were the only people down there fishing. Drost had a tank and an aerator in his garage, so we put the night's catch in there for safekeeping. "These are for the Escoffier feast," I told him. But then the next day we got invited to a party at a buddy's beach house and we took the crayfish along. We caught more crayfish the next night, but then Drost and Rachel had some friends over for a barbecue and ate those. So after three nights of crayfish catching, I still hadn't saved shit.

On my last night in town, Drost and I stayed out extra late, slaying the 'dads. We caught a half bucketful, well over a hundred of them. By then it was clear that none of the pedestrians would be joining us. They were all talk, no action. It was like they thought talking about catching crayfish was more fun than actually catching them, which definitely is not true. When we got done, we stashed our half bucket of crayfish next to our bicycles and went into the Union for one last hurrah. The only thing keeping me from really whooping it up was I knew I had to go frog gigging in the morning. So instead of waiting around until last call, we went home and boiled our catch. Since I was freezing them, I wanted to cook them only halfway, like Ron Leighton taught me to put up crabs. We dropped the crayfish into salted, boiling water until they turned pink, like zinfandel. Then we chilled them in ice water, packed about forty crayfish in each bag, and froze them.

In the morning I lay in bed thinking, Fuck it. I won't even get frogs. Who cares if I don't? I decided I'd just get out of bed and pack my stuff, because I was heading off alone to New York while Diana finished out her job in Traverse City. But lying in bed, I started thinking again about what a lame-o adult I'd become. I wondered what had happened to me. Why had frog hunting become so unappealing? Lying there, I got this horrible feeling that I was old now—an old curmudgeon nearing the inevitable. Now that I no longer had the vigor of my youth, I was going to fade away and die.

Apparently Drost was having some of the same feelings, because when I got up and walked out of my room, he was already dressed in his camouflage shorts and rubber boots, drinking a cup of coffee.

"You up for a little frog gigging, for old times' sake?" he asked.

We stashed the bikes in the cattails on the edge of the pond at the Commons and sneaked to the water's edge to look for frogs. In the *Handbook of Frogs and Toads of the United States and Canada,* by Albert Hazen Wright and Anna Allen Wright, there is a wonderfully vivid description of what a green frog looks like. The description was taken from the notes of two amateur naturalists, A. M. and C. C. Deman, concerning a green frog they observed in New Jersey on April 30, 1928:

> Upper parts forward rainette green or parrot green. Below eye and forward, calliste green. Rear upper parts olive-citrine. Tympanum Saccardo's olive, with center yellowish citrine. Barred with black on hind legs and feet. Side of body has seafoam yellow interspaces between citrine-drab areas. Throat barium yellow. Rest of under parts white, groin with cream color cast. Under parts of hind legs dark vinaceous-brown. Front of hind legs with a line of Hay's brown. Line under tympanum neva green, becoming viridine yellow over shoulder. Line on upper jaw and lower jaw medal bronze. Front part of lateral fold blackish, a blackish bar back of tympanum, a raw umber line on front of foreleg. Iris black, pupil rim greenish yellow. Iris above and below pupil with much xanthine orange.

Judging by the description, you'd think that a green frog in a swamp would stand out like a clown on a golf course. In fact, the military could produce good swamp camouflage by reproducing on a set of fatigues the color pattern of a green frog. Drost and I crouched on the edge of the pond. We were right where Drost's friend Matt sees the most frogs when he's chasing his dog. I could hear frogs all over the place. It sounded like a banjo player was tuning up in the pond. *Twang, twang, twang, twang.* He was hitting all the notes. The sun shone through the cattails and cast a tiger-stripe pattern of shadow and light. The water was coated with a skin of algae. I looked and looked, but I couldn't see the frogs. I looked at Drost and shrugged, but he was so busy watching for cops and his students' parents that he wasn't even looking at the water. I studied one square-foot section and then another. After a minute or so, I spotted a frog's barium yellow throat patch only six feet away. Above the patch were two eyes and a nose.

The gig was lying behind us. I raised my body a little, so I was looking down at the frog. Then I slowly lifted the gig and moved the tip out over the water until I was holding the gig's shaft in my left hand, my right index finger curled over the handle's end. Drost saw the frog now and gave me a nod—an all-clear signal. Moving as slowly as possible, I moved the tip of the gig toward the frog. The frog stayed put; it must have thought it was still hidden.

Once the point of the gig was ten inches from the frog, I paused, suddenly hesitant. I was still perfectly open to eating frog legs, but now that I had the chance, I couldn't decide if I really wanted to kill a frog. I thought about it good and hard. I realized that if I wasn't willing to kill this frog, I'd never be able to eat a frog again in good conscience, even at a restaurant. I refused to be that kind of hypocrite. If I ever decide that I can't pull the trigger or release the arrow or throw the frog gig, I'll be forced to ask myself a question: Are you willing to become a vegetarian? If the answer is no—and I believe it always will be a no—then I'll have to continue to see my own desires for what they are, and be willing to do my own dirty work.

So I aimed. Steadied my hands. I opened my left hand slightly, so it fit around the spear like a barrel around a bullet. Simultaneously I used my right finger to drive the gig down hard. The frog disappeared as the spear tip swept it beneath the surface. The spear burrowed into the sand on the bottom. I waited a few seconds, then pulled the spear back in. The frog was on there, still kicking a little. Drost gave the frog a sharp whack on the head with a stick we'd selected just for that purpose. The frog went still, and I put it into a wet gunny sack. Once I'd done it, I couldn't remember why I was so reluctant in the first place. It felt perfectly natural and organic, like the behavior of a child before his head gets all screwed up with everyone else's ideas about what he should be doing with his time.

We moved along the shore, creeping and looking, creeping and looking, and taking turns with the spear. Some of the frogs spooked before we could take a poke at them. Others spooked before we even saw them; we'd hear a splash and there would be nothing to see but disturbed rings of water.

When we got around to the road side of the pond, we hunkered low and watched the water. We had six frogs, which was plenty. We'd seen nineteen. We could hear cars passing. We were careful to keep the gig handle down, so passersby couldn't detect our presence. I took out my Leatherman tool to clean the frogs, because I wanted to get the nasty part over with before any frog-sponsored nausea kicked in. I moved as quickly as possible. I first snipped off the frog's feet, then removed the legs with a cut near the lower abdomen, slicing all the way through, so that each pair of legs stayed joined at the waist. With the pliers on my Leatherman tool, I pulled the skin off like I was removing a doll's pants. All cleaned up and skinned, the meat was translucent and glossy. A long, elegant bone ran through each leg. In this form, the frogs were extremely appetizing. I could have popped the leg right in my mouth. I held up the legs and compared the meat to a whole frog. It's just one and the same, I reminded myself: you can't have one without the other.

## CHAPTER FOURTEEN

# The Hairbag by the River

I WENT LOOKING FOR RAY TURNER, AKA THE EEL MAN, BECAUSE of a mystery that I'd encountered within the pages of *Le Guide Culinaire*. The mystery had to do with the sorts of things that Escoffier did *not* cook. Although Escoffier claimed to know his business "thoroughly down to its least details," he often sought the expertise of others. His breads were produced for him by artisan bakers using large, wood-fired brick stoves. He purchased cheeses from *fromagers* across France and Europe. He bought pâtés from producers in Strasbourg, sausages from Italian butchers, butter from Normandy dairies, and smoked hams from a variety of sources, though he preferred the hams produced in the cities of York and Prague.

Escoffier never bothered to explain why he outsourced the things he did. Depending on the individual circumstances surrounding each item, his decisions probably had to do with convenience, the need for unwavering consistency, or an admiration for regional flair. Because he did not explain the thinking behind his methods, his readers are left to wonder why they shouldn't go ahead and attempt certain dishes on their own. After all, Escoffier does not come right out and say not to try something. Instead, he simply omits any description of how to do it. For instance, he offers a dozen recipes for veal heads, but about pig's head, he says only that it is "usually utilized for the preparation of fromage de tête," or headcheese. He does not include a recipe for headcheese; he doesn't even explain that it's a jellied loaf made from the chopped cartilaginous parts of the head. So the reader is left to assume that Escoffier bought his headcheese, ready-made, from someone else.

Escoffier takes a slightly different approach with turtle soup. He provides his standard, lengthy segment on turtle soup, but he qualifies the passage with his observation that turtle soup "is more generally obtained ready-made, either fresh or preserved, and as a rule of exceptional quality, from firms whose specialty it is to make it, and who usually deliver it in excellent condition." He goes on to say that a firm at 137 Beekman Street, New York, New York, has a good reputation for this soup. Curious, I looked the address up, but that street number no longer exists. They knocked the building down and changed the street numbers around, and now there's a dude on that same piece of real estate who sells custom neckties. His name is Joshua Bach. He told me that he's been in that building for years and hasn't seen any turtles around.

As for smoked eels, Escoffier is enigmatic. He offers a number of preparations for fresh eel, from soups to main courses, but all he says about smoked eel is that it should be cut up and served. I noted this particular omission with disappointment, because I was interested in reading Escoffier's thoughts on eel smoking. While I've never attempted to smoke an eel myself, I have done a bit of fish smoking over the years in my Little Chief, which, being one foot wide and two feet high, is the smokehouse equivalent of the Easy-Bake Oven. When I realized that even the mightily proficient

Escoffier entrusted others with the chore of smoking eels, I lost my own confidence to properly execute the job. So I canceled my plans to go eel fishing on my own, and instead I made arrangements to catch and smoke eels with a trained professional. It seemed that I couldn't do better than to find the guy known as the Eel Man.

Though the location of Ray Turner's business may be geographically prohibitive, his business's sign is almost universally inviting. It is nailed to a post in a patch of tall weeds next to a turnoff on Route 17, in the Catskill Mountains near Hancock, New York. At the top of the sign is a stenciled drawing of a leaping trout, and beneath the trout are four words: Delaware Delicacies Smoke House. If a motorist isn't fluent in English, chances are still pretty good that he won't miss the turnoff. Beneath the leaping trout, the words "smoke house" appear in Chinese, Japanese, Italian, Greek, Hebrew, Swedish, and Spanish.

After I hung a right at the sign, I remained unconvinced that I was going in the right direction. The road narrowed after a mile or so and became very noncommercial-looking. I passed Hancock's municipal dump, where old refrigerators and broken lawn chairs jutted out of a bulldozed pit. After passing the dump, I curved to the right, down into the floodplain of the Delaware River's east branch. The foliage on the trees was so thick it looked like you could land an airplane on the canopy. The road swung left again, following the contours of some marshy backwaters that sprouted with cattails. Cottages sat at the end of little side lanes. The lanes were pocked with potholes, and the potholes were full of water.

Every time I thought I might have screwed up and taken a wrong turn, a little painted sign egged me on. One of the signs was about a foot long and said Eels. Another sign said Smoke

House. I proceeded. Trees blocked out the sun. Just when I was finally sure that I'd missed it, I drove down a narrow, heavily wooded lane, past an emu standing in a wire pen, and into a clearing in the trees that contained Delaware Delicacies Smoke House, or *casita de ahumar*.

Upon first glance, the smokehouse looked like little more than a shack, and Ray Turner's home, next to the smokehouse, looked like the entrance to a coal mine. It was built of rock and buttressed with heavy wooden beams. As I pulled up, Ray stepped outside the mine to greet me. He had a jungle of a beard. It came to a rounded point at his chest, like a digging spade. Some of the hair in his beard was pure white. Other strands tended toward smoky shades of gray. The hair on his head had similar colors, though much of it was collected in a loose ponytail. What the ponytail had missed sat atop his head like clumps of hair cleared from a shower drain. By way of introducing myself, I made a predictable comment about his place being hard to find. He said, in a pat tone that suggested years of recitation, "My geography culls the timid and the shy. I get a better clientele."

While Ray Turner might not have the ideal location for retail sales, he does subscribe to the old business maxim of "location, location, location." In his cutoff blue jeans and soiled T-shirt, Ray said he was "dressed for the office," and gestured with his thumb toward the river. We walked along a dirt path leading behind his house and down the river bank to a small dock. A fourteen-foot Old Town canoe was tied to the bank. Ray found the canoe in the river when it came floating past his house during a spring flood a few years back. He now uses the boat for his morning commute.

Ray stepped out onto the dock and waved his arm up and down the river. "Generally," explained Ray, "the Delaware

runs southeast. Right here, it runs dead nuts north." Upstream from us, we could see Ray's office—an eel weir. At a
distance, the weir looked like a low, funnel-shaped dam made
of head-sized rocks. The funnel accepted the downstream
current of the river and forced it through a five-foot-wide
spillway, which was blocked with a colander made of nar-
rowly spaced wooden slats. The colander let the water pass
through but filtered out the eels like spaghetti. Ray referred to
the colander as "the crib."

Ray's eel weir and his smokehouse work in tandem every
summer and fall to produce smoked eel—the signature product of Delaware Delicacies. While Ray smokes a wide variety
of products, including trout, shrimp, salmon, chickens, and
turkey breasts, his specialty is smoked eel. Every year, from
about July to October, he traps and smokes roughly one ton of
eels, meaning he individually handles over two thousand eels
a year. He's been trapping eels commercially for twenty years
and sportfishing for eels since shortly after he was born, in
1948. There's no denying it: he's the Eel Man.

AFTER POINTING OUT HIS EEL WEIR, RAY THOUGHT THAT I
should meet an eel. The eels he catches in his weir do not go
directly to the smokehouse. Usually they have a layover period in the holding tank, which sits near the end of Ray's
driveway. I had never seen an American eel before I looked
into the tank. I had eaten eel, or *unagi,* in Japanese sushi
joints, but *unagi* looks as much like an eel as steak looks like
a cow. I've often read that eels resemble snakes, but I was inclined to disregard the comparison because it seemed too
weak and general. I looked inside the holding tank, trying
hard to think of a better line. The almost black eels were lined
up nose to tail along the bottom perimeter of the tank. The

longest one was about the length of my arm. "They look like snakes," I said.

Ray challenged me to grab an eel out of the holding tank with my bare hand. The tank was a shallow wooden barrel the size of an economy car. The top was screened to ward off birds of prey. I reached under the screen and made a few attempts at grabbing an eel. It was impossible. They're way too slimy. Anyone who claims that it is possible, says Ray, is either full of it or else they're grabbing the eel hard enough to injure it. Which would be bad, because Ray wants his eels to stay alive and healthy until he's ready to process them.

Killing an eel is almost as hard as handling one, and Ray solves both problems by removing the live eels with a net and putting them into a tub of coarse salt. The salt quickly kills the eels by suffocation and begins to strip off their slime. When Ray removes the eels from the salt, he puts them into an old cement mixer along with some sand and turns the mixer on. The eels come out as nonslippery as a dry stick.

Ray pulled an eel out of the gravel and rinsed it off with a hose. To prepare the eel for smoking, he uses a knife and a spoon. The end of the spoon is sharpened and has small serrated teeth cut into it. It looks like a souped-up grapefruit spoon. Ray gutted and scraped the eel's body cavity clean in the time that it took him to say, "You gotta come all the way down here like this, so you can get at the shit sack. You always have to remember, too, the easiest place to get under the guts is right under the liver, otherwise it's pretty well attached, you know. And then you stick your thumb down underneath there, and go down here like that, and pop off the top. That's how that works."

He picked up the grapefruit spoon and held it to the light. "This is my own innovation," he said. He took the innovation and gave the inside of the eel's chest cavity a good scraping. "It sounds like an old lady's washboard," he said. Ray described the process of cleaning the eel's chest cavity as "tricking it out," a phrase popularized by car fanatics to describe customizing their vehicles, and used frequently by Ray, generally to describe the final few steps of a procedure.

With the exception of his cold-smoked salmon, or lox, which he covers with a dry mixture (heavy on the crushed white pepper), everything Ray smokes, including the eels, is brined in a solution of water, brown sugar, salt, and dark honey. The eels go into the brine in batches of sixty-eight and soak for two days. He put the gutted eel into the brine, then walked me through the rest of the smoking procedure.

Ray's two smokehouses are built from cinder blocks, each about the size of an average walk-in closet, or fifty-six times bigger than my Little Chief. The smokehouses are powered by barrel stoves, which sit outside the smokehouses, beneath a wooden lean-to with plastic tarps for walls. Ray won't burn a thing in the stoves except apple wood. An orchard's worth of split apple logs is piled along the periphery of the lean-to. "I got a lot of friends who like smoked salmon," explained Ray. "You bring me a load of apple and I'll take care of you. You just got to get it here; I'll split it."

Each stove is rigged to a system of chimneys. "All of this there, except the damper, I found at the dump up the road. Stove included." He pointed to a chimney that rises up through the roof of the lean-to. "This one is a starter tube," he explained, "to get the fire going. That way it's not putting any smoke into the smokehouse until I want it to."

While the fire builds, Ray removes his eels from the brine and dries them off, until they feel a little tacky. He then hangs the eels inside the smokehouse from small strings.

"And then what happens is, when the meat is in there, I shove in a damper that's homemade—and that works very well—and the damper diverts smoke directly into the smokehouse rather than straight up and out."

Ray made a ghostlike *whoo-ooo-ooo* noise and rose to his tiptoes while lifting his arms and waving his fingers, demonstrating how the smoke enters the smokehouse and fills it up. I tried to open a little flap on the door to peek inside, but the flap wouldn't lift. "That didn't work," he said, "so it's been sealed in place. It was going to be so you could look inside there and see the thermometers, but you can't see shit in there. Too smoky."

Instead, Ray drilled three small holes through the door, and he shoves long meat thermometers through the holes to monitor the temperature. The eels get smoked for four hours at temperatures between 160 and 180 degrees. I opened the door to take a look inside. Years' worth of wafting smoke had colored the insides of the smokehouses a deep charcoal black and caked the walls and ceiling. Ray demonstrated how he occasionally scrapes the residue with a putty knife; watching the flakes come off the ceiling was the first time I've seen smoke fall instead of rise.

Ray has no problem selling all his eels. He moves his two thousand or so eels every year with an absolute minimum of advertising. He won't send out product to delis or restaurants without getting direct payment with a credit card. Sixteen bucks a pound. His refusal to work with thirty-day invoices has cost him business with such places as Dean & DeLuca. Or, as Ray sees it, the refusal of Dean & DeLuca to pay up front has cost them business with Ray Turner.

"You know the Ferris wheel philosophy?" he asked.

"Like what goes up must come down?" I guessed.

"No, that's Isaac Newton," he said. "I'm Ray Turner. And I say, 'You want to take a ride, buy a ticket.'"

While we were checking out the smokehouses, a retail client came in. She was an old woman, perhaps German, with two American granddaughters and a luxury sedan. She bought an eel, four smoked prawns, and one pound of lox. She asked Ray if the kids could look at the river and the weir. "Just because they're on vacation doesn't mean they shouldn't learn something," she said.

Ray said, "Please, please do."

The retail shop is small and homey. Photographs from Ray's eel weir decorate the walls and a fish spear leans behind the glass display case. The refrigerated case holds a variety of smoked products: salmon, Cornish game hens, trout, eel, fryer chickens, turkey breast, shrimp, duckling. One wall of the retail shop is formed by the walk-in cooler, where Ray stores finished products and brining solutions. "I'm not dealing with a bread, butter, milk clientele, you can see."

An old Italian man came in alone. He looked to be about halfway through with losing all his hair. Purple splotches dotted the top of his head. He wanted five pounds of Ray's smoked salmon. As Ray cut and wrapped the fish, the old man said, "You should know: these are for the doctor who saved my life. For him and his secretary. His secretary is Russian. Your salmon is the best salmon they've had. Ever. Anywhere."

While Ray waited on the Italian man, a delivery guy called to say he was lost. He was trying to deliver some pickled garlic and Dutch sweet relish. Ray likes to stock a few extra niceties on his shelves. The delivery guy was unamused by Ray's location. A while after the Italian man left with his doctor's salmon, an eighteen-wheeler squeezed down the narrow road. The driver got out, stepped inside, and looked at Ray. He seemed to disapprove of something. "You're off the beaten path," he said to Ray. "Makes me wonder what exactly you guys are smoking out here."

Ray Turner says that he was conceived in his own house. More precisely, he was conceived on the location of his house, because his family's cottage that was built on the same spot burned down years ago. He and his family used to come to the river every weekend and catch eels, using fishing poles and worms as bait. His father, Ray Turner Sr., had himself fished for eels since he was a kid.

Ray enlisted with the army during the Vietnam War. He was trained as a civil engineer, then stationed in Panama from 1969 to 1971. After his discharge, he worked a hodgepodge of jobs back in the States, running construction projects and doing his own masonry work as a private contractor. Without blueprints or a floor plan, he rebuilt the family cottage from stone and moved in. "I've had a few women move through here over the years, but never had a wife," Ray said. "No kids."

Inside the cottage was the coolest-looking stone fireplace I've ever seen. Ray cooks his dinner in it every night. He described the fireplace to me, pointing to each individual rock that he had cemented into place. "Geode glass; green jade; volcanic glass; that's a type of glass produced when lightning strikes beach sand; that's a fossil from Utah; there's a piece I took from Plymouth Rock; that piece of rock is from the northernmost lighthouse in the lower forty-eight; that's a rock from the grave site of an Indian princess; that granite's from an interstate curb. My friend crashed his car into the curb and knocked it off."

RAY'S EEL WEIR IS BUILT FROM ROCK TOO. INSTEAD OF AN ECLECTIC variety of stone, though, Ray picks up the rocks, one by one, from the bottom of the river. He builds the weir every summer.

The labor wears his fingernails down to nothing and gives his fingertips a callused, bulbous look. Every winter, ice floes on the Delaware smash the weir down and grind all his work into the river bottom.

One day I went out to help Ray work on his weir. It was operating, but it wasn't yet "totally tricked out." Before we started moving rock, we checked the catch from the previous night. Eels are nocturnal; they feed and travel under the cover of darkness. As we stood outside the crib, Ray said, "We got a good flow coming in here. The buggers come in, get banged by that hydraulic pressure, and they'll come up into here. We got stuff in here. Let's look."

Seven eels were slithering around in the crib alongside four shad, five rock bass, a trout, and a bluegill. Everything but the eels went back in the river. Ray keeps a log of all the creatures that turn up in his weir. Along with the stuff we caught, the list includes bullhead, sunfish, suckers, pickerel, bowfin, striped bass, needlefish, northern pike, chubs, lampreys, shiners, catfish, horned dace, carp, walleye, catfish, water snakes, a bar of Ivory soap, a bowling ball, and a dead rat.

Ray begins his annual work on the weir when the spring floods in the river begin to subside, usually in late May. He doesn't like to build the crib until early July, because he doesn't want to catch the shad that come upriver to spawn in the spring and early summer. Once the shad are mostly cleared out of the river, he hauls the dismantled crib upstream on top of his two canoes, which he lashes together to form a small barge. A stone cofferdam helps to hold back the current while he works. Once the crib is built, he tears down the cofferdam and lets the current flow through.

The rock walls of the weir are each three hundred feet long. There is a ten-foot-wide opening between the banks of the river and the point where the walls begin, to allow upstream fish passage and downstream boat passage. The walls diverge from the banks of the river, running at a thirty-degree angle toward the river's center.

"Basically," he explained, "the wall's got like four parts: you break the top of the water with big rocks to cut down the hydraulic pressure; you get a little backing of rock downstream of that so it stabilizes it during higher water; you chink the front of it with small rocks and gravel, so it curves the front of the rock wall like the bottom of the river, and the eels bounce along it; the last part is paving, on the downstream side." Ray "paves" with large, flat rocks, some so big he uses a pry bar and fulcrum to move them.

Once Ray gets the V-shaped weir built into its basic shape, he'll start catching eels in the crib. He might get 5 or 10 eels a night, even though the rock walls of the weir are months away from being completed to his satisfaction. The 7 eels that Ray caught with me boosted his summer's catch to 109. On that exact date one year before, he had 119. These first eels he gets in the summer are locals. "They're just hanging around, feeding along the bottom," explained Ray. "They're not migrating yet."

Our day's work took place on the left bank of the river. (The left and right banks of a river are determined by facing downstream. So if you're walking upstream, the left bank of a river is on your right.) I peeled large rocks off the bottom and fit them together, trying to get the wall high enough to break water. When I put a rock in place and released it, I had to be ready to jump back to avoid the rock if it came loose in the current and tried to roll back on my toes. Once, I worked my hand under a rock and felt my sore fingertips brush against an eel. I reached in farther and tried to grab the eel, but it slipped right out of my grip. I watched the eel retreat quickly upstream. As it swam, its shape would come into view against the light-colored rocks and then disappear against the dark-colored rocks.

As I broke the waterline and stabilized the wall, Ray tricked my work out. We fell into a quiet, pleasant groove of labor. An hour passed without our saying anything to each other. I watched Ray hold a rock in place on the weir, change his mind, then prop the dripping rock on his knee. He rearranged a few stones, then slid the piece from his knee into the slot, as smoothly as if he were replacing a library book on its shelf.

I asked Ray, "Does it strike you as peculiar that you worked for years as a stonemason, making fireplaces and whatnot, and then you started making your living by building an eel weir out of stone?"

"It doesn't strike me as peculiar," he answered. "It does strike my fancy."

"Are the stones what drew you to this work?"

"No, the fish did. And the battle. Me and Mother Nature fight pretty hard. We have some battles, but we play clean."

What Ray and Mother Nature are fighting about is whether or not Ray's eel weir will be functioning properly during the massive eel migration that sweeps down the Delaware River one night out of every year. The migrating eels are headed for the Sargasso Sea, between Bermuda and Puerto Rico. For a female eel, the journey to the Sargasso may take up to a year. Once she arrives, she deposits about 20 million free-floating eggs, then dies. The eggs hatch. As larvae, the young eels look like transparent willow leaves. The larvae get carried on oceanic currents for a year, eventually arriving off the coast of North America. By this time they have become elvers, which look like smallish versions of their parents. The elvers congregate at river mouths before heading upstream to complete the long, complicated cycle.

The eel migration occurs on September 27, give or take a week, depending on such variables as the moon phase and water clarity. (Migrating eels like their privacy; a new moon over slightly turbid water makes for ideal migrating conditions.) The migrating eels are sexually mature specimens, usually between seven and twelve years of age. Ray can tell when the migration is about to happen, because he sees an initial scattering of large, darker-than-usual eels coming downstream in the hours before the main run. That's when he knows that all hell is about to break loose.

The fate of Delaware Delicacies depends on the eel weir and the crib's being in good shape when the migration passes through. Mother Nature has been known to bust out some nasty moves. There's always the threat of a flood; if the water gets high enough, the eels just blow right over the weir and the crib. Another threat is drift logs, which often knock the shit out of Ray's weir. "A big log coming down that river is my arch, most deleterious nemesis," explained Ray. "I've seen whole trees come down that river. You want to see what a whole tree can do to wood slats? I don't think so."

If everything goes smoothly, if Mother Nature doesn't play too rough, Ray stands to make a good catch on the night of the migration: usually about a thousand pounds of eels in eight hours. He works through the darkness, scooping and transporting eels. "I just do my best to be ready for them when they come, so I can get what I can get. Whatever Mother Nature can offer. I get maybe one in fifty that come downstream. Remember, the weir only suggests where the eels should go. Some go around it, on the boat passages. Or they hit the weir and slither over the rocks like the dam ain't even there. They can absorb oxygen on dry land. They'll cross dams and slither through wet grass. They don't give a shit."

Hanging out with Ray, I became fond of the peculiar amal-
gamation of scientific thinking and spiritual pondering that
comes out of his mouth. He took a long time explaining how
frustrating it can be to maintain a weir during high water,
speaking fluidly in the hard-edged parlance of engineers. He
went off about "vortexes," "cross-triangulation supports,"
"calibration," and "hydraulic dynamics." Once he exhausted
the technical side of floods, along with a catalog of curses, he
atoned for his own blasphemies. "You can't get mad at
Mother Nature," he warned me. "If you do, she'll only make
it worse. You'll pull your hair out."

While we moved rocks together, building up the wall and
tricking it out, Ray told me that scientists used carbon dating to
age the remains of a nearby eel weir; the weir was 5,800 years
old. Ray said, "Any red-blooded American Indian would see
this kind of food coming down. You can bet they'd be out here.
The whole tribe would be out here!" Telling me this, Ray tried
to replicate the facial expression that might have swept across
an Indian fisherman's face upon discovery of the massive eel
migration. It was an expression of complete glee, wide-eyed
and open-mouthed.

Except for some metal screws in his crib, Ray's weir wasn't
terribly different from its predecessors from previous millennia. Keeping a weir requires a tolerance for routine and repeti-
tion and drudgery. But that tolerance has to be tempered with
some love for the rhythms of nature, or it would never last. Indeed, weirs or no weirs, the eels have come down the river
every year for thousands and thousands of years. That's amazing. But it's especially amazing when you consider Ray Turner,
and the hundreds of Ray Turners before him. Picking up rocks,
setting them down. Collecting eels, preserving meat. Once I
watched Ray place a rock into the weir's wall, then stand up to

admire how well it fit. He wiped his hands on his shorts. He looked up the river, then back at the weir. "I just want life to go by in a calm and collected way," he said. He reached down and touched the rock again. If he moved it at all, it was an imperceptible amount. He stood back up and admired the rock again. "I go to my eel weir," he said, "and everything's cool."

## CHAPTER FIFTEEN

# A Scavenger's Freezer

AT ANY GIVEN TIME, MATT AND I HAVE A BUNCH OF STUFF HANG-ing out in our freezer: fish, a whole porcupine, a couple of geese, a loaf or two of zucchini bread, salmon fillets. Mostly, though, the freezer is packed with our red meat. Matt and I butcher about eight or so big game animals a year. We get elk, mule deer, antelope, black bear, caribou, and occasionally one of us will have a permit for moose, bighorn sheep, or moun-tain goat. Matt is my left side. "Left side" is a term I borrowed from the writing of Vilhjalmur Stefansson, who spent many years traveling with Eskimo hunters in northern Canada and Alaska during the early twentieth century. Stefansson writes that Eskimo hunters often maintain a partnership with a hunting companion. A hunter may have his partner selected for him upon birth, by his mother. Throughout life, but espe-cially during the winter seal-hunting season, the partners col-laborate and share the meat of their kills. One partner gets the left side of the animal, the other gets the right side. They refer to each other accordingly: my right side, my left side.

Matt and I do not literally split our animals down the back and then go our separate ways. All the meat goes into our freezer, with no regard for which of us killed what. In total, we'll put up hundreds of pounds of meat. We help ourselves and give stuff to friends throughout the year, but we each practice discretion. Neither of us hogs all the good cuts, and neither of us refuses to eat the not-so-good cuts. Ideally, by the time we make our first kill of the new fall—usually in Alaska in August, hunting with Danny—we are nearly through with our meat from the year before. The system works pretty well.

When organizing our freezer, we attempt an out-with-the-old/in-with-the-new system. Sometimes I make an itemized list of the freezer's contents and tape it to the door, but the list always gets screwed up. A friend will grab stuff and not cross the items off, or Matt will add stuff and not record it. Or I'll take out low-grade cuts of meat and make jerky for back-country hunting trips, then fail to record that the items have changed form. The result of all this laxity is that I never really know what's going on in the freezer. Periodically I'll just empty the entire thing out, take stock of what's in there, and start from scratch.

When Diana finished teaching at the summer camp in Michigan, she drove out to Miles City with the fish that Drost and I had caught. Everything arrived safely and frozen stiff, and I went out to the garage to organize the freezer and make room for the frozen frog legs, crayfish, a whole carp, and fillets from smallmouth bass, bluegills, perch, walleye, and a northern pike. When I opened the freezer, I found a disorganized mess. Little bags of frozen sparrows were lying here and there. Matt was just beginning to harvest his garden, which was proving to be as prolific as Eden; containers of tomato puree and blanched green beans were mixed in with boxes of frozen shrimp and crab. The last few packages of burger from a bull elk I'd killed the year before had gotten mixed in with the meat from my freshly killed wild pig. I emptied the freezer out.

As I packed it all back in, I organized the meat into two sections. One section was the stuff for the Escoffier feast. The other section was red meat from the past hunting season. I kept an eye out for things that fit both categories—that is, red meat from the last hunting season that would work for the Escoffier feast—but there wasn't much. We were pretty much down to hamburger, jerky, and summer sausage. Such items would not jibe with Escoffier's style of big game cooking.

Escoffier considers whitetail deer, mule deer, reindeer (a domesticated caribou), and roebuck suitable for fine cuisine, and he endorses the flavor of elk above all else. Rather, I should say, he endorses the flavor of the American elk's close cousin and genetic ancestor, the European elk, which is commonly known as a red deer or stag.

I was happy to read that Escoffier admired the various forms of venison, because venison happens to be one of my favorite foods as well. I will probably never repeat many of the journeys I made during my search for the ingredients of *Le Guide*: I doubt that I will go down to Iowa to trap sparrows with Floyd Van Ert again. And I've almost certainly killed my last frog. But as I prepared for fall hunting in the mountains, I felt as though Escoffier's life and tastes had melded quite naturally with my own. I had gone out searching for classic French cuisine. Now, for once, I felt as though classic French cuisine had come looking for me.

Even so, I knew that I would encounter a lot of weird and new things as I tried to replicate the meat-handling methods of Escoffier's day. I had a long list of organs that I wanted to try: kidney, bladder, liver, heart, tongue, thymus gland, and caul fat, even though I didn't know what caul fat was or how to find it. I also needed to altogether rethink my butchering technique to start making better use of bones.

In *The Escoffier Cookbook,* a condensed, Americanized translation of *Le Guide Culinaire* that first appeared in 1969, the editors printed an addendum in the game section intended for the American hunter. The addendum begins with the observation that "furred game is not nearly so plentiful in the United States as in France and other parts of Europe." One has to assume that this observation relates to the availability of furred game in restaurants and butcher shops, not the wilderness. The editors suggest that the scarcity of game is due to an American lack of knowledge about preparing and cooking it. They advise the reader that "the following recipes often mention cuts of venison not used by American hunters . . . the hunter may follow the directions in the recipes and butcher his own kill."

The recipes that follow use cuts of game in which bones dominate; think of Georgia O'Keeffe's bones and skulls paintings. Escoffier says the bones add significantly to the flavor and appearance of the cut, and bones are indispensable for making stocks and sauces. He liked whole legs, known in culinary terms as haunches. He liked rib chops, which are cuts of loin with long handles of bone. He liked the whole saddle. The saddle is the midsection of an animal's backbone, with the loins and upper ribs still connected.

Escoffier would probably be bored by the modern supermarket meat section. We've got boneless pork roasts, boneless chicken breasts, boneless top sirloin steaks. My own personal butchering technique doesn't exactly highlight the bones; I don't even use the bones. Basically, my method amounts to filleting all the meat off the carcass in the simplest, least imaginative way possible. The little pieces get ground into hamburger and the big pieces get cut into steaks. The bones get discarded.

I had never really asked myself why I butcher the way I do, but I guess my method is born of laziness: it's convenient and easy. For starters, it's difficult to transport a large cut of meat, such as a saddle, when you're up in a remote area with nothing more than a backpack. Aesthetics play into it too. When I have friends for dinner, I don't want to hand them a big ol' bone; bones tend to remind people, in a vivid way, that what they are eating used to be able to stand up and walk around.

Recently, there's an added incentive to toss the bones away: chronic wasting disease, the deer and elk version of mad cow disease, is carried in the animal's central nervous system, including the spine. The disease was first observed in captive game animals in Colorado in the 1960s. It seems to spread most readily where deer and elk are confined in close quarters and are fed in designated areas. In several instances across the West, the disease has spread from captive animals to wild animals. Currently there is no evidence that the disease can be transmitted to humans, though questions about chronic wasting disease seem to outnumber answers. So, besides looking like a Neanderthal when you're nibbling on a deer's spine at a dinner party, you may also look like a fellow who's not afraid of contracting a degenerative, invariably fatal brain disorder. I'd be reluctant to change my eating habits, however, even if CWD was linked to humans. Rather than interpreting the disease as a warning to stay away from game meat, I interpret it as a sign that game farms and captive wildlife facilities should be shut down and banned before they further compromise America's wildlife.

I made my first and least successful attempt to collect some large, bone-in cuts of meat when I was up hunting mountain goats in Alaska. I talked Moisan into coming up with me, to help pack meat. He and I flew into Fairbanks and joined up with my brother Danny. The three of us drove south and parked the truck alongside the Richardson Highway, north of Valdez. We hiked about six miles back into the Chugach Mountains, and made our first camp along a northern fork of Ernestine Creek. The creek flowed with the gray, chalky water of glacial runoff. We were on the edge of the alpine zone. Below us, the valley was overgrown with impenetrable mats of head-high alder and willow and mountain hemlock. Above us, glaciers filled the valleys and basins. In the rare cloudless moments, the sunlight would turn the glaciers a perfectly unnatural blue. The tops of the glaciers were as smooth as roads, and ridges of mountain rose up between the glaciers like highway dividers. The crests of the mountain ridges were bare rock, but the slopes were grown over with an abundance of ankle-high vegetation—crowberry, blueberry, cranberry, bear berry—and topped with a thin layer of snow. As we walked around, the berries burst under our boots and stained the snow with bright blotches, as if someone were shooting at us with a paintball gun. A heavy cloud cover blew in on our first day and snow fell on our first night. Finding a goat became a serious challenge: we were looking for white animals against a white backdrop. The tops of the mountains, where goats hang out, were hidden behind gauzy clouds. We hunted for several days. The first five goats we found were inaccessible, perched on the ledges of sheer cliffs, where you'd think only an eagle could land.

One morning the low clouds broke apart and we had a couple of hours of sunlight. First the valley became clear, then the peaks of the mountains came into focus. Danny worked his spotting scope along a mountain peak that had been hidden from view for days. As he scanned the peak, he saw the heads of two mountain goats that were lying down and chewing their cuds. We spent the morning stalking the goats. After climbing for a couple of hours, we got up to where we thought the animals would be. I peered over a rock and spotted the goats moving away from us on a windswept ledge. On one side of the animals was a gradual slope; the other side was pure nothingness, just sky and cliff. I waited until the closest goat moved more toward the gradual slope, so that it wouldn't go over the cliff when it fell. I meant to hit the animal in the front shoulder, which would have dropped it in its tracks. Instead, I hit it too far back—in the lungs—and it took several steps toward the ledge before falling.

It bounced, slid, and somersaulted 1,200 feet, the equivalent of four football fields. That's a long way to drop your dinner. It took us two hours to get down to the goat's elevation, and then another hour to find the carcass. The horns were gone, busted off at the skull. Every bone in the goat's body was shattered. We butchered that animal, though we didn't retain much besides hamburger. After cutting away bone fragments, we had to cut away blood clots. The organs were gone, the saddle was gone: we filled our backpacks with scraps.

We were pretty bummed out. Since our packs weren't totally full, we stayed in the mountains and looked for black bears. We'd been seeing bears every day. They were getting ready for hibernation and feeding on berries in the high, open country. With the snow on the ground, the bears' black coats looked almost iridescent. We spotted one bear from two miles away. Danny stalked the bear to within a hundred feet and killed it with a clean shot.

We made the opening skinning cuts along the bear's legs and up its abdomen, then started peeling off the hide. The bear's loins were covered in a two-inch-thick layer of fat. The fat was pure white and it smelled good, like blueberries.

The animal had obviously not been feeding on dead salmon, which can make the meat and fat almost unapproachable. I started cutting away long, thick strips of fat and laying them on a boulder.

If it hadn't been for something that happened a few years ago in these same mountains, I would have never thought to save that fat. My brothers and I had been up in the area looking for Dall sheep and we hadn't packed enough food. After a week of reduced rations, we were starting to suffer from mild malnourishment. One night we cut our last piece of hard candy into three sections with a skinning knife. The next afternoon we killed a black bear; we were feeding on the bear within a couple of hours of skinning it. Since we didn't have oil, we melted bear fat and used it to deep-fry pieces of the meat. The next morning Matt poured himself a mug of the warmed bear oil and drank it. He thought it was pretty good, better even than olive oil. I watched him all day, waiting for him to suffer the gastrointestinal problems you'd expect one to suffer from drinking a mug of fat, but he was fine.

The memory of that is what made me want to keep the fat of this new bear. Escoffier used a lot of lard and saltpork made from pig fat, and I was thinking that I might be able to make the same thing from bear fat. Our packs were now overloaded with meat and two hides, but I piled on an additional ten pounds of fat and we started picking our way down out of the mountains.

A few days later I was back in Montana trying to rearrange the freezer again. As I packed away the meat in a somewhat organized fashion, I tried to imagine what Escoffier would have done if his meat purveyor had shown up at the Ritz Hotel with a cartload of smashed goat meat and some bear fat with a handful of dried crowberry leaves sticking to it. Would he have seen potential or disaster? As I pondered this, I worried that I may have taken the substitution thing a little bit too far. It's not easy to look at a glob of frozen bear fat and imagine the world's greatest cuisine coming out of it. I knew that only time would tell, but first there was a lot more hunting that needed to happen.

## CHAPTER SIXTEEN

# The Stinkhole Mountains

Matt and I were glassing for elk in the Stinkhole Mountains of southwest Montana.

Actually, that's a lie. As far as I know, the Stinkhole Mountains do not exist outside my and my friends' imaginations. The fact is, I am not at liberty to reveal the name of the mountains where I really do hunt elk. Matt and I have a pact of silence regarding our elk spots. To find an elk spot that no one else hunts, we have suffered mind-boggling heat and bone-chilling cold, blistered feet and torn ligaments, sprained ankles and chapped asses, and we're not going to start advertising the location.

So anyway, we were sitting on a bluff above the Stinkhole River, glassing the Stinkhole Mountains. The sun was nearing the western horizon. As it dropped toward the ground, the clouds in the sky turned the color of salmon fillets. The mountain range rose abruptly from the foothills on the edge of the valley. The mountains were so steep that they looked like a long, straight wave folding over on a beach. From where we were sitting, we were a two-mile walk from the edge of the mountains; the distance allowed us a panoramic view covering many miles of slopes. We could see five miles to the north, five miles to the south. The air was cold enough that I had to pull my shirtsleeves down over my hands to keep them warm as I gripped my binoculars.

Finding elk involves a lot of just sitting and looking. Elk live in the wildest, remotest tracts of wilderness in the lower forty-eight. The cows weigh around four hundred pounds and the bulls weigh up to twice that, but they can vanish into the mountains like little birds. They have bodies the color of dried grass and necks the color of pine bark. In thick timber, you can get close enough to smell an elk and still not see it. The trick to hunting an elk is finding it before it sees you.

I mentally divided the vast expanse of land into little sections and then began picking those sections apart with the binoculars. When glassing long distances, I spend a lot of time examining suspicious shapes and colors that usually turn out to be stumps and rocks and patches of shade. To be good at finding animals, you have to resist boredom when you're looking around. If I can't positively identify an animal-shaped object that catches my attention, I'll come back to it later and see whether it moved. Or I'll just watch it, then watch it some more.

Hunting in the Stinkhole Mountains for elk, Matt and I have glassed mountain goats, bighorn sheep, black bears, wolves, coyotes, whitetail deer, weasels, martens, mule deer, moose, antelope, mountain lions, and loads of other animals. Next to elk, we're most interested in the whereabouts of grizzly bears. These mountains hold one of the highest concentrations of grizzly bears in the lower forty-eight. Every year a hunter or two will get scratched up by a grizzly. Or severely mauled. Or killed. Being close to grizzlies requires that you be wary but not too wary. If you're thinking about bears too much, just about anything can start to look furry and alive. Rocks take on menacing characteristics. Stumps stand up. You always think you "might have seen something." But when it really is a bear, even if it's two miles away, you instantly realize, binoculars or not, "Holy shit! There's a grizzly!"

As we glassed, Matt guided my eyes to a small herd of mule deer he spotted grazing on a grassy plateau. "Do you see the third peak on the north side of the second valley?" he asked. "Okay, go down from that peak to where the juniper gets sort of thick, and then look below that little patch of lodgepole pines to the right. Okay, go down from there, and you'll see a little rock slide. The rock is grayish, with a white strip. Well, just below the end of that white strip and to the right—"

"Oh, shit. There they are. Good eyes."

The sun was low and bright. From miles away, we could sometimes see the quick flashes of sun shining off birds' wings as they passed from tree to tree. The flashes reminded me of flipped coins.

After a lot of looking, we still hadn't seen any elk. It had been a dry summer, and warm. We discussed the possibility that the elk were still way up in the high country, on their summer range, though the animals usually move into this area in the early fall. We kicked around the idea of heading over to the eastern side of the range, or just going up into these hills and hoping we'd find something.

As we discussed our options, I was glassing far to the north, up behind the Lone Butte Ranch. As I looked, something caught my eye. "I got elk," I said.

Matt turned his binoculars toward where I was looking. "Where?"

"Well, hold on a minute. Maybe I'm fucked up. Oh, nope.

Loads of elk. Maybe forty or so. Up on the ridge above Badger Creek, behind Lone Butte Ranch."

Matt always says that, from way far away, elk look like little maggots crawling around on a hillside. The first time he said that, I thought it was a stupid comparison. But after he'd gotten the image in my head, anytime I looked at elk in the distance, I couldn't help but agree. They do look like little maggots. Even so, I don't like to compare elk to maggots. Looking at maggots usually makes me feel a little nauseated, but looking at elk makes me feel hungry. In my mind, elk are the supreme animal—the biggest, best-tasting animal around. You might get a mule deer that is more tender, or an antelope that is more flavorful, but for consistent, good eating, elk are unrivaled. The closest comparison to elk meat is beef. I hesitate to compare a native animal that can run full-throttle up a one-thousand-foot incline to a slovenly, Old World creature that walks around a fenced pasture with its own green shit caked on its body, but elk and beef do taste somewhat similar. However, wild elk has more flavor, has far less fat and cholesterol, and is 100 percent organic and free-range.

The Lone Butte Ranch is one of those gorgeous, sprawling ranches that have gone in recent years from a hardworking cattle operation to a celebrity trophy ranch. The Lone Butte covers a stretch of grassland and rolling hills along the Stinkhole River, bordered on the backside by high mountain passes and snow-covered peaks. At the time Matt and I started hunting the Stinkhole Mountains, the Lone Butte was owned by an action-adventure movie star. We entertained the idea of sneaking across the ranch to get into the mountains behind it, but rumors had spread that the movie star traveled with a Samoan masseur, a ninja warrior, and a machine gun. It seemed that we'd have better luck walking unannounced into the Playboy Mansion than we would trying to traipse across his property. Over time, we figured out a seven-mile route of footpaths and game trails that would get us on the other side of the fence, back behind the ranch. A Samoan masseur with a set of keys to the Lone Butte's gates could make the drive on a four-wheeler in the time allowed between cocktails and dinner. But past that fence is federally designated wild land, protected by a ban on all motorized vehicles and equipment. In short, the other side of the fence is like the edge of the known world.

It was getting dark. The elk herd seemed calm and relaxed, not likely to travel any great distances. In the morning, they'd probably be in that same area, or at least close by. We picked up our backpacks and started hiking downhill through a stand of Douglas fir. We hit a footpath at the base of a bluff. By then it was dark. The path followed Dry Creek up toward the mountains. As we walked, we went through stands of trees and patches of sagebrush. In his earth-toned clothes, Matt looked like nothing more than a shadow in the darkness in front of me. As we entered one patch of trees, a spruce grouse blasted out from some limbs above our heads and nearly scared the shit out of us. Getting startled like that got me thinking about bears, so I pulled my headlamp out of my pack, just in case (I didn't turn it on), and released the safety latch on my pepper spray. My bow and arrows would be essentially useless against a charging grizzly, because it takes time to load, pull, and aim a bow. Besides, I'd be reluctant to shoot and injure a bear with an arrow unless I really thought it was going to fuck me up. The spray gave me a sense of security, though probably false. A couple of years before, we were heading up a trail like this and came face to face with a grizzly. I nocked an arrow on the string of my bow *and* pulled out my pepper spray, but once we started hollering and screaming at her, she dropped down on all fours and headed back up the trail.

Over the next two hours, we followed Dry Creek, zigzagging through sagebrush flats and sparse patches of aspens, until we'd climbed up to a large bench of grassland. The bench spread toward the mountain and then ended where the rocks and timber on the slopes took over. From there, the mountain rose a couple of thousand feet, forming a network of ridges and peaks rarely visited by man. We walked up to the edge of the bench, then headed northward until we entered a sheltered stand of aspen.

"What do you think?" Matt asked.

The ground in the aspen stand was rough but flat.

"I guess it's all right."

We took off our packs and unloaded our gear: I had a sleeping bag, a plastic tarp, cutlery, archery equipment, a small cooking pot, rope, basic first aid stuff, a compass, long underwear, a rain jacket, a collapsible canteen, a water purifier, candy bars, and freeze-dried food. I found a stout stick and pried up some rocks, forming a relatively flat spot for my sleeping bag. The air temperature was above freezing, so I laid out my clothes beneath my sleeping bag for padding instead of keeping them on my body for warmth. Matt has a much higher tolerance for rough ground; he laid out his sleeping bag right where it landed and started cooking us some Italian sausages on an alcohol stove. We had made the sausage from a moose that we had killed right in those same mountains. After dinner we hung our food way up in an aspen tree, out of the reach of bears, and were asleep within ten minutes.

Birds started making a racket long before daylight. The

white-bark pine nuts were coming into season and loads of birds—gray jays, Clark's nuthatches, Steller's jays—had moved into the area to feed. They sounded anxious to get on with their day. Matt and I were a little slow to crawl out of our bags. The air temperature had dropped radically. Checking my water bottle, I found the mouth crusted with ice. I pulled it into my sleeping bag to thaw it out. We lay there, talking quietly and listening for elk bugles. Generally, bulls bugle during their breeding season, which runs from early September to late October. Bugling has something to do with attracting females and challenging rival bulls, but there's probably more to it than that. I don't like to act like I understand it very well. The classic, picture-perfect bugle is a three-note sequence that lasts four or five seconds. It sounds sort of like a long, drawn-out *Gloria*—minus the *G*. Just as likely, though, a bugle will sound like an outrageously loud belch, grunt, scream, or sob. Bugling usually intensifies at dawn, and then again right before dark. If you listen to the bugles as you doze off in your sleeping bag, the sounds will infiltrate your dreams.

Aside from the birds, the mountains above us were quiet. We skipped breakfast. Our gear was packed up and we were walking north by the time a thin band of light had formed at the tops of the eastern mountains. I checked the trail for animal tracks, a habit of mine. I saw coyote and deer tracks. The tracks formed clean, definite marks in the dry dust, so I knew the animals had recently passed through, probably that night.

The trail cut through a few meadows and then down into a timbered drainage. The creek at the bottom was just a rocky trickle of water. We stopped to fill a couple of bottles. On the edges of the stream, small patches of claylike dried mud adhered to the tracks like plaster. You would miscalculate the number of animals passing through an area if you relied on the mosaics of tracks formed in this kind of mud; the tracks can last for months and it takes major rain or runoff to wipe them away. The most recent-looking track was from a small bear, but it wasn't clear enough to show whether it was a grizzly or a black bear.

We crossed two more creeks, and then the trail we were following began to split apart, like the frayed end of broken rope. We believed that the herd of elk was still north and east of us. As the trail ended, we had two options: either head into the mountains up a narrow canyon and then climb through a pass, or else climb another steep ridge and continue moving north along the face of the mountains.

We decided to keep heading north. The going was slow, with scattered boulders and thick sagebrush. After we topped the ridge, the properties of the Lone Butte ranch were down below us. The ranch ran all the way up to the foot of the mountains, so we'd have to go uphill to dodge the private property line. It's not that I was morally opposed to passing through private land; I just didn't want to get caught by some hired hand out riding the ranch's fence lines. We decided to keep uphill of the property line, which meant we had to travel along the steep face of a mountain slope. Eventually we came to a V-shaped opening in the face of the mountain. It was Badger Creek. We dropped down into the creek bed and then began following it up. We were leaving the Lone Butte's property line behind us.

Badger Creek does not have a good footpath, so the going was rough at first. We passed through some thick stands of lodgepole pine with lots of fallen trees that we had to climb over. Then we hit a game trail and picked up the pace. The ground got rockier and the trees started to thin out. As we got into the mountains a ways, we started to notice more and more elk droppings. Steep slopes rose up on either side of us. Looking up Badger Creek, we could see glimpses of snow-covered peaks a couple of miles in front of us, up near the range divide. The wind was coming down the valley, and we caught a few whiffs of elk. Elk smell like horses, only sweeter and wilder. When the animals are using an area heavily, the odor permeates the area and hangs on for days after the animals leave. But the odor we were catching was fresh, like it was still connected to its source. The sun was high in the sky and the air had warmed up to the midfifties. The elk were probably bedded down on the slopes, in the shade of the timber.

At the creek Matt and I stripped our clothes and washed up, then rubbed our armpits, crotches, and feet with Dr. Scholl's Original Foot Powder. An elk might not be familiar with the smell of Dr. Scholl's, but it damn sure doesn't hate that smell as much as it hates the smell of a man. We got dressed again and started working our way up Badger Creek, very slowly.

Every so often we'd climb out of the creek bed to look around. On both sides of the creek, scattered across the valley floor, head-sized rocks had been turned over by foraging bears looking for bugs. The soil at the bottoms of the indentations was still moist.

"I'm trying to decide how much money you'd have to pay me to spend the night here with a bucket of honey strapped to my head," whispered Matt. It's a favorite topic of ours when in bear country.

Here and there, among the turned-over rocks, we could see large piles of bear shit. One way to determine the age of bear shit is to see what's in it. A grizzly's scat reflects its current diet more accurately than that of any other animal I know.

The shit we found along Badger Creek was packed with the green leaves of knick-knick, a low, berry-producing shrub. Knick-knick grows so low to the ground that bears seem to pick up a lot of extra goods when they graze it. Mixed in with the leaves were berry seeds, pine needles, and dirt. Later in the fall, into October and November, most of the bear shit we find contains white-bark pine nuts. A grizzly's stomach cannot break down the shells of the nuts; the bears pass large cylinders of the crushed shards, packed together like particle board. I've picked through the scat and found whole, individual nuts inside that were still in good-enough condition to roast and put on a salad, if you were in a pinch.

If a grizzly's been feeding on a dead deer or elk, its scat will resemble a supersized hairball from a domestic cat, with bone fragments mixed in. In the spring, grizzlies eat various grasses and pass greasy, greenish black balls resembling horse manure. One time I was hunting black bears in the spring, in Montana's Cabinet Mountains, where a lot of grizzlies live. I found a pile of bear shit made of dark, glossy hair. As I turned a piece over in my hand, I was startled to see that the hair was actually a small black bear's finger and claw. I have a collection of wild animal shit, and I added that specimen as the centerpiece in my display case.

As Matt and I worked upstream, our view of what lay ahead was blocked by trees. The timber on each hillside extended down toward the center of the valley in long fingers that touched at the creek. When we entered the trees, an eruption of angry pine squirrel chatter filled the air as the squirrels raced to the tops of the trees. I often wonder if other animals rely on pine squirrels as an alarm system. I tend to doubt it, because pine squirrels' warnings are too indiscriminate. For example, I've watched them bark at grouse. In this case, though, the squirrels' barks were warranted; I've shot pine squirrels with my bow and shredded their meat for burritos.

We crept to the upstream edge of the trees and found a comfortable place to sit and glass. The squirrel chatter faded as they forgot about the disturbance and went back to knocking pine cones out of the trees. Beyond the edge of the timber, the valley spread out into a large bowl, shaped like an amphitheater. The amphitheater was made of grass-covered slopes, with small patches of white-bark pine and subalpine fir—maybe three or four trees per patch—sprouting here and there.

Say it really was an amphitheater; Matt and I were crouching where the band would play. In the half circle around us, where the back row of cheering fans would be, we could see scatterings of elk. Maybe thirty animals in all, in groups of three or four, formed the amphitheater's rim up on the ridges. Those were probably the same animals we'd seen the night before. We'd arrived at our destination.

Off to our right, the north-facing wall of the amphitheater had much thicker timber than the other walls. Long, wheezy elk bugles came down from the timber, but the trees were too thick for us to see what was going on up there. We could see a vertical slash through the timber where an avalanche had swept the trees away. The path of the avalanche had grown over in grass and flowers and was strewn with bleached, barkless tree trunks that had been uprooted by rushing snow. We glassed the avalanche chute but couldn't see any elk. It sounded like at least three of them up there, screaming their heads off. One of the bulls sounded like it was up and over the rim, maybe even in the next drainage to the south.

We discussed our options.

"If we step out of here," I said, "we'll freak out those elk on the rim. But maybe we could go straight up after those bulls. Get in on them by coming in from below."

"That won't work," Matt said. "As soon as we start up that hill, they'll be downwind of our scent."

He was right. A slight thermal current was moving uphill. Every few minutes, a breeze swayed the tops of the trees on the slope. To kill an elk with a bow, you've got to get within forty yards of it. If an elk is downwind, it will smell you coming three hundred yards away, easily.

Many hunters carry an elk bugle, a tubelike tool that you can blow through to mimic the sound of a bull. When bow hunters first started using bugles, in the 1970s and 1980s, they worked really well. But the elk in many areas, particularly on public land, have wised up, and most bulls now treat a bugle with suspicion unless they can see that it's coming from another elk. Matt and I used to bugle for elk, but we gave up on the calls and started silently stalking and ambushing the animals instead.

The creek wound its way through the floor of the amphitheater. It was lined on each side by aspens and willow, the way maples line the boulevards in university towns. The trees shaded the water, which was so cold it cooled the air above it and caused a slight downhill breeze to move along the creek bed. As a makeshift windsock, I had a grouse feather tied to the limb of my bow with dental floss. The downstream breeze above the water was stiff enough to make the feather stand out horizontally on its leash. We decided to continue moving upstream, with the hope that the air current along the water would carry our smell back downstream instead of up into the hills.

We stayed low, moving slowly and keeping an eye out. The stream bed climbed rapidly like a staircase, sometimes spilling over its path in small waterfalls. After an hour of creeping along, we had moved up through the amphitheater. The walls of the valley closed back in on us like a canyon. When we turned around, we could see the place we'd been sitting when we initially spotted the elk, way down below us. We had passed to the upwind side of the animals, so that we were almost eye level with the elk on the rim.

It was getting into the afternoon, and the sun had passed its midway point in the sky. We stashed some of our gear. Matt tied a rock to a string and hurled it over a high limb, then pulled our food up into the tree. He marked the location of our gear on his GPS. We were eight miles from the truck, 9,200 feet above sea level.

We moved to where we could get a good look around. As evening approached, we expected the elk up on the ridges to move down into the bowl of the amphitheater to feed on the grass. The slopes there were carpeted in a common bunch grass called Idaho fescue, which elk seem to prefer above all else. From where we were, we could see some familiar peaks where we'd hunted mountain goats in the past. We looked up there with our binoculars to kill time, but it was too far to tell if any animals were hanging around.

Every ten minutes or so, the bulls on the thickly timbered slope would let out some bugles. For an hour, the source of the bugles didn't seem to move. As the sun dropped toward the horizon, and the trees started to throw long shadows, the source of the bugling seemed to travel downhill toward the creek.

"We should probably move down," said Matt.

"Yeah, in a minute."

I was watching the opposite side of the valley. The herd on that rim, at least twenty elk, was moving slowly downhill, feeding along the way. The lower the elk came, the better we could see them. There were lots of cows, and a few young spike-horned bulls. A spike-horn is one and a half years old—not yet sexually mature.

We decided to split up. Matt would move into the timber and try to get in front of the bugling elk. I'd try to move toward the elk that were moving down the open hillside. Each move was a challenge. Because Matt couldn't see his elk, he might unknowingly stumble into some cows and spook the whole herd. Because my elk were out in the open, I had the advantage of being able to keep an eye on them. But they had the same advantage on me; they could potentially see me coming from hundreds of yards away.

We each packed up some basic gear: food, water, jacket and rain pants, flashlights and matches, meat bags, and plenty of strong cord.

As soon as we split up, I got the same uneasy feeling that I always get when Matt and I split up in the mountains. I worry that something will happen to him. Matt doesn't worry about himself, he says, because he's too busy worrying about me. Neither of us is likely to get lost, but there's plenty of other stuff to go wrong. Rocks fall. Trees fall. You could twist a leg or get stuck between shifting boulders. Hypothermia happens fast, and it kills many mountain hunters. There are rattlesnakes. And then there are things you'd never expect. One time we were heading up a mountain through some thick brush with one of Matt's old girlfriends. All of a sudden she started screaming and flailing her arms. We couldn't tell what had happened. I thought she was having a stroke or something. Then we saw that a porcupine had nailed her from above. Her shoulder bristled with quills. The porcupine climbed down from its tree and walked away, as nonchalantly as someone stepping off a bus.

And there are bears, of course, although a bear attack is the least likely potential disaster. But we sometimes get careless and ask for it. Once we were taking a nap on a ridge and woke up for a moment when a black bear came running by. After our nap, we happened to travel in the same direction the bear had gone. We walked a ways down the ridge, then heard the unmistakable scratching sound of a bear climbing a tree. We thought it was the black bear, and Matt still had a bear permit, so we ran over there. But it wasn't the black bear. It was a sow grizzly and her cub; the cub was scratching the tree all right, but the sow was on solid ground and looked about ready to come at us. She didn't, but it reminded me of how easily something bad could happen.

By using the contours of the land, and clumps of trees, I quickly closed the distance on the elk that I was after. I found a few places where elk had pissed in the past day or two, little saucer-sized circles of wet dirt. The piss smelled musky and elky. I scooped up the dirt in my hand and rubbed my clothes with it. I rubbed some of the urine and dirt on to my face. I scanned the area for grizzlies.

Soon I was lying prone in a patch of subalpine fir and had elk both above me and ahead of me. I'd moved about as far as I could without being detected. The closest elk was two hundred yards above me. A cow. I could see the top of her back and glimpses of her head. I could see bits and pieces of other elk behind and ahead of her, obscured by trees and rocks and folds in the land. I could see an ear, a patch of orangish-colored fur on a rump, a leg from the knee down. At least one of the elk was a young bull; I caught glimpses of white antler tips every time it lifted its head. The breeze was more or less in my face, but I watched the feather on my bow carefully. Time and again, a faint wisp of air tugged the feather uphill, toward the elk above me. I worried that a stronger gust would carry my scent up there and freak those elk out. I decided to hold tight until the wind made up its mind about which way to blow. I was on my belly. Slowly, without moving more than an inch at a time, I pushed myself up to a sitting position with a tree to my back.

The elk that was closest to me lifted its head and stared downhill, right in my direction. Shit. Had it seen me? I stayed superstill, holding my breath and avoiding eye contact. The tree's lower limbs camouflaged my form. The elk looked like a young cow. I've had young elk look me in the face for five minutes, then start feeding again. They don't always trust their eyes. And older animals don't always trust the judgment of young animals. I've watched younger cows and spikes get spooked by a movement and then run off alone, the other elk just watching them go. If a lead cow—an old, mature cow who's been around for a few years—gets nervous and trots away, the whole herd will trip over themselves to follow her.

I couldn't hold my breath any longer, so I let it out in a slow exhale without moving my chest too much. The elk lowered its head and had another munch of grass. I took a long, deep breath. Maybe it never even saw me. Either way, I was trapped. I knew I couldn't move until that elk did.

At times it feels as though killing an elk with a bow is an impossible feat. So many things can go wrong, it seems like there is no room left over in the world for something to go right. When I get discouraged, it's helpful to remember those rare occurrences when things fall into place in the mountains. Just the year before, over a ridge to the south, I was trapped in a similar situation. I'd been crawling down a mountain with the wind in my face, trying to get into a herd of elk that I could hear below me. I made it down the mountain a ways, but then I ran into a group of cows that were bedded down. I couldn't go down any farther without their seeing me, so I was trapped. I waited about half an hour and the elk wouldn't move. I was finally getting ready to crawl back up and go look for a different herd when a bull walked up and smelled one of the cow's asses. She jumped up, stepped toward me, and then disappeared behind a tree. The bull walked after her and paused, broadside to me, at thirty yards. My arrow cut into him right behind his shoulder blade. He took a few steps down the mountain and then stopped. He looked around, stumbled a bit, then tipped over dead.

As I watched these elk in Badger Creek, I hoped for a similar piece of luck. I watched several more cows emerge over the crest of the rim and start feeding down into the amphitheater. A bull emerged along with them. He was hundreds of yards away. I could have killed him with a rifle, but he was way beyond the range of a bow. He had six tines on each antler; he was a big, breeding-age bull. He stepped up behind one of the cows and got too close to her. She trotted away. The bull straightened his spine, stretched his neck out, tipped his snout up, and let out a horrendous noise, like he was trying to clear a cactus thorn out of his throat. I was so far away that the bull had already closed his mouth and lowered his head by the time the complete bugle had traveled to my ears. The animal was huge. It seemed that when an elk got that big, it should switch from grass and start eating meat. Another bull, up and over the rim, answered him with a three-note falsetto call.

I'd lost track of how many elk were above me and ahead of me. The cow that had looked in my direction had moved down a bit, but I was clearly not going to get a shot at her. She was out in the open and I didn't have any cover to use while sneaking up on her. The small bull behind the closest cow had turned around; he was walking one way and the rest of the herd was walking the other way. He seemed intent on something that I couldn't see. Maybe he was going to check out some other elk. As he moved along the hillside, he walked down into a slight gully and dropped from view. That was my chance. I moved to my belly and tried to inch up the hill to close the distance while the elk was out of sight. I kept checking on the other elk, who were facing away from me.

The sun was halfway gone behind the western peaks. I could feel the air temperature plummeting. I didn't have much time, but there was no point in rushing. So long as we didn't spook these elk, we could sleep nearby and hunt them again in the morning. The breeze stiffened. It was perfect for me. I crawled on all fours until I was close to where the small bull had disappeared into the gully. The bottom of the gully was covered in young aspen trees. Several large boulders were strewn about. I figured the bull could be anywhere. It might have turned back while I was crawling, or it might be standing in range but out of sight. I removed an arrow from my quiver and slipped the nocking point over my bowstring. I was up on my knees. I waited.

A minute passed. Then I heard the unmistakable sound of hooves clacking on rocks and thudding into dirt. The sound was above me. At first I thought the hooves were coming toward me, but they were actually heading away from me. I sat up a little more and saw elk asses moving uphill. The whole slope was going into motion. The elk were heading up, running over the top of the rim. Then, right in front of me, an elk ran out of the aspen and started hauling ass uphill, leaving a trail of dust. It was the bull. His head was held improbably high, like a running camel. His body looked stiff and taut as he ran. Within seconds, the whole amphitheater was cleared of elk.

All I could think was, What the hell happened? I checked the feather. The wind was perfect, blowing away from all the elk. I stood up. What the hell?

When I caught another glimpse of movement out of the corner of my eye, I ducked back down quickly. Something just below me, something much darker than an elk, was coming my way. Was it a bear? I lifted my head. It was Matt, strolling across the valley like some tourist in Yellowstone Park. *Matt* had scared off all the elk? What a moron. I stood back up. He was walking toward me. I shrugged my shoulders and lifted my palms toward the sky in a "What the fuck are you doing?" gesture.

Matt lifted his bow and acted like he was shooting an arrow. I stood up and let out a yell of excitement. He'd gotten a shot.

WHEN MATT AND I HAD SPLIT UP, HE HAD GONE INTO THE TIMBER and begun working his way toward the bugling elk, who were moving downhill at a fast pace. Pretty quickly, Matt could tell from the bugles that the herd was down along the creek, so he followed them there, backtracking along the same path that we'd walked a few hours before. The wind along the stream had reversed from its earlier direction and was blowing upstream. As he crept downstream, he could hear and see elk on both sides, but he couldn't tell where they had all come from; we'd just walked through there together and hadn't seen any elk that low.

Every time he poked up his head for a look, he could see the backs of elk, but none of them were close enough for a shot. He crawled downstream some more, sometimes right in the shallow, rocky trickles of water that branched off the main stem of the stream. When he got to a spot where he could see several elk feeding in a meadow, he contemplated taking a shot but decided he was too far away. As he watched them, he noticed that four cows were actually coming toward him. He got an arrow ready. The cows walked right down toward the stream, like they were going to cross. The second cow in the line was clearly the biggest. The first cow took a step down into the stream bed, and Matt let her pass. When the second, larger cow got even with him, he drew back his bow. She was twenty-five yards away. He took aim right behind her front shoulder, a little lower than halfway up her body. He released the arrow. It sank into the brown hair and disappeared.

All four of the elk bolted back out of the creek bed and headed back the way they had come. At first, the arrowed elk didn't act any differently than the healthy elk. Matt watched them run out of view behind a slight rise of land. But when the elk reemerged on the other side, there were only three of them. Matt walked up to where he figured I would be, hoping to intercede before I killed another one; we already had more than enough work cut out for us.

We followed the creek down to where Matt had made his shot. It was getting dark. He pointed to where he'd tied a strip of plastic ribbon on a twig to mark where the elk had been standing. We walked about sixty yards and there it was. The elk was lying on its side, two legs folded beneath it and two legs stretched out. It weighed more than Matt and me combined.

Up until the point when we had a dead animal lying on the ground, I'd been thinking about all sorts of stuff: I'd been thinking about elk, and how they live in constant fear of wolves and then get added stress from us hunters; I'd been thinking about the way the wind changes when the sun sets;

I'd been thinking about how a gray jay will clean pine pitch from its beak by scraping it on a limb, just like a person cleans extra peanut butter from a knife by scraping it along the rim of the jar.

Once the elk was dead, though, I only had room in my mind for the carcass. When I thought about the wind, I thought of how the smell of the elk's blood was already blowing off into the mountains and perhaps getting the attention of a grizzly. When I thought about gray jays, I thought of how they'd quickly find the carcass in the morning and start squawking about the good fortune and then probably draw the attention of a grizzly.

The year before, two of our buddies were hunting in these same mountains, not far from us, when they lost one-fourth of their elk to a grizzly. A couple of years before that, a hunter to the north and west of us was killed in the Swan Mountains, on Cottonwood Creek, when a sow grizzly caught him in the act of gutting a cow elk.

After the hunter in the Swan Mountains was killed, state and federal wildlife officers went out there and killed the grizzly along with her two cubs. I found the whole situation depressing as hell. That bear had probably stolen dozens of carcasses in the course of her life, from wolves and coyotes and other bears, but that time she stole from the wrong species. The hunter's widow later sued the government agencies, basically for allowing grizzly bears to exist. The way I see it, you shouldn't go into the largest piece of contiguous wilderness in the lower forty-eight and spend your day butchering a warm pile of protein if you and your family can't accept the potential threats. Matt and I have an agreement that if one of us ever gets mauled by a grizzly, we'll keep the location of the incident a secret. When I die, I want my brothers (or whatever kids they have) to quarter out my carcass and dump it up in the Stinkholes. They should nail a small wooden plaque to a tree that says Here Lies Meat.

Keeping game meat safe from scavengers is one of the oldest chores of mankind, and we took to the job quickly. We pushed on the elk together, as though we were trying to get a barrel rolling along, and got it up on its back. The four legs were pointing up.

With the elk on its back, I took my knife and cut around the elk's anus, then made a neat incision all the way up to the throat. With a bone saw, I cut through the center of the rib cage. The chest cavity was flooded with blood. The diaphragm was holding the blood back like a dam. I could see the stomach, the coiled intestines, the liver, all clean and bloodless. It was a vivid depiction of what I'd look like splayed open. I reached up into the chest cavity and, blindly, severed the esophagus. Doing so, I pricked my finger on something sharp. I reached back in there and pulled out a six-inch section of carbon arrow shaft that had snapped off inside the body. I pulled the heart out too. It was the size of a small chicken.

Once I sliced through both sides of the diaphragm, the guts were lying loose inside the elk's body like soup in a soup bowl. Everything was freed up. I reached under the stomach and peeled away the kidneys, which I set aside with the heart. Matt lifted up on the neck of the animal and I rolled everything out in a great sloppy heap, leaving the bowl of the rib cage clean and glistening with blood.

At that point, it was like we'd released a massive advertising blitz promoting an all-you-can-eat elk special. As we continued to work, we took turns scanning with our flashlights for approaching bears. I removed the two tenderloins from inside the body cavity. A tenderloin is about the size of a hoagie roll: it's one of the most primo cuts of meat. We rolled the elk onto its side and skinned half of the animal. As Matt lifted the rear leg, I cut through the joint. Then I climbed about fifteen feet up into a nearby tree. I draped a piece of parachute cord over a limb and lowered the ends down to Matt. He tied one end of the cord to the leg and then pulled the other end, hoisting the leg into the tree. There it was safe from coyotes and grizzlies, but black bears, which can climb, were still a threat. Anything else that got at it, such as a marten or bobcat, wouldn't eat too much. Lions like to kill their own animals and generally don't mess with carrion.

We repeated the process with the front leg, then boned out the ribs and the neck and removed the loin. The loin was about the size of two pieces of firewood laid end to end. All the boned-out meat went into a meat bag and up the tree, along with the heart, liver, and kidneys. Once the left side of the animal was done, we rolled it over and repeated the process on the other side.

After about three hours, all of the usable parts of the elk were up the tree, and the carcass was just guts and bone and hide. We knew our leftovers wouldn't last long. We've seen bears eat every part of an elk carcass except for the base of the skull.

We turned off our flashlights and waited for our eyes to adjust to the dark. Matt took a waypoint marking the carcass on his GPS. Then we headed back up to where we'd stashed our food and gear. We were totally exhausted. We ate some freeze-dried soup, washed our hands in the creek, raised our grub back into a tree, and went immediately to sleep.

At dawn we could hear bulls bugling all around us. We probably could have killed another elk, but we first had to get one out of there. Every time we come up into these mountains, we like to pretend to ourselves that we have the balls to backpack our elk meat across the Lone Butte properties and then stash it along the highway. Doing so would cut our walk in half. That plan has multiple problems: We'd have to wait until dark, and flashlights would be out of the question. We'd have to walk to the highway and then get back into the cover of the mountains in the time allowed between sunset and sunrise. A few times we'd gone so far as to stash a car at a place where we might emerge if we did make a midnight run with a load of meat. And we thought of what we'd say if we got caught: "We're lost."

Every time we get an elk, though, we have a conversation that goes like the one we had the day after Matt killed the cow along Badger Creek.

"I don't know, man," I said. "It almost seems like less of a pain in the ass to just hike this bastard out of here. I don't feel like dealing with some irate landowner . . . or worse, the sheriff."

"We should get going then, if we're going out the way we came in."

We walked to a vantage point from where we could see if any bears had found our kill. We could see about ten magpies feeding on the gut pile, but otherwise, the coast was clear. At the carcass, the bones were all scattered here and there. The stomach was mostly eaten away, and the elk's last meal was lying there like someone had dumped a bag of grass clippings. The ground was peppered with coyote tracks, but there were no visible bear tracks.

We went over to the tree and lowered the meat bags and the four whole legs. Because we had to pack the entire animal on our backs, we were forced to bone out the legs. Packing out a haunch or a saddle was out of the question. With the bone in, an elk's back ham will barely fit into a large backpack. A whole saddle would almost be a load in itself. By cutting the meat off the bones, we could reduce our total load of meat down to just over 200 pounds. That's 120 pounds apiece, including the heart, liver, kidneys, drinking water, and the weight of the backpacks themselves. After I've walked a few miles, 120 pounds makes me feel like dying. A few more pounds and I probably would die. So the bones were staying in the mountains for the bears and coyotes.

Once we got done boning the elk and putting the meat into mesh game bags, we stashed all of our gear and our extra clothes under a tarp to make room in our packs. Later we'd have to come back up to get our stuff. Sometimes we leave our gear in the mountains for a couple of weeks like that.

The packs were so heavy, we had to help each other get to our feet. Once we got under way, we started popping ibuprofen like trail mix. The miles dragged along. We walked until we couldn't walk anymore, then sat down and bitched and moaned about having to walk more. To go up steep hills, we took baby steps and no rest stops, which is better than moving fast and then having to stop for air halfway up an incline. Our other brother carries a little weed for these sorts of situations up in Alaska. Just when you can't stand to carry meat another foot, you have a quick smoke. Then, within minutes, you're back to thinking about how tripped out and crazy it is to be hiking through the mountains with a load of Dall sheep meat on your back.

We made it to the truck before dusk. I lay down in the dirt for ten minutes. When I stood up, my legs had already cramped. We'd left our sleeping bags in the mountains because we didn't have room for them. It was getting cold, down near freezing, and neither of us relished the idea of suffering through a night in the back of the truck with no sleeping bag.

We walked down to Dry Creek and washed out our backpacks, so that we didn't smell too much like a dead elk. Then we started walking back into the mountains.

It was a totally moonless night, and thick black clouds were settling in. We couldn't see shit, so we had to use our flashlights. With a flashlight, your whole world is reduced to whatever's in the beam. It's frustrating to travel long distances with the seemingly myopic vision of a flashlight beam; I feel as though I'm going to walk right up on something that I may not want to get that close to.

When we got to Badger Creek, we tried to travel up along the mountain face so that we wouldn't go near the elk carcass. We didn't want to get close to the carcass and surprise a grizzly. We got a little screwed around on our route; when we came down to Badger Creek, we couldn't tell where we were.

"We better cut back uphill," Matt said. "I'm not sure we made it far enough past the carcass."

"Sure we did. I think it's way the hell down from here."

"No, I don't think so."

"Take a look with your GPS," I said. "You took a waypoint at the kill site."

Matt pulled the GPS out. He waited a couple of minutes while the unit conferred with the satellites to figure out where it was. When the GPS found its position, Matt pulled up the kill site waypoint. He pointed at the digital reading. I took a look.

We were forty feet away from the carcass and whatever might have been eating it.

I felt my stomach rise up toward my throat. "Holy shit," I said.

We walked quietly backward. I half expected to hear the

*woof* of a pissed-off bear, but it never came. We slipped back up the hillside and continued on our way.

That night we got six inches of wet snow by morning. At sunup a mist settled over the hills. We couldn't see any farther than we could shoot our bows. In the early morning the temperature dropped some more and the snow froze to a crust. Walking on it sounded like we were dancing on potato chips. We packed up our wet shit and headed back down. By the time we got to the truck, we were walking on dry ground and it was sunny. Looking back, we could see that the Stinkhole Mountains were still socked in with haze and covered in a crust of icy snow. The wave that was folding over the valley two days before had frozen in place.

# CHAPTER SEVENTEEN

# Mixed Bag

PUTTING AN ELK ON THE GROUND GIVES ME A TREMENDOUS sense of relief. It feels good in an immediate way, like shaking an all-day hangover. And it feels good in a long-term way too, like knowing you've got some money in the bank. Once Matt and I had his elk out of the mountains and in the truck, we holed up in a motel for the night. When we woke up, we went out to the truck and took another long look at all that meat. It felt as though our whole fall was stretched out ahead of us, free and clean. Now we were free to do whatever kind of hunting and screwing around we felt like without having to worry about whether or not it was productive. To celebrate our freedom, we launched a trip for bighorn sheep.

In Montana, bighorn sheep permits are given out in a lottery; a hunter who puts in his name only has about a one percent chance of drawing. Matt got lucky; he picked up a tag while I was putting together the Escoffier feast. I'd be excited to hunt sheep no matter what, but Escoffier happened to use a bit of mutton. The rare chance to eat bighorn would be complemented by some help from the King of Chefs.

Matt's sheep permit was for a hunting district in the southeastern Gallatin Range, near Cinnabar Mountain. The sheep down there tend to spend their summers in the high country of Yellowstone National Park, up near Electric Peak, and then migrate out of the park as the snows get deep. As they come down, they cross over Cinnabar Mountain.

Now, man has been hunting in the land that encompasses Yellowstone National Park for something like ten millennia, but for the last hundred or so years it's been off-limits to hunters. So hunting for a bighorn around Cinnabar Mountain is a waiting game. You've got to watch the weather carefully. As soon as the snow in the high country starts to stack up, the sheep will begin coming down. That usually happens around late October, just when the sheep season around Cinnabar Mountain ends. It's a gamble.

We made our first trip to Cinnabar Mountain the day after killing our elk, so we still had the animal's meat in the back of the truck. We were hoping that the snow we saw in the Stinkhole Mountains had fallen in the Gallatin Mountains as well. It had, but not as much. That night we slept in a beautiful meadow beneath a crumbling thousand-foot cliff. The meadow was strewn with car-sized boulders that had broken free and landed in our campsite over the years. When I woke in the morning, I thanked Mother Nature for not squashing me. We then spent a day hiking around Cinnabar Mountain and glassing the ridges for sheep. By the end of the day it was hot as hell, the snow was gone, and we hadn't seen shit for bighorns. We determined that the sheep weren't coming down yet, so we went back to Miles City to process our elk.

As soon as we turned the garage lights on, two things happened. First, the pigeons started cooing. The coop is positioned near the garage window, so the birds thought morning had arrived and woke up to resume their ongoing battles over who got which perch. The second thing that happened is Wes Munsel came over. Wes is the old fellow who lives with his wife, Agnes, next door to Matt. Wes is eighty-seven years old and retired. Whenever Wes sees the garage light on after Matt and I have been out hunting, he comes over to see if we're butchering an animal. He can't resist the temptation; a butchering job lures Wes Munsel in like a siren's song.

"What do you know?" asked Wes. He was carrying a bottle of beer for each of us. As usual, Wes was all dressed up. He was wearing Western-cut, brown polyester pants. Agnes had ironed a razor's edge crease down the front of each leg. He had on a brown satin jacket and a button-up dress shirt. Up on top, he was sporting his beige cowboy hat and trifocals. His face was lined with age, but he stood erect and bright-eyed.

I think Wes likes me and Matt because he's hard of hearing and we talk really loud and clear for him. We like Wes because he's a walking meat encyclopedia. He knows about wild game animals and domestic animals. He used to invest in livestock and he founded his own slaughterhouse in Miles City back in 1946. He's butchered about everything that ever walked or crawled, and he's done a lot of other bizarre, meat-related stuff. Back in the 1940s, Wes bought lame horses for five dollars apiece. He was fattening hogs back then. He'd take the horses into the pigpen and shoot them dead. Then he'd make all the skinning cuts on the hide, tie the horse's head to a fence post, and pull the hide off with a tractor. Horse hides were going for three fifty. The hogs would take care of the rest. They could eat a horse down to bone in a few days. When the pigs were done, Wes would go in and gather the bones up, because the pigs would wind up carrying the bones around and would eventually choke on the splinters.

Another thing I like about Wes is that he doesn't pass judgment on our informal butchering methods, which may not be up to the specifications of the USDA. Wes watched us pull the elk meat out of the game bags, and there were some pine needles and hairs that needed to be picked off. Wes didn't comment; instead, he helped us pick the meat clean. This wasn't as easy as it would be for your average eighty-seven-year-old man, because Wes is missing his right thumb. That's a silly way to put it, because Wes knows damn sure where his thumb is. When he was in his twenties, he and a brother were cutting firewood on a saw blade powered off a pickup truck's driveshaft. When Wes's thumb fell to the ground, his brother picked it up and tossed it into the pigpen. Now Wes can grab a piece of hair by pinching it between his index finger and the base of where his thumb used to be.

As we worked with Wes on the elk meat, I said, "Wes, as long as you're here, I've got a couple questions for you."

"What do you need to know?"

I described to Wes how some types of rabbits, especially jackrabbits, have this weird sort of membrane beneath the hide that you have to peel away before cooking them.

"That membrane is called the 'fell,'" said Wes.

"Oh, cool. Do you know what caul fat is? It's not the intestine, like a sausage casing, is it?"

"No, it's the peritoneum—a membrane that surrounds the internal organs. It's run through with strands of fat, so that it looks like a web. People used to wrap roasts in caul fat, to keep them moist while cooking. Agnes used caul fat on beef roasts. Now we sell all the caul, along with the entrails, to a rendering plant over in Spokane, Washington. There's no market for it. We sometimes have to pay to dump it in a landfill."

"Could you get caul fat off of, like, a deer?"

"Of course you could."

"I've got one more question for you, Wes." I went to the freezer and pulled out the bag of bear fat that I'd brought down from Alaska. "Do you think I could use this bear fat to make salt pork? And what exactly is salt pork?"

"It's generally made from the back fat on a hog. Or the belly. The best salt pork comes from back fat, just like you got there. But it's cured, with salt. People don't cook with salt pork much anymore, you know."

"I know." I explained what I was up to with the Escoffier meal, and how I needed a whole bunch of salt pork to pull it off. Wes thought that the bear fat would work just as well, and he helped get me started on making it. I cut the pieces of back fat into long, one-inch-thick strips. I then made a brine of salt and saltpeter and put the fat to soak in the refrigerator.

"You can leave that in there for months," said Wes. "It's very stable with the high salinity, and the saltpeter helps cure it and give it color."

Matt and I thanked Wes for the help, and I wrapped him up an elk roast to take home to Agnes. He folded the package under his arm and used his cane to walk back home.

In Montana, winter doesn't usually begin in earnest until December. Starting in September, though, winter has a lot of false starts. These false starts are punctuated by blasts of Indian summer. As hunting season progresses, I'm always trying to anticipate the weather so I can decide what to do next. If it happens to snow really hard in both Canada and Montana, the ducks and geese might just fly through Montana without stopping for long. When that happens, I don't get a chance to hunt them. If it gets supercold in Canada but stays mild in Montana, a lot of waterfowl might come down along the Yellowstone and Missouri Rivers. Once the waterfowl do show up, the weather stays just as important. If it's overcast and rainy, ducks and geese will fly low to the ground, and they'll stay active all day long. If it's sunny and warm, they'll fly high, out of gun range, and tend to move only in the early mornings and late evenings.

If the weather is bad for waterfowl, it's not the end of the world. Instead it's probably a dandy time for antelope. Antelope live in flat, open country, and good visibility is essential to finding them. I went out for antelope during a warm, dry spell in mid-October. I drove an hour west of Miles City and then caught a ranch road that led me up to a high plateau on the north side of the Yellowstone River. Montana's pronghorn antelope season had already been open for about a week. The sagebrush on the plateau was low and stunted. Cattle had overgrazed just about every square inch of ground. The only places where the grass hadn't been munched to the dirt was where prickly pear cactus kept the animals away. The soil was reddish-colored, with long, white, meandering streaks of dried salts on the surface. The road was dusty, and clouds of dirt kicked up off the tires. From the air, my moving vehicle must have looked like a solid dot at the tip of a long, dusty exclamation point.

From the truck, I quickly spotted a herd of seven antelope moving in single file, way out across a sagebrush flat. They were paralleling the road well over a mile out. Their heads were down and they were moving at a slow walk. I could tell they were traveling. Unless something fucked with them, they'd probably keep going like that for a while. I drove the vehicle down the road until I was a mile ahead of the animals, then pulled over. The sun made the ground hazy with refraction waves. Despite the disturbance in the air, I could still see the white patches on the sides and throats of the antelope. I drove further, until I couldn't see them at all, until I was way out in front of the animals. I parked, grabbed my backpack and my spotting scope, loaded my rifle. I headed out across the sage flat, jogging toward a place that I thought the animals might pass when they came through. I was roughly the same distance from the road that they were, but I was a long ways ahead of them. I lay down behind some sagebrush, propped my rifle on my backpack, laid my binoculars next to it, folded my arms, and rested my head.

After fifteen minutes I started watching for the antelope. Nothing. Fifteen more minutes passed. I saw a white patch emerge on the horizon. It was the first animal. The rest of the animals came into view behind it, one, two, three. . . . They were still in single file, but it was clear that they wouldn't pass within range. Either they had altered their trajectory, or I had screwed up my positioning. I'm comfortable with shooting three hundred yards, but I don't like to make longer shots than that. I started to crawl along, dragging my backpack. I thought I might be able to get ahead of them still. I moved a ways and then stopped again. I raised myself up on my elbows to scan the horizon. I saw several antelope heads poking up from the sagebrush, much closer to me than the antelope I was originally after. These new antelope were bedded down. Three of them. On one I could see a blackish cheek patch and two stubby horns. It was a buck.

The antelope were out of shooting range, but if I'd stood up they would have taken off. Antelope are ridiculously fast for any four-legged predator that lives in North America, but they've learned to run from man and his long-range rifles. If I was going to go after them, I'd have to belly-crawl the entire distance.

It took over an hour. I'd reach ahead of myself with my rifle, my arms outstretched and my chin to the ground, and then I'd pull my body up. By watching ahead of me for prickly pear cactus, I was able to veer to the left and right of most of it. Every so often, I had to reach back and pluck a quill or two out of my knees. I cursed myself for not sewing leather knee pads to my pants, which is something I always think I'll do but then I never get around to it.

By staying down below the sagebrush and using thick clumps to block my outline, I got within easy range of the antelope. Two hundred yards. But they were still lying down. I moved closer. One hundred fifty yards. The animals were still lying down.

Old-timers used to carry a white flag with them while antelope hunting. The animals are curious-minded and gregarious. Supposedly, if you flash a white flag at them, they'll come in to see if you're an antelope. I've had caribou walk hundreds of yards out of their way in the Arctic to see what I was, but most caribou live their whole life without ever seeing a man. They don't know any better. But antelope live in cattle country, which means they know all too well about people.

I got a few yards closer. One of the does finally saw me. She stood up and stared at me. I centered the crosshairs of my scope on her brisket, but I didn't want to hit her there and ruin a lot of meat. It's better to shoot clean through the ribs on broadside shots. After staring at me for a while, she folded her legs and lay back down.

If I were to stand up, those antelope would have run to the next county before I could have made a shot. But because I was staying low, they couldn't tell what I was. Once the doe lay down, the buck stood up. He was acting nervous and agitated, but he still couldn't see me. He walked a little closer and turned broadside. I slowly, slowly moved the barrel of my rifle toward him. I found the center of his rib cage in my rifle's scope and touched the trigger. The antelope disappeared. The other two jumped up, unsure of where the noise was coming from. They paused just long enough for me to fix the closer doe in the scope. I found the center of her rib cage and touched off another round. When the recoil settled, I could see a couple of legs and hooves poking up from the sagebrush.

Antelope are smallish; the buck weighed under a hundred pounds. I gutted and skinned it where it fell, and cut it into quarters. I put three of the quarters into my backpack and fixed the fourth to the outside with bungee cords. I packed that load to the truck. I went back for the second animal. A turkey buzzard was already circling overhead. As I gutted the doe, I remembered something that I was supposed to do. Before I sawed through the pelvis bone, I pulled the bladder up through the gutting incision. Once I snipped it off and drained it, the bladder didn't seem big enough to hold a tube of lipstick. How the hell was I supposed to fit a whole duck inside there? I bagged it up, along with the heart and kidneys, and then walked over to the other gut pile and looked for that bladder. I had nicked it when I split the pelvis. I went back to the doe. I put on my raincoat, to keep my shirt clean, and lifted the whole doe up to my shoulders. I carried her to the truck as the sun set.

An hour later I was back in Miles City. I flicked the garage light on. The pigeons cooed. I covered a workbench in butcher's paper and started working on an antelope saddle with a large hacksaw, trimming the spine down to a size that might fit into a roasting tray. Just as I got started, someone knocked on the door.

"Smells like antelope in here," said Wes Munsel. He was wearing his beige cowboy hat and carrying two beers.

It's common for old-timers in Montana to be prejudiced

against antelope. Often old-timers call antelope goats, and they won't eat them. I don't understand why. Maybe old people ate too many antelope during the Depression and got sick of them.

I could tell by the look on Wes's face that he was just that sort of old-timer. He had no desire to butcher an antelope. Undeterred by this display, I asked Wes about sweetbreads. The word *sweetbread* is a more appetizing way of saying thymus gland. Sweetbreads are considered to be a great delicacy. Escoffier says they are "one of the finest delicacies provided by the butcher and may be served for any meal, no matter how rich or sumptuous." I knew the thymus was located along the esophagus in the animal's neck, but I hadn't had any luck in finding one. I gestured to the antelope and asked Wes how to extract one.

"You get sweetbreads from veal," said Wes. "From steers that are less than six months old. My God, are they good. Any later than that, the sweetbread turns to wax. *Fatty* wax." He contorted his face into a look of disgust and nodded his head toward the antelope. "You don't want to eat any sweetbreads from that thing."

I didn't want to push the topic of antelope any further than necessary. I acted like I was conceding to Wes's opinion and that I appreciated his sparing me the wasted effort. I asked him what the different types of sweetbreads are. He said the thymus gland is it. That's the only one that's any good. I opened up my copy of *Le Guide Culinaire* to ask him to look at something for me. I pointed to a passage. Wes adjusted his trifocals on his nose and followed the text with his finger. It read, "Veal sweetbreads are of two kinds, unequal in shape as in quality. They are the *Noix* (heart sweetbread) which is round and plump in shape and of superb quality and the *Gorge* (throat sweetbread) which is longer in shape and inferior in quality to the former."

This puzzled Wes. He stood there and ran his finger across the passage about five times. He lifted his hat and scratched his head.

"Is there a sweetbread next to the heart?" I asked. "Like some other kind of gland?"

"No, there's not. But I think I might know what he's talking about."

A couple of days later, Wes called to tell me to meet him at his slaughterhouse the next morning at nine a.m. "We're doing ten steers tomorrow," he said.

I drove over. The slaughterhouse sat on the bank of the Yellowstone River. Outside, there were loading chutes and stockades. I could hear cattle bellowing. Inside, the floors were bare concrete. Wes wouldn't let me walk to the killing floor, because of safety rules about nonemployees. As I waited, a fresh dead steer came swinging through the door. Its head was gone, but it was still steaming hot. I watched one of the meat cutters give his knife a quick flick with a sharpening steel and then remove the four legs. He did in seconds what would have taken me five minutes. He reached into a slit along the animal's throat, near where the head had been removed, and made a couple of quick cuts with his knife. He walked over to me and Wes and tossed two thymus glands into a tub. The glands nestled in with six other sweetbreads that Wes had already collected. He admired the tub.

"My God, are these good," said Wes. He said it as though he was humbled by the sweetbreads.

"What do you guys usually do with them?" I asked.

"Ninety-nine percent go to the rendering plant."

"What about the other one percent?"

"I eat some, but that don't amount to much. We keep a box here, in case someone orders a case. When they do go, they go to Indian country."

"What do you mean, Indian country?"

"Around Indian reservations, south of here. Crow, Northern Cheyenne. Indian people will eat sweetbreads. Indian people will eat beef tongue. They know how to cook it. Whites don't. Or won't."

Wes lifted one of the glands from the tub and placed it on a clean cutting board. The gland was white, about half the size of a chicken breast. It was run through with thin veins of purple. All in all, it resembled brain.

"Here's what that book of yours is talking about," said Wes. He showed me how the gland is actually in two parts, connected by a translucent membrane. He separated the glands by pinning one down with the back of a boning knife and pulling the other one away from it. One of the parts was heart-shaped. The other part was longer, like a cylinder. "Your book must treat these two halves as different. That's what he calls the *noix* sweetbread, and that must be the *gorge* sweetbread. I've eaten many, many plates of these, and I've never noticed a difference. Agnes cleans them and cleans them, and gets all that gristle and connective tissue off. My God, she cleans them nicely. Maybe that's why I can't taste the difference."

Wes gave me the sack of sweetbreads to take home and see what I thought about them. In return, I extended an invitation for him to come to the Escoffier feast.

"You're not going to make me eat that antelope, I trust."

I shrugged. "I don't know. I haven't completed the menu yet."

Wes's sweetbreads were the only thing I'd collected so far that weren't wild. I thought about just cooking them up for a regular ol' dinner and getting some other sweetbreads from a young deer. But Wes had given me the sweetbreads as a gift; he'd think I was a lunatic if he came over and found my friends and me eating sweetbreads out of a deer after he'd gone through all the trouble of getting us some real ones. I pondered the situation, then decided that the spirit of the do-it-yourself meal wouldn't be too compromised by one farm-raised addition. Especially an addition that came from such a culinary authority as Wes Munsel.

RED THE PIGEON HAD NO WAY OF KNOWING IT, BUT WHEN I brought those sweetbreads home, he had already entered the final month of his life. Thanksgiving weekend, the official date of my Escoffier feast, was just four weeks away. I was essentially finished collecting ingredients; I had pretty much exhausted my resources, and my time was running out. It was hard for me to comprehend that I only had one squab after all that effort. A couple of months had passed since Matt had allowed all the birds to escape. After the two yellow-banded birds were reunited, they continued to ignore each other and never again joined up in the nesting box. Even if two of the adult birds in the coop had decided to breed at that very moment, there wasn't enough time for the egg to hatch into a squab before the beginning of the feast. My attempts at animal husbandry had officially failed.

I set a goal to at least double my squab population before the feast. That might not seem like an overly ambitious goal, because doubling the population meant catching just one squab. But I had learned by then not to be too optimistic about squab hunting. Nonetheless, I went out for several nights in a row, using a ladder to survey all the known pigeon hangouts around Miles City. After flushing a few pigeons from atop a sheet metal box that housed an air-conditioning unit, I pulled myself up there to take a look. There was a nest, and in that nest was a squab. The bird looked almost old enough to be on its own; I had it weaned and eating solid grain within two days. After fitting the new squab with a red band, I named him Lil' Red and moved him into the coop with Red. Then I poured on the feed, just like the old witch in the Hansel and Gretel story.

I once knew a guy from Arkansas who trained falcons to hunt game birds for him. He could tell when a falcon was ready for a hunt by testing the bird's body fat: a skinny falcon hunts harder than a fat falcon. The guy tested the fat by feeling the bird's keel, which is the ridge of the breastbone. I pulled Red out and palpated his keel. Rather than testing him for how good he'd hunt, I was testing him for how good he'd taste. He felt plump and tender. For the sake of comparison, I pulled H&G II out of the coop and felt their keels. They were not as fat as Red. I quickly put the two birds back in the coop, because Jen would have had a fit if she'd seen me touching them. Whenever I tested Lil' Red's keel, I felt nothing but skin and bone.

I wasn't too sure how far the two squabs would have to stretch, because I still hadn't finalized my guest list. I'd put so much effort into scrounging ingredients that I hadn't thought too much about who was going to eat it all. With the date drawing near, I started an aggressive promotional campaign. Initially, I'd been reluctant to set the date for Thanksgiving weekend. I was concerned that the traditional, Pilgrimesque trappings of Thanksgiving would overshadow the highbrow theme of my Escoffier feast. But I wound up using the holiday weekend because everyone had the time off from school and work.

As I called friends around the country, trying to rally attendees, I manipulated the Thanksgiving date for varying effect, depending on who I was talking to. For my less-traditional friends who are easily bored by routine, like Anna Baker, I argued that the feast would be a good break from the boring blahs of the standard turkey dinner. I guaranteed a once-in-a-lifetime dining experience that would never be replicated in the history of the world.

For more traditional folks, like Wes and Agnes Munsel, I promoted my feast as being in tune with some of the less-acknowledged facets of the true Thanksgiving story. For example, the original Thanksgiving of 1621 lasted for three days. The Escoffier feast would last exactly that long, not just the one paltry day that modern, time-strapped Americans give it. Also, I argued, it's quite possible that the turkey tradition of Thanksgiving is a sham. There is no solid evidence that the Pilgrims actually ate turkey. At the time of the original Thanksgiving, American colonists tended to refer to all wild-fowl in the same way—as turkey. So, in essence, we would be having many kinds of turkey: ruffed grouse, pheasant, chukar, Hungarian partridge. One thing the Pilgrims certainly ate was venison, which my Escoffier feast would include in ample portions. Also, the Pilgrims ate a variety of seafood from the waters around Plymouth Rock, such as clams and lobster. The Escoffier feast would include ample seafood.

For anyone who remained reluctant to violate their own traditions by coming to the Escoffier feast, I had this one final clincher to seal the deal. "For argument's sake," I would say, "let's say the Pilgrims did actually have turkey as we know it. Well, you can guarantee that they didn't have a goddamn Butterball. They would have had a wild turkey. And it just so happens that I have a wild turkey on the menu. Matt killed a nice young turkey here in Montana this April, and he's graciously donated the bird to the feast."

Even this rigorous logic of mine couldn't convince some people to come to the feast. Moisan, newly married and relocated to Seattle, wouldn't budge from his obligation to go to the new in-laws for the holiday. Dee, who originally gave me the copy of *Le Guide Culinaire* when I needed a turtle soup recipe, couldn't bear to separate from her aging parents. Still I had about fifteen more-or-less confirmed attendees, so the pressure was on.

The Thanksgiving legend has it that the Pilgrims were overwhelmed by how many Indians showed up for the feast at Plymouth Rock. The Pilgrims invited the "family" of several friendly Indians, but the Pilgrims and Indians had different definitions of the word. Scores of Indians showed up. Once it was determined by the Pilgrims that their stores of food could not sustain everyone for three days, Massasoit, the chief of the Wampanoags, dispatched his own hunters to bring in the necessary amounts of food.

As October went into November, Matt and I launched a last-ditch gathering excursion of our own. We'd finally gotten some snow in the high country, so we went again to look for bighorn sheep on the eastern slopes of the Gallatin Range. On our second morning in the mountains, we found five rams. They were bedded down on the edge of a grassy bluff, almost a wide ledge on the side of the mountain. A craggy ridge rose above the bluff. Beneath the rams, the land broke away into gullies and steep drops. We stalked the sheep for hours, crawling on our bellies in the fresh snow and coming at them from the same elevation they were on. The rams were gearing up for their breeding season. As we stalked the rams, a couple of them would now and then stand up and square off. They'd rise to their back legs, fold their front legs against their chests, and tip toward each other, running, until their curled horns smacked together. The crashing of the horns sounded like rifle shots. The largest ram would try to sit these fights out, but the smaller rams would hook his horns with their own and drag him to his feet. Then they'd crack his horns, and he'd lie back down.

When the big one stood up, he never walked clear of the younger rams. We waited and waited for a clean shot. An hour passed. We were getting wet from the snow, and Matt was afraid that he was getting too cold to make a good shot. We wedged an extra jacket under his body for insulation.

The big ram finally stood, and the two rams behind him started fighting a little and dropped down the hill. The second they were clear, Matt touched the trigger. The ram staggered and then stopped. Matt shot again; the ram tipped over. It started sliding down the snowy mountain, leaving a trail of bare grass in its wake. It vanished from sight. The other four rams chased after it and vanished as well. Then the four came running back up the hill. When they got to the bluff, they formed a single file and headed up toward the ridge, back toward the safety of higher ground. Matt's ram was just down the hill, hung up in a patch of sagebrush. When we climbed down to it, Matt said, "That's a lot of mutton laying there." The animal weighed over three hundred pounds.

After getting a ram, we made our last big trip of the year. Eric Kern and Pooder came out to canoe down the Breaks with us. The Breaks are a long string of badlands in the upper-central part of Montana, along the upper Missouri River, where the land of the Great Plains "breaks" away into the canyon of the river. The Breaks are one of Montana's most famous places. The renown comes from the fact that nothing ever really happens there, and hardly anyone goes there. Long after horse rustlers were exterminated from most of the West, a few renegade thieves were able to hide out in the Breaks and continue their business. The land is desolate and heavily eroded. It looks just about the same as it did before Lewis and Clark traveled up that stretch of river on their military excursion from Saint Louis to the Pacific Ocean. One big difference, of course, is that the buffalo and the wolves are gone for now.

But at least there are still mule deer. Lots of them. We glassed for deer from the canoes, and we hiked up to sandstone outcroppings and looked for deer from up there. We followed herds of deer through canyons and stalked groups of deer that came down toward the river at night. Matt and I killed a buck and a couple of does. We cut pieces of caul fat from the animals before butchering them, and we saved the bladders. We put the meat in nylon mesh sacks and stacked the sacks in the bottoms of the two canoes. The water that dripped from our paddles collected in puddles in the sterns of the boats. At night we dumped the water out, or else it would have frozen solid while we slept. We hunted pheasants on islands that were carpeted in willow shoots and crisscrossed with beaver trails. We shot mallard ducks as they whistled up and down the river. I killed a Canada goose that waited on the water a few seconds too long before deciding that it should fly away.

We got to the takeout on a Wednesday afternoon. We passed a familiar cluster of islands and rounded a familiar bend, and there was the road and the bridge and Matt's truck. I snapped a few end-of-trip photos. We chased after a cottontail rabbit that was hiding under the truck. We loaded gear and scrubbed mud out of the canoes. As we worked, I was surprised by how good I felt. Usually the end of a hunting season settles over me as a heavy melancholy. The sadness lasts for a month or so, as I adjust to regular ol' life and sleeping indoors all the time. I guess I thrive on the uncertainty and the labor of hunting. And that's why I was feeling so good this time: the uncertainty and labor of hunting was passing seamlessly into the uncertainty and labor of cooking Escoffier. The greatest challenge of the year was still to come.

# CHAPTER EIGHTEEN

# The Enigma of Vatel

WHEN MY DAD COOKED WILD GAME, HE FOLLOWED A STRICT ritual. First off, he'd dispatch me or one of my brothers to run up to the garage, which sat on a hill above the house, to turn on the deep fryer. To turn the fryer on, you just had to plug it in. The fryer did have a dial, so you could, in theory, turn it off and adjust the temperature. However, my brothers and I weren't allowed to touch the dial. My dad kept it locked at a trusty 375 degrees Fahrenheit, which he believed was the ideal temperature for all applications. By avoiding contact with the dial, he could reduce the chances that human error might have an impact on his cooking. So long as the fryer was plugged in, he knew what temperature that son of a bitch was going to be.

The fryer had a red light, about the size of a human eye, that clicked off when the oil reached operating temperature. Usually my dad would make one of us kids stay next to the fryer until the light blinked out. Then we were supposed to run down to the house and notify him that it was time to start cooking.

Upon receiving word that the oil was ready, my dad would make a vodka martini and stir it with a wooden dowel. He'd then line a ceramic crock with paper towels and put whatever fish or game he was preparing into an orange Tupperware container with a white lid. He put his drink, the crock, and the container on a bamboo serving tray and marched up the sixteen steps to the garage. Watching him march up those stairs was like watching an alchemist, one of the medieval protoscientists who attempted to turn various metals into gold, disappear into the smoke of his lab. The difference between my dad and the alchemists, though, is that my dad succeeded. He could turn just about any meat into crispy little squares that were the uniform color of swimsuit models.

Over the years, we ate venison steaks and goose breasts out of the fryer. We ate perch and bluegill and pumpkin seeds (a cousin of the bluegill) and goggle eyes (another cousin). We ate coho salmon, chinook salmon, pink salmon, and steelhead. We ate lake trout, brown trout, rainbow trout, brook trout. We ate smelt and sheepshead. We ate cottontail rabbit, snowshoe hare, black squirrel, gray squirrel, and fox squirrel. We ate wood duck and mallard. We ate black duck, black bear, and black sucker. We ate rainbow sucker and redhorse sucker, two species of bullheads, two species of catfish. We ate largemouth bass, smallmouth bass, speckled bass, and rock bass. We ate perch roe and bluegill roe. We ate deer hearts cut into cubes, and deer hearts sliced like onions. And we ate snapping turtle. All of it fried.

As the date of my Escoffier feast closed in, I longed for the simplicity of my father's own wild game cooking procedures. With the industrial-strength deep fryer at my disposal, I could have cooked all of my wild game in a few hours, tops. Instead, I had over a week's worth of work to do. And I *wanted* to do it, for sure. It's just that I was having a hard time actually getting started with the project. The transitional period was killing me. After so many months of having my senses tuned to the whereabouts of fish and animals, I couldn't bring myself to stop gathering food.

One day I sat down at my laptop with the intention of drawing up a menu and a plan of attack for the feast's preparations. Just as I was getting started, Matt came home from work and said that he had just seen at least five hundred Canada geese fly down the Yellowstone River. I thought of how a few more goose livers might come in handy. That got me thinking about whether I had any goose loads for my shotgun. After digging though my boxes of shotgun shells, I played with my goose call. I let out a few toots, then remembered that I was supposed to be planning a menu. I went back upstairs and opened the new file on my laptop called "Tentative Menu." I sat at the kitchen table and stared at the screen. In my peripheral vision, I saw a sparrow flit past the window. I ran out to see where it went. After looking around for the sparrow and checking the telephone wires for any pigeons that might be hanging about, I went over to the coop to palpate Red's breast. He seemed to be putting on weight. Lil' Red was growing a little fatter as well. I'd been gone long enough for the laptop to switch to sleep mode. Rather than start the computer back up, Matt and I drove down south of town and killed a few game birds.

My problem, I began to realize, was that the contents of the jam-packed freezers amounted to abstract, unknowable quantities. At night I started going out to the garage for the sole purpose of staring at all the boxes and shelves of ingredients. I couldn't imagine where to begin. I thought it might be fun to make a list of my ingredients:

*Fish:* bluegill, burbot, carp, eel, flounder, green ling, halibut, northern pike, Pacific ling cod, pompano, rockfish, smallmouth bass, sockeye salmon, Atlantic ray, walleye, whiting, yellow perch

***Shellfish:*** butter clams, blue mussels, coonstripe shrimp, crayfish, Dungeness crab, horse clams, manila clams, spotted prawns

***Fowl:*** Canada goose, chukar, English sparrow, European starling, Hungarian partridge, mallard, pheasant, ruffed grouse, squab, wild turkey

***Red Meat:*** antelope, bighorn sheep, black bear, black-eared jackrabbit, cottontail rabbit, elk, moose, mountain goat, mule deer, wild boar

***Innards:*** bladders, caul fat, head, hearts, intestines, kidneys, livers, sweetbreads, tongues

***Miscellaneous:*** frog legs, snapping turtle

With everything listed, building a menu was much easier. I just had to come up with forty-five or so dishes—fifteen courses per day—that would account for every item I had written down. There were some minor complications, or rather, considerations. For instance, I wanted as wide a variety of dishes as possible for each night. I didn't want too many shellfish or too many organs to appear on any one night's menu. Starting with appetizers, I would move into soups and sides and then on to main courses, alternating from fish to meat to shellfish to keep things interesting. Also, I thought it would be cool to end each night with a pièce de résistance, something big and glorious. For the first night's finale, I'd serve a braised wild turkey galantine rolled with pistachios and sausage. For the second night, we'd have a venison saddle garnished with whole pears poached in red wine. For the third night, I wanted a finale that could serve double duty; along with being the pièce de résistance of its own meal, it needed to be the pièce de résistance of the entire festivity. These were demanding requirements for a dish. I decided that *carpe à la ancienne* was up to the task. Of all the dishes in *Le Guide,* a creamy, truffled carp's body with a real head most perfectly embodied the grand luxuries and artistic achievements of Escoffier's brand of cookery.

For the third prong of the sacred trinity of classic French cuisine which includes caviar, foie gras, and truffles, I opted for a combination of morels and a type of truffle that is less swanky than the Perigord but also way less expensive. The jobbies I purchased, an Italian type of truffle, were only about twelve dollars an ounce. I ordered four ounces of them over the Internet from an importer in Miami. The truffles arrived in Miles City in decorative, fluted bottles with gold seals. A few years ago I had some hardened cysts cut out of my head. The extracted cysts were pretty cool-looking, so I saved them in a glass cylinder of formaldehyde and brought them home for a decoration. Floating in their clear liquid, the little truffles didn't look a hell of a lot different from the cysts. I was mildly disappointed in their appearance. But, I thought, if that's what it takes to make a carp taste good, so be it.

I knew that all of the screwing around—the making of lists and creating of computer files and ordering of things over the Internet—wasn't going to be worth a shit if I didn't get around to doing some cooking. Still, I screwed around and made computer files for a few more days. Then, when I only had a week to go before Thanksgiving, I realized that I'd better get my ass going.

The next morning I was ready to start. I had just over a week to prepare forty-five courses, and here I was, ready for number one. Diana and Jen were out of town, and Matt was working twelve-hour days; I had the house and garage completely to myself. My knives were honed. The stereo was cranked. I had a pig's head sitting in a bucket. I was wearing an apron. Nothing could get in my way.

But I was stuck. Next to the pig's head, I had two translations of *Le Guide Culinaire* laid out on the workbench in Matt's garage: the complete translation by Cracknell and Kaufman, and the truncated Americanized version put out by Crown Publishers. But I couldn't find a lick about headcheese. I had looked through the books before, hunting for information about pig heads, but all I had found was that a pig's head is "usually utilized for the preparation of fromage de tête," or headcheese. I was holding out some hope that the information was hiding somewhere in the book, perhaps a casualty of sloppy indexing. However, a thorough search did not turn up any headcheese information whatsoever.

I could see that cooking from *Le Guide* was going to be like studying Shakespeare in college. To study Shakespeare, you need to have the actual play in front of you, which scholars refer to as "the text." To ferret out the deeper mysteries and arcane innuendos of the Shakespeare text, it's essential to have on hand a copy of the *Oxford English Dictionary*.

With *Le Guide Culinaire* as the text, I would discover that the equivalent of the *OED* is the good ol' *Joy of Cooking*. The authors of the *Joy of Cooking*, Irma S. Rombauer and Marion Rombauer Becker, say that headcheese comes from a calf, not a pig. But at least they explain the process. So I carried on, in spite of the head's species of origin. Since I'd already skinned the head at Anna Baker's ranch, I just needed to take a meat saw and cut it into quarters. I did so, then I cut out the eyes and removed the top of the esophagus. In the throat, I found some pieces of green clover—remnants of the pig's last meal. I removed the tongue. With the tongue in one hand, I flipped through *Le Guide* for tongue instructions. Escoffier spells it out, plainly and thoroughly. I brought the tongue into the house, boiled it until the skin peeled off (about forty minutes), then submerged the tongue in a bowl containing *Le Guide*'s recipe 269, which is "Brine, pickling for tongues." The brine contains water, salt, saltpeter, brown sugar, peppercorns, juniper berries, thyme, and a bay leaf. I picked the juniper berries from a juniper growing up against Matt's garage, and then put the tongue in the fridge.

I went back to the quartered head. As I worked on the next step, "clean teeth with a stiff brush," I couldn't shake the feeling that a passerby would think he'd stumbled onto some kind of occult devil-worshiper ceremony. Once I had the head quartered, cleaned, cut up, and its teeth nice and shiny, I put the pieces into a large tub of cold water to soak. The water was supposed to draw out excess blood. I set the tub on a workbench. The temperature in the garage was hovering around the freezing point.

The next morning I was feeling so enlivened by the previous day's small successes that I began working on the holiest of culinary holies—stock. Basically, stock is a liquid created by boiling meat, bones, water, and seasonings together. Sounds simple enough. But according to Escoffier, stock is the foundation of the house, the binding of the book, the keystone of the archway. In fact, he opens his book with a dire warning on the matter of stock:

> Indeed, stock is everything in cooking, at least in French cooking. Without it, nothing can be done. If one's stock is good, what remains of the work is easy; if, on the other hand, it is bad or mediocre, it is quite hopeless to expect anything approaching a satisfactory result. The cook mindful of

success, therefore, will naturally direct his attention to the faultless preparation of his stock, and, in order to achieve this result, he will find it necessary not merely to make use of the freshest and finest products, but also to exercise the most scrupulous care in their preparation, for, in cooking, care is half the battle.

I tried to estimate how much game stock I'd need. Many dishes, such as the sparrows baked inside a polenta and risotto cake, would need just a dash of stock. Other dishes, such as the wild turkey galantine, would need to be poached in copious amounts. And there were countless sauces to make, most of the them built up from a base of stock. After fiddling with various calculations, I decided that I'd do what my mother always did when she thought a recipe wouldn't yield an adequate amount: I'd make a double batch.

The preferred meat for stock is not the preferred meat for eating; because the meat is being simmered to extract its flavor, it doesn't matter if it's tender or not. In fact, Escoffier suggests using older animals and tougher cuts, which have a greater potential for deep flavor. I needed four rabbits. I had killed two cottontails a few days before, and they were still hanging in the garage. I gave their ears a tug, as though trying to tear paper, which is Escoffier's recommended rabbit-aging technique. The ears didn't give, so the rabbits were old. I pulled two more out of the freezer that had already been skinned and cut up. Back when I had killed those two rabbits, near Thermopolis, I had failed to properly test their age. So I didn't know if all four rabbits were old.

But I did know that my sheep meat was damned old. By counting the growth rings on Matt's bighorn ram, we could tell that the animal was eleven years old. Matt had also killed an old antelope buck. I needed two old pheasants too. A pheasant can be aged by the spur on the back of the bird's leg, right above the foot. A young pheasant has a short, rounded spur. Older birds have a developed, pointy spur, maybe a quarter-inch long. A couple of the pheasants I killed in the Breaks had long spurs. When I froze them, I had written Stock on the label. I dug through the freezer and pulled them out. I also took out a ruffed grouse that I had shotgunned in Alaska.

I set up my scale on the counter and began weighing out the red meat. I was supposed to use cuts from the brisket, shoulders, neck. I boned out five pounds of antelope trim. From the mountain goat that fell over the cliff, I selected eight pounds of scraps. I then set to work on the neck of Matt's bighorn sheep. It weighed almost twenty pounds. I didn't need that much of it, so I roasted the neck in the oven for a couple of hours. Then I shaved off half the meat, chopped it, and mixed it with some Stubbs Bar-B-Q. I set the other half aside and began browning the rabbits, grouse, pheasant, mountain goat, and antelope on roasting trays. While that cooked, I ate a couple of barbecue sandwiches.

I put two stockpots on the burners and stirred some chopped carrots and onions into a touch of hot oil. To each pot, I added water, sage, and a bouquet garni of parsley, bay leaves, and thyme, tied together with kitchen string and wrapped in little sacks of cheesecloth. I selected thirty more juniper berries from an upper limb of Matt's tree and tied the berries into two pieces of cheesecloth and tossed them into the pots. Once the meat in the oven was browned, I dumped it into the stockpots as well. I deglazed each of the roasting trays with a bottle of white wine and poured the wine and pan drippings into the stockpots. Once I had the stock cooking at a low simmer, I checked the clock. In three hours I would pull the pots off the stove, cover them, and move them into the garage to cool.

In the morning I went out to the garage to check on my projects. The stockpots were capped with a layer of fat that had hardened and risen to the surface, just like it was supposed to. The layer lifted up as easily and solidly as a Frisbee. Escoffier sometimes mentions using bouillon fat, and I assumed that's what it was; I broke the fat into pieces and saved it. Then I ran the stock through a fine screen into clean, empty milk jugs. The skimmed stock smelled of roast meat. I froze the jugs.

The quartered pig's head had turned white in the water, like something that had drowned. Surprisingly, it was almost completely odorless. When I carried the head inside the house, the teeth scraped on the bottom of the tub with the rhythm of my steps. I boiled the head until it was so cooked that I could pluck out a tusk from the jaw. I put the plucked tusk on the kitchen windowsill, for a souvenir. Then I peeled all the meat and cartilage and fat off the head, leaving the bones as dry and white as a bone out in the desert. I minced the meat and gelatin to the texture of hamburger, covered it with the cooking liquid, and popped that into the freezer.

I worked on stuff every day, getting dishes as far along as possible. I made fish stock with whiting from the Gulf of Mexico. I made some more fish stock with freshwater fish. To clarify fish stock in order to make fish jelly, or aspic, Escoffier says to crack egg whites into the finished product. I did this. As the eggs cooked, they pulled the impurities to the surface and left the stock as clear and golden as lemon-lime Gatorade. The stock smelled of fish, but not like old fish or fresh fish. Instead, it smelled ageless, almost synthetically stable. With the stock ready, I boned out two mallard ducks, ground the meat, and cooked it into a portion of the game stock to make a duck consommé. Then I laid a complete leg of boar into a cooked marinade of white wine, vinegar, oil, and loads of seasonings and veggies.

Working along, I liked to taste things to see what they were like during their various stages of preparation. The stock wasn't salted, so it tasted bland but showed definite potential. I dropped a piece of salted bear fat on a skillet. It gave off considerable oil and tasted delicious, like bacon, minus the smokiness. After mincing the pig's head, I tried a little nibble. It wasn't seasoned yet, so it resembled hand lotion without the flowery undertones. The duck consommé, on the other hand, was fantastic. After tasting it, I called some friends to say that I'd just made the best thing I'd ever eaten. I hadn't gotten as excited about something since I learned how to ride a bike. The flavor was rich and layered, like a mild, buttery beef broth at first, but that taste quickly faded and was replaced with a deep roast duck flavor that hung on for several seconds. I'd eaten scores of ducks over the years, but I suddenly thought of a mallard in a completely different light. It was like learning that your girlfriend, whom you already love anyway, just won a million dollars on a slot machine.

As for the turtle soup, I resisted the impulse to taste it. Just looking at the turtle meat made my lip curl. My memories were still fresh from my last batch of turtle soup, which stunk up my apartment and turned all my friends off to the idea of ever eating turtle again. In the months since that initial experiment, I had developed a number of theories about what went wrong with that first turtle: first, the turtle was fed ground meat while it was in captivity, which I believe tainted its flavor; second, I failed to flush the turtle in fresh water before slaughtering it; third, I cooked the turtle's plastron and bones before picking

the meat off, which I believe added to the off-taste of the finished product.

For this new turtle, I'd already remedied two of the problems. I didn't feed it anything during its two days of captivity,
and I continuously flushed the turtle with fresh water. At
first, the water in the turtle's tank would turn cloudy almost
immediately. But after a few changes of water, I could have
dipped a glass into the tank and had a drink if I was thirsty.
After dispatching the turtle with a hatchet, I removed the
shell and skinned it. Still on the bone and uncooked, the meat
was the color of raw, skinned chicken. I froze it under a layer
of water in large plastic tubs.

Now I was ready to perform the next step on the turtle, so
I thawed it out. With a small fillet knife, I removed all the
meat from the bones in thin strips. Cleaned off, the bones
were rubbery and flexible. I discarded them. I simmered the
strips in water until they were lightly cooked, then stored the
meat in the cooking broth. Escoffier says that meat can be
kept like that "for some time." To finish it off for the snapping
turtle à la Baltimore presentation, I would simply reheat the
meat, color it in butter, add seasonings and broth and arrow-
root, then finish the dish with sherry. Voilà!

By Wednesday, the day before Thanksgiving, I'd done as
much of the prep work as I could. I was limited by concerns
with freshness; I wanted the fish to remain in the deep freeze
until I was ready for them; I couldn't thaw a fish out, mess
around with it, and then put it back into the freezer. If you do
that, fish will get mushy and old-tasting.

Throughout the day, I received a number of packages for
which I'd arranged last-minute delivery. I had accidentally
left my pig's ears and tail at Anna Baker's mom's house, so I

had to make an embarrassing call and ask her to dig through the freezer in search of the pig's appendages, then ask her to spend forty dollars to send them to me. My two pounds of American golden caviar arrived in perfect shape from Michigan's U.P. I received two boxes from San Juan Island. The first was a package of smoked Pacific salmon that Pooder had made in his fish smoker. The second was a cooler full of five dozen oysters. Pooder was supposed to collect the oysters for me and send them out, alive. He's got a good oyster spot on a small island near his home. Before he could get out there, though, a red tide (a naturally occurring biotoxin) had rolled into the area and Pooder called to say he couldn't go collecting. I *had* to get oysters, I told him, because I'd already been flapping my mouth about them; I didn't want my friends to accuse me of false advertising. Pooder gave me a number for an oyster supplier on an island that didn't have red tide. I called her and ordered five dozen oysters, and they arrived in a cooler, layered atop soft ice packs and still very much alive. In Matt's garage, I used a bench grinder to modify a screwdriver into a serviceable oyster-shucking tool.

As I looked over my menu, I could see that I needed a helper. I had initially imagined the feast as a great, magnanimous task that I would tackle single-handedly for the enjoyment of my friends. I would swish in and out of the dining room with dish after dish of crazy shit, and the inner workings of the kitchen would be a mystery to all. But now, with my menus coming into shape, it was clear that I wouldn't be swishing into the dining room with much besides half-finished recipes if I didn't have a coconspirator.

My sous-chef would need to be someone with an unwavering temperament, someone who could handle long, tedious hours and seemingly arbitrary instructions. Diana was out of the question; she'd been off working in California where she had a writing fellowship at San Jose State University. She wouldn't be coming into town until that night. I didn't want to drop a bombshell on her when she showed up. Besides, I wanted her to enjoy herself as much as possible so that she'd come away with a positive image of eating meat. Most of my other friends would be out hunting during the day, not cooking. Besides, this was their vacation. It would be rude to impose on them.

It occurred to me that my friend Nina Lynch was the perfect person. Nina had recently taken a job as a technician for the Agricultural Research Services, where my brother Matt works. She moved to Miles City from Nevada, and we became instant buddies as soon as she arrived in town. She'd already pitched in to help with the feast a few times. She made several attempts to catch the sparrows at the bird feeder in her yard, and she went pigeon catching with me. When Matt and Jen and I were out of town, Nina would look after the pigeons. But there was more to Nina than her willingness to chase birds. She possessed the perfect credentials for the demanding labor of cooking Escoffier, because she's very meticulous and artistic. At the time, she was working on a series of paintings depicting battles among space-age robots, all done on the pelvis bones of elk. She also makes ceramic mosaics of iconic figures. She designs and paints greeting cards with cryptic, existential, and sometimes insulting messages stenciled on the inside. Once she collected hundreds of yellow butterflies from the front grilles of cars and laminated them onto white poster board in neat rows. She did another series with daddy longlegs. I reckoned that her animal-related artistic skills would come in handy for molding and styling such complicated and ornamental dishes as *carpe à la ancienne.*

The only problem with Nina is that she's so mellow and easygoing you can never tell what she's thinking. When I called her to ask if she wanted to be my sous-chef, I was hoping she'd jump up and down and scream with excitement, like the people who get called down on that television program, *The Price Is Right.* Instead she said, "Sure. That might be fun." I suspected that she didn't appreciate the magnitude of what lay ahead. To convince her how exciting this was going to be, I printed off a copy of the first day's menu and called Nina over for a staff meeting. She drove up in her white sedan, which was still bearing Nevada plates and had a few Elvis bumper stickers plastered on the trunk lid. Nina's in her early thirties and dresses like a high school stoner. She was wearing a red T-shirt with a faded and peeling horse decal across the breast. Her hair is short and tousled; she had it clipped above her forehead with insect-shaped barrettes. When she sat down and got comfortable, I handed her the menu. "Go ahead and peruse that," I said, "and tell me what you think."

Nina adjusted her glasses and studied the sheet carefully as she fiddled with her barrettes.

*huîtres natives au caviar*—raw oysters with whitefish caviar

*côtelettes de saumon*—salmon, prawn, and morel cakes shaped like lamb chops

*fromage de tête*—wild boar headcheese

*Cyrano consommé*—duck soup with mallard quenelles

*matelote à la marinière*—smallmouth bass, walleye, eel, bluegills, and crayfish in a broth of white wine, brandy, and fish velouté

*mousse froide d'écrevisses*—crayfish mousse

*soufflé de foie gras*—soufflé of goose liver and pheasant

*fritot de raie*—marinated and fried stingray

*sweet meat*—Escoffier does not offer a cool French name for this dish, a loaf of sweetened, fruity meat baked inside a crusty puff paste.

*mauviettes à la piemontaise*—sparrows baked inside a polenta and risotto cake

*anguille fumée*—Ray Turner's smoked eel

*caneton rouennais en chemise*—ducks poached inside bladders

*pâté de lièvre*—pâté of brandy-marinated cottontail rabbit and salted black bear fat

*pigeonneaux crapaudine*—grilled squab with *diable* sauce and gherkin garnish

*dindonneau en daube*—a rolled galantine of young wild turkey, venison sausage, and pistachios

When she finished perusing, she had a puzzled look on her face. "And there are three of these? Three days like this?" she asked.

"Yeah. Three."

She didn't say anything.

"I've done a lot of that already, you know. Like prep work," I said.

"How much of it?"

"Well, I made the duck consommé. The headcheese is about halfway done. And I made all the stock—fish stock and game stock. The tongue's ready. The turtle's coming along. That's about it, though."

Finally Nina said, "There's no way two people are going to get all that done. Three days in a row? No way. I mean, wow." She shook her head.

When Nina left, I thought of another potential helper whom I might enlist. One of my buddies, Julian the Hairy Hedonist, was coming from Helena, Montana. Among my friends, Julian the Hairy Hedonist is known for two things. First, he's known for being hairy. When Julian's drinking, he sometimes strips off his shirt and flaunts his pelt for the enjoyment of any women who happen to be around. We were all loaded one night, playing charades, and Julian was supposed to do Curious George, the monkey. He simply took off his shirt and scratched his head. One time he stripped down and wrapped a bear rug around his waist like a caveman. When he did this, my brother Matt observed that he could tell where the bear ended and Julian began because the hair got thicker.

Second, Julian's known as a crack commando of a chef. Julian just plain loves food. He's worked in several pretty nice commercial kitchens. He grew up on a hydroponic vegetable farm near the coast in Northern California, so he knows veggies and seafood inside and out.

When I called him, I said, "I need your help, Jules, badly. There's no way I can get everything done without you."

"Just tell me what to bring," said Julian.

"Your knives and your talents," I said.

The last thing I did, before Miles City started to shut down for the holiday, was make a massive liquor run. Escoffier wasn't shy about pouring the spirits into his recipes. I bought a truckload of liquor that Al Capone would have been impressed with: Madeira, port, Grand Marnier (César Ritz named this orange liqueur after its creator, a friend of his named Monsieur Marnier Lapostolle), bottles and bottles of red and white wine, sherry, cognac, stout beers.

Matt's house started filling up toward evening. Diana and Anna Baker and Drost all came in from the Billings airport. Eric Kern and his wife, Deirdre, arrived. Danny and his girl-friend, Lauren, had driven up with them after flying from Alaska into Denver.

In the days leading up to the arrival of all my friends, I thought that I'd party my ass off once everyone got to town. Instead, I found myself to be in a reclusive, abstemious mood on the eve of the first day of the feast. When everybody went out that night to hit the Montana Bar, down on Main Street, I hung back in order to worry and fret. The cool and collected feelings I had been having that morning were long gone, and I was feeling as though I'd invited all these people out to wit-ness a culinary flop. I had pulled several trays of stuff out of the freezer to thaw, and as I looked at the ingredients, I just couldn't fathom how that stuff was going to turn into what I wanted it to turn into. I ran recipes and measurements and procedures through my head as though I were cramming for a chemistry exam, but my hands felt tied by the overwhelming nature of what lay ahead. I couldn't get a grip.

And where was Julian the Hairy Hedonist? I wondered. He should have gotten to Miles City an hour before. I called his cell phone.

"Julian? What's up? Why aren't you here yet?"

"I'm running late."

"How far are you?"

"I'm not. I haven't left."

"Damn Julian. Get it together."

"I'll be there. Probably real late. Just don't lock me out of the house tonight."

There was nothing else I could do, so I went down to my bedroom and thought about the enigma of Vatel, who ran him-

self through with his sword rather than face the embarrassment of a botched banquet. I could sympathize. I fell asleep
waiting for the sound of Julian coming through the door, but I
didn't hear anything. Diana came sneaking in real late and assured me that everything would go slick. I tried, but I couldn't
believe her.

## CHAPTER NINETEEN

# *Brigade de Cuisine*

I WOKE UP TWO HOURS BEFORE DAYLIGHT AND RAN UPSTAIRS.
Julian was racked out on the couch, snoring, with a cowboy
hat tipped over his face. I never felt so happy to see someone.
"Holy shit," I said. "It's Julian the Hairy Hedonist."

Julian sat up. He was wearing his wool hunting pants and
a pair of Danner boots.

"What the hell you dressed like that for?" I asked.

"Deer hunting."

"Deer hunting? Come on, Jules, we had a deal."

"No way," he said. "All I got is one antelope this year. I
need a deer, bad. I'll be back. Early afternoon, the latest."

Escoffier had a routine for this sort of situation. When he
was pissed at an employee, he would tug at his own earlobe,
and say, "I am going out for a while. I can feel myself getting
angry." Then he'd take a stroll and come back when he cooled
off. I tried a similar move on Julian. "You bastard," I said.
"You'd better hurry up."

Then I stomped back downstairs.

Escoffier may have handled himself better, but he was ac-
customed to staffing problems. He even had Ho Chi Minh, the

communist revolutionary, working for him. At the beginning of World War I, Ho Chi Minh, whose real name was Nguyen That Thanh, was scrubbing dishes at the Carlton Hotel in London. He was in his twenties and very poor; dishwashers would eat scraps of steak and chicken from the plates. At the time, Ho Chi Minh was becoming involved in labor organizations formed by overseas workers. (According to Ho Chi Minh, Escoffier suggested that he forget about his revolutionary ideas and concentrate on becoming a cook, because he'd make a lot more money.) Ho Chi Minh doesn't say so, but one has to assume that his political opinions about the plight of the laborer came from his experiences working amid the rigors of the early twentieth-century kitchen. In those days, cooks worked in horrible conditions. Hotel kitchens were usually in the basement. Floods and fires were common. During mealtime rushes it was customary to close off the ventilation system, so the ambient temperature would be sufficient to keep the prepared entrées warm. Chefs spent twelve-hour days in these one-hundred-plus-degree kitchens, breathing toxic, unventilated fumes from burning charcoal and seasoning dishes with their dripping sweat. At dinnertime in the Carlton, Escoffier's *brigade de cuisine* would number sixty people, all crammed into the kitchen. At the turn of the century, a medical journal reported that chefs suffered more work-related maladies than miners. Well into the twentieth century, the average chef was dead by his mid forties.

When I climbed up from the basement and entered the kitchen, I took a look at the menu. It was six thirty a.m. I was exhausted. There were fifteen courses to make. Half of my staff had just vanished. The other half, Nina, wouldn't be showing up for hours. Ho Chi Minh never knew such pain.

Each dish had so many steps and preparations, selecting

any one of them seemed arbitrary in the extreme. After staring at the list for a few minutes, dumbfounded, I picked the most complicated dish and decided to begin working on that. So I went to the fridge and pulled out the wild turkey. To skin a turkey for a galantine, you have to remove the entire skin in one piece, making only one cut. The bird was already plucked. I laid it, breast down, on a cutting board. I had a basic understanding of what I was trying to make, though I couldn't really visualize what it was supposed to look like. I began cautiously. With a fillet knife, I made an incision up the bird's back, from the fatty flab of a tail, known as a parson's nose, toward the neck. My phone rang as I was passing the wing joints.

It was Julian. He'd just left twenty minutes ago.

"What," I snapped.

"Hey, you lucked out. I just hit a deer with my truck."

"Are you kidding?"

"It jumped right in front of me. Put a good dent in the hood, but I hit it in the head so the meat's not messed up. I'll be back in a minute."

I thought my staffing crisis was over, but Julian's minute turned into an hour. I worked the turkey's skin free and spread it out across a piece of cheesecloth. The skin was the size and shape of a medium pizza. There were four holes, from the wings and legs. I was getting ready to sew the holes shut with a needle and thread, as instructed, when Julian came in. He had to stash the deer in a ditch, because it's illegal to possess roadkill animals in Montana. You're supposed to leave them to rot on the highway, for some reason. My buddies and I see this as a matter of moral law versus civic law, so Julian would go back at night to tag his deer and bring it home.

Julian started to relay the story again: "It just jumped

right out. I never even saw it until . . . you should check out the dent."

I interrupted him to say that the dent in the truck wasn't going anywhere, but the thawed crayfish in the fridge might go sour. Julian changed into a clean T-shirt, skimmed through the recipe, then got busy on the early steps of the crayfish mousse. He sautéed the whole crayfish in butter with a mirepoix of carrot, onion, thyme, bayleaf, parsley, and white wine, then started peeling all the shells and tails. As he worked, I noticed that he had that smooth fluidity of motion that you can only get from working in a fast-paced commercial kitchen. It was a fluidity that I didn't have, so I was glad to have Julian at my side.

I continued working on the turkey galantine. I removed all the meat from the skinned carcass. After slicing the breast fillets into long, thin strips, I put the strips into a bowl of brandy along with some equal-sized strips of bear fat. The rest of the turkey meat went through the grinder, along with some venison and bear fat. The result was a smooth paste. I stirred it together with a few eggs, seasonings, and brandy. I spread the sausage in an inch-thick layer over the entire skin. Then I removed the strips of turkey breast and bear fat from the marinade and arranged them in alternating rows down the center. I topped the breast strips with crushed pistachio nuts and chopped parsley. Escoffier calls for chopped truffles, but I sprinkled in some sautéed morels instead.

Escoffier also says to put a pickled pig's tongue down the center of the galantine. It seemed to me like a good-enough idea, but I left the tongue out. Sure, I was committed to authenticity, but I was also committed to making my dishes somewhat appealing to the quasi-vegetarians in my life. Diana had agreed to try as many of the dishes as possible. This was my big chance to show her the joys of meat eating, so I was trying to be diplomatic. And I wasn't going to kid myself; if there was one thing that would keep Diana from sampling a wild turkey galantine, it would be a pig's tongue running through the middle of it. Working together, Julian and I rolled the galantine into a cylinder the size and shape of a piece of firewood. Julian tied the ends with kitchen string and wrapped the whole log in a layer of cheesecloth. He tied the package shut with several more wraps of string. I put the galantine in the fridge. Julian went back to his crayfish mousse; I opened the door of the fridge back up, to admire how kick-ass the galantine looked. It was tidy and precise, the most efficient packaging that a turkey could hope for.

By then we had an influx of people running through the kitchen. Everyone was getting up to go pheasant hunting. They were all passing to and from the bathroom, looking for coffee and borrowing toothpaste and trying to find their boots. I tried to head off the run on the kitchen by pulling out some zucchini bread that I'd made just for the situation. I was a good host for about ten minutes, then I started swinging my chef's knife around and yelling, "Get out! Get out! Get your coffee at the gas station."

When things got quiet again, I realized it was time to make rabbit pâté, but Matt and Danny hadn't shot the rabbit yet. The pâté called for a layer of bear fat soaked in brandy, so I put that together. The only other step we could do ahead of time was the crust. Nina was supposed to handle all dough-related substances, and she hadn't shown up yet. As I was punching in her number on my phone, she walked through the door.

"We need puff paste!" I said. Nina took a seat at the back corner of the kitchen table and spread cookbooks in a half-circle around her. Pretty soon she was measuring flour.

We were operating as a crude, pared-down version of Escoffier's own *brigade de cuisine*. To speed processes along and ensure consistent quality, Escoffier broke the preparation of dishes down into individual steps and assigned those steps to qualified practitioners. For our *brigade,* Nina was in charge of dough and making things look artistic; I was in charge of the rough work, basically converting things from animal form into ingredient form; Julian was in charge of finessing dishes through the difficult stages and creating the sauces. It also seemed as though Julian was in charge of being confident. While Nina and I constantly consulted cookbooks and second-guessed all of our moves, Julian went efficiently from chore to chore.

While Nina worked the puff paste, I cranked a few mallard breasts through the grinder. I worked on plucking the sparrows that I had in a box by the door. Then I trimmed and skinned a salmon fillet and peeled some shrimp tails. When that was done, I went over to help Julian finish up the crayfish mousse.

The crayfish were all peeled, and Julian had sliced the tail pieces into thin ovals and reserved a dozen of the best shells. He was supposed to pulverize the rest of the crayfish meat with the shells and bodies and cooking mirepoix, so he put everything into the bowl of a food processor.

"I bet Escoffier didn't have a food processor," I said.

"But he wishes he did," said Julian.

When the crayfish were crushed into a mush, Julian added fish velouté, melted fish jelly, and melted butter that he colored red with paprika. He passed the whole mixture through a piece of cheesecloth to separate out the bits of shell. The liquid emerged a beautiful red.

I set a mixing bowl in the sink and packed crushed ice around its sides. Julian poured the crayfish liquid into the bowl, then quickly folded in some half-whipped cream and the reserved pieces of sliced tail meat. I lined a charlotte mold with parchment paper and filled it with the mousse. Julian shaped spoonfuls of mousse into the emptied crayfish carapaces, then we put them into the fridge to set.

When Nina had her puff paste ready, she kept saying, "I don't know if it'll puff. We might want to try again."

"I have no clue," I said.

Julian looked over his shoulder at the dough. "It will puff," he said.

"Good. Roll that shit out, Nina."

Nina took a rolling pin and pressed out a twelve-inch, circular base of puff paste on a cookie sheet. While she rolled, I pulled out two pounds of ground mountain goat for the sweet meat. I mixed the goat with currants, red currant jelly, salt and pepper, and ground ginger. When Nina was done with the base, I piled the loaf of sweetened and spiced mountain goat on top of the disk. Then Nina built a dome of puff paste to cap over the meat. She sealed the dome to the base by pressing the edges together with the tines of a fork. She rolled out a reserved piece of puff paste dough and used a paring knife to cut out the shapes of two mountain goats for a decoration on the dome. She gave her goats horns and long beards. Using egg white as glue, she attached the goats to the roof of the dome. I was thrilled. She was capturing the spirit of the Escoffier feast.

I had pulled the headcheese fixings out of the freezer the night before. I added salt, pepper, and herbs and put the pot on the stove to simmer. In thirty minutes the stock was reduced and had started to gel. I scooped the headcheese into a mold, covered the mold with parchment paper, capped it with a weighted lid, and put it into the fridge. It was ready for the table.

When Nina finished mixing the short paste, she rolled the

dough into a thin oval and used it to line a mold for the rabbit pâté. She put the mold in the fridge.

It was already afternoon.

Julian was cruising on the soufflé de foie gras, one of the most complicated dishes for the day and also the most mysterious. He was swigging from a bottle of Grand Marnier and mashing five ounces of Canada goose livers in a ceramic mixing bowl. He minced an equal amount of pheasant flesh and a couple of ounces of cooked morels.

I turned my attention to the mallard breasts that I had run through the grinder earlier in the morning. I weighed out two and a quarter pounds of the duck flesh and made it into a quenelle mixture by stirring in butter, egg whites, salt, and pepper. The quenelles were a garnish for the duck consommé, which was thawing on the counter. I placed the mixture on the crushed ice and stirred in a little cream. Over the next two hours, I added more cream and worked the mixture over the ice, so that it stayed firm and cool.

I'd been thinking that the stingray would be a simple, last-minute job, but then I remembered that it was supposed to marinate for a few hours. I asked Nina to put together the marinade and a light batter for the stingray. The marinade called for fresh lemon juice, oil, onion rings, bay leaves, parsley, thyme, salt, and pepper. Once she started working on that, I realized that our organizational system had already collapsed. The kitchen had turned into a free-for-all; the three of us were just trying to do whatever needed to happen next, with no regard for Escoffier's prescribed division of labor. The man would not have been pleased.

I began the final processing on a tub of thawed fish. I prepped the stingray and cut it into finger-sized strips. The stingray's meat was textured with a washboard pattern, like

Ruffles potato chips. I started to prep fillets of eel, small-mouth bass, walleye, and bluegill for the white wine matelote, but then abandoned the job when I realized that I'd forgotten to put the stingray into the jar of marinade. I didn't want to forget about it again, so I used the jar to prop open the cookbook on the counter.

Nina made polenta. She molded the polenta into a greased cake pan, let it cool, then tipped it out. She took a long knife and cut a one-inch slice off the top of the mold, like she was removing a lid. Using a spoon, she hollowed the mold out, so that she had a bowl made out of polenta. All that dish needed was sparrows and risotto.

As the three of us worked, we discussed our plans for table service. Decisions about table service were no joking matter to Escoffier. When he was an up-and-coming chef, the preferred method of table service was something called *service à la française,* which involved setting all the courses out on the table in elaborate displays at the beginning of the meal. *Service à la française* probably came into vogue during the reign of Louis XIV, when royal dinners were arranged like still-life works of art. Carême, Escoffier's hallowed predecessor, endorsed the *française* method because he considered himself to be as much an architect as a cook. He would sometimes pile 150 dishes on a table in tiered arrangements resembling Greco-Roman structures. Diners couldn't pass the dishes around, either. They just ate whatever was within reach.

In Escoffier's lifetime, a new form of service gained some popularity. At first Escoffier thought *service à la russe,* or Russian-style service, was a passing trend. The chief proponent of the new method was the chef of the king of Prussia, a guy named Félix Urbain-Dubois. With another chef, Emile Bernard, Dubois coauthored a book that began with a three-page rationale for *service à la russe.* They argued that each patron or guest should have a chance to sample each dish, and that footmen, or waiters, should play a more important role in dining. Escoffier eventually converted. As his reason, he cited his belief that each client deserved individual attention.

We were going to use *service à la russe,* but with a twist. Some of the dishes were going to look so cool, we wanted to bring them to the table whole. Then, while the guests observed, the dishes would be divided into individual Russian-style servings. As for the order of meals, we were largely going to wing it. Escoffier was adamant about beginning a meal with oysters and caviar and soup, so we knew how to begin. As for the rest, we'd play it by ear and serve things as they were ready. It might not be perfectly to Escoffier's liking, but it was the most practical way for inexperienced chefs like ourselves to keep the hot stuff hot and the cold stuff cold.

I rinsed out a large roasting pan and filled it with game stock. I brought the stock to a simmer. After placing the turkey galantine on a wire rack, I lowered it into the stock and moved the roasting pan to the oven. It needed three hours to cook and a couple of hours to chill.

We set ourselves up to start working on the duck quenelles. Nina boiled a saucepan of water and set it on the table next to us. By dipping the teaspoons into the hot water, we could use them to mold the creamy quenelle mixture into olive shapes without the mixture's sticking to the metal. We formed about forty quenelles and laid them in a lightly greased baking pan. It took us over an hour to finish the project.

When we were done, I baked a salmon fillet and sautéed some shrimp, then minced the meat together with cooked morels. I added three eggs to this mixture along with some béchamel sauce that Julian made. Julian was terribly displeased with how his sauce turned out. He scalded the milk slightly, and it came out tasting a little like burned almonds. I cooked the entire mixture on a low burner. Once it thickened, I spread it out in a buttered Pyrex baking dish and chilled it in the freezer for a few minutes. When the mixture firmed up, I cut it into fourteen individual cakes and placed them on a platter. At that point we had twelve dishes started. It was getting dark out. I told Julian that now would be a good time for him to go pick up his roadkill deer. Nina thought it would be a good time for her to go home and shower. While they were gone, I figured that I'd work on the thirteenth dish. I'd been soaking a couple of antelope and mule deer bladders in cold water. I was supposed to stuff ducks inside them, but I couldn't imagine how I'd ever get a duck to fit.

I instead tried to get a half duck inside the antelope bladder, but there was no way it would go. I figured that Julian might have a good idea how to do it, so I busied myself with some other chores. I prepped a few more fish for the matelote, then went out to see if my brothers had gotten back with the rabbits. I went back inside and started plucking a few more sparrows. Diana came into the kitchen to check on me and see if I needed help, but I shooed her away so she wouldn't have to witness any unnecessary gore. Moments later the hunting party got back with the rabbit loins I'd been waiting on. I put the loins to soak in some brandy, then stepped outside with a hatchet.

Someone had turned a yard light on. As usual, Red took the light to mean that morning had arrived. He was cooing. I walked across the yard to the coop. Everyone who'd been out pheasant hunting was milling around in the yard, but they all went inside rather than watch me kill the "pets." Maybe I was looking for an excuse to postpone the pigeon slaughter, but it occurred to me that I shouldn't leave the kitchen unmanned.

Julian and Nina were gone, so there wasn't anyone around to protect our space and guard our ingredients from anyone looking for a quick snack. I dropped the hatchet next to the coop and ran back in to find that everyone was digging through the cupboards in search of mixers and appetizers.

By the time I got everyone herded into a couple of cars and headed down toward the bar, Julian was back with his deer. As we hoisted it up on a joist in the garage, I gave him an update on where we were. I explained that I was feeling a little cowardly about Red and Lil' Red. I wasn't quite sure how to go about slaughtering them.

When Julian was a kid, his family raised chickens for food, and he said he had a good method for dispatching fowl. He started two nails into a plank with a claw hammer. The nails were a half inch apart, and he left them sticking out an inch. We set a wooden bar stool next to the coop and placed Julian's block of wood on the seat. He had a hatchet in his hand.

"All right," he said. "We're all set."

I opened the door of the coop and snatched Red by the feet. I had recently read an essay in *The New Yorker* magazine by a woman who had to kill a chicken for dinner. Before lopping its head, she described taking the bird by the feet and twirling it around like a windmill, to confuse it. I gave Red a few twirls out of pity.

"What are you doing?" Julian asked.

"Getting him dizzy."

"Give me that poor bird," he said.

Julian took Red by the feet, slipped the bird's neck between the two nails, pulled the bird taut, and brought the hatchet down in a smooth swipe.

"All right," he said. "Next bird."

I pulled out Lil' Red. *Whap.*

Julian's moves were so quick and efficient that I didn't have time to feel bad for the birds. They were cooing one moment and then, at least for them, the next moment simply vanished. As we plucked the two birds into a trash can in the yard, I came up with an idea for the bladders. I pulled out two of the adult pigeons and tried to visualize them without feathers. It might just work, I thought. Escoffier warns his readers against adult pigeons, but I was in a pinch; it was either these two birds or nothing. We plucked all four pigeons and brought them into the house.

Nina was back, and she was making risotto for the sparrow cake. While she worked on it, I removed the breasts from the plucked sparrows and sauteed them in the bouillon fat that I had saved from making stock. Nina laid a layer of risotto in the bottom of the bowl that she had molded from polenta. I topped it with sparrow breasts. She laid down another layer of risotto and I topped that with breasts. Once we filled the bowl, we pasted the lid on with a glue made from egg and forcemeat. Nina buttered the outside of the polenta bowl and placed it back inside the mold. She popped it into the oven.

At seven p.m. we were just about ready to start serving. Julian was popping open the oysters and applying dollops of whitefish caviar into the shells. It was time to call down to the bar and tell everyone to come home for dinner. After placing the call, I stuffed the two adult pigeons inside the bladders. I filled the empty spaces with a mixture of sautéed goose liver, minced bear fat, chopped onion, parsley, salt, and pepper. The pale, elastic sacks looked as full and tight as occupied condoms.

## CHAPTER TWENTY

# The Tastes of Escoffier

I THOUGHT IT WOULD BE COOL IF DIANA HAD A NOTEBOOK ON her lap during the meals, so she could record the reactions of everyone sitting at the table. I asked her to make a special effort to record her own reactions. I thought that reading her personal notes would be like getting a glimpse into her meat-eating diary. Since Diana had starting eating fish almost six months before, I knew she was ready for the next steps: red meat and fowl. If I had notes about her likes and dislikes concerning those items, I could tailor my future meat-cooking accordingly.

Long after the three-day feast was over, I wound up using that notebook to solve a mystery. The mystery had nothing to do with Diana's favorite recipes. Instead I wanted to determine exactly when, during the first night, Diana had gotten sick. The notebook was an invaluable source of information, because her own memories of the evening were blurred.

While I had been cooking all day, Jen had been busy converting the living room into a swank dining room. She had agreed to oversee the decorating job on the condition that I grant Hansel and Gretel II permanent amnesty. I agreed, and she recruited Diana and Anna to help her. They purchased candles, flowers, and a special Thanksgiving-themed cloth for a banquet table they rented at the hardware store. Because we didn't have enough plates and glasses, Jen had also purchased paper plates, plastic champagne flutes, plastic wine glasses, and plastic silverware. Escoffier probably rolled over in his grave because of all that paper and plastic, but I thought the temporary nature of the place settings conveyed the special-ness of the feast: instead of using the same old worn-out plates we normally used, we were using plates that would never suf-fer the future stains of lesser meals. When Jen lit the candles that night, the living room looked fantastic, like something from a movie set.

As Julian and I prepared to begin serving the meal, I took a look into the living room. Except for Moisan, all of my hunt-ing partners were sitting in a complete circle around the room. Diana was sitting close to the kitchen door, a notebook in her lap. It was a beautiful sight.

The only blemish at the table was a newcomer who had shown up in town just before the meal was served. Her name is Sarah. She's the girlfriend of my brother Matt's friend Kevin, who drove up from his home in Jackson Hole, Wyoming. Kevin's in his mid thirties and looks like the sort of all-American guy who would work at a golf course. He was ready for some hard-core eating. His girlfriend, Sarah, is the last girl on earth you'd expect him to be dating. She's the same age as Kevin but was dressed that night like a punky adolescent. Her hair had more dye in it than a Grateful Dead T-shirt, and her wardrobe accessories numbered in the dozens: neon-colored trinkets and jewelry and a special, glitzy belt. Her wardrobe looked incredibly, well . . . intentional. When I saw her, I felt a strange obligation to compliment her on her hair or something. It was like she was ready for a costume party.

In retrospect, I don't care if Sarah looks like a seventh grader. She's an aesthetician, and to be an aesthetician, I suppose it's important to look like you care a lot about your aesthetic, no matter how ridiculous it is. My wrath toward her is based solely on the fact that she tried her damnedest to sabotage the feast. I'm not really sure why she came; I guess she just wanted to spend the holiday with her boyfriend. Once she was there, though, she decided to wage holy war. Sarah is an extraordinarily self-righteous subspecies of vegetarian, the kind that's usually opposed to all forms of animal subjugation. What makes Sarah unique among self-righteous vegetarians is that she wears leather and eats cheese. Her vegetarianism stems from her belief that due to some complex, yet ill-founded health concerns, it's important for her to live a healthy lifestyle. Her healthy lifestyle includes smoking a lot of cigarettes and other materials, regularly stripping layers of skin off her face with something called "chemical peels," and drinking a dietary supplement of liquified clay. (I'm not sure why a person would drink clay, which, followed by a diuretic, turns the colon into petrified rock.) Anyway, she's got it in her head that meat is lethal. So she showed up armed with refried beans and lettuce. She even brought her own water, as if Matt's faucets dripped meat. Then, as if all that wasn't annoying enough, she sat herself at the head of the table with a grizzly-sized snarl on her face.

Otherwise, the atmosphere was exciting and charged. Everyone was a little drunk from the bar, which was good; reduced inhibitions couldn't hurt. I dismissed Nina from the kitchen so she could sit at the table. She and Jen were going to make sure the wines and drinks were served at the proper times.

Once everyone was seated, I gave Jen the nod to pour out fourteen flutes of bubbly. After a quick toast, Julian and I rolled out the oysters and caviar. I also passed out a bowl of caviar atop crushed ice, along with a gorgeous little seashell caviar spoon that Jen had bought for the occasion.

From where I stood in the kitchen, I could hear the exclamations of approval in the living room as the oysters and caviar made the rounds. Diana recorded her own response to the oysters and caviar as "paradise on the half-shell." While the oysters moved through the dining room, I was heating a skillet of oil to a smoking-hot temperature. I lowered each salmon-and-prawn cake into the oil for a ten-second flash fry. I had to support the fragile cakes with a spatula as they cooked, to keep them from falling apart. Julian whipped up some more béchamel sauce to accompany the cakes. Escoffier said that a sauce should fit a dish "as a tight-fitting skirt fits a woman." Julian and Escoffier must speak the same language. When he finished his sauce, Julian took a taste. "That's it," he said. "That's what it's supposed to be."

We presented the salmon-and-prawn cakes to the table. Julian and I kept one of the cakes and broke it into two. I was pleased. "That salmon did not die in vain," I said. I overheard Diana say that the cakes were the best thing she'd ever eaten, and I thought, You ain't seen nothing yet.

I wanted to mix up the land and sea dishes, so as the salmon-and-prawn cakes disappeared, I busted out the headcheese, along with a vinaigrette dressing Nina had mixed up in an empty vodka bottle. At first the headcheese prompted a lot of caution. No one in the room had ever seen headcheese, so no one had any idea what it was supposed to look like. I didn't know either, until that day when I finished making it. It looked mottled and brownish, and shiny. I had molded it into the shape of a large stick of butter. I handed it to Diana, whose Jewish upbringing had taught her that pig is filthy. She refused it. I wasn't shocked. Diana passed the dish to Anna, who will eat anything. (I once watched her open a fridge and pluck out a slice of rare, pink moose heart for breakfast.) She took a dinky little slice of headcheese and tried it. Everyone watched her. "I've never tasted anything like it," she said. She took a bigger slice.

Kern was the next to sample it. "It's delicious," he said. "It's tough to describe. The consistency is really good . . . It's much milder than I would have thought. It's not like cheese. It's more like a thinking man's lunch meat." The headcheese made the rounds like that: most everyone greeted it with apprehension but ended up liking it. Even the couple of people who didn't taste it thought it looked cool.

Except, of course, Sarah. During the courses of caviar and prawns and salmon, she seemed to be wondering how to handle herself. She must have recognized those dishes as standard restaurant fare and had probably heard from her acupuncturist that seafood is good for the brain or something, so she refrained from scoffing too loudly. The headcheese was a different story. She rolled her eyes and scrunched her nose up so violently that I half hoped/half feared the expression might stick.

Cooking the quenelles was a tricky business. Earlier in the day, we'd formed the creamed mixture of raw duck flesh and butter into olive-shaped dumplings. Escoffier wanted us to poach them using an odd method. I brought a pot of water to a boil, then poured the water into the shallow baking pan containing the raw quenelles. The hot water cooked them a little bit, but not much. I ladled the water back out of the baking sheet and poured in another pot of boiling water. Escoffier doesn't specify how many pots of water the quenelles might need, so after three pots, I started to worry. But after the fourth pot, the quenelles magically stiffened and rose to the surface, poached. I scooped the already-warmed duck consommé into some glass bowls that Jen had bought at a second-hand store, and added some quenelles to each bowl.

The duck consommé proved to be the biggest hit of the first day. The quenelles were creamy and rich; they had a mousse-like texture and exploded with the taste of medium-rare duck. I had sampled the duck consommé a few days before when I made it, so I already knew it was pretty damned good. Now my friends agreed. Diana's notebook filled up with rave quotes: "Oh wow . . . Oh, that's so good." "It's so subtle . . . it's not something that overwhelms you initially . . . I just like the combination of textures." Before tasting it, Kern reminded everyone that duck is the one game bird he doesn't like. (He calls mallards "flying liver.") But after tasting a quenelle, he said, "This kicks ass." Even Diana liked it.

The foie gras soufflé was one of the least popular items. When it came out of the oven, it was perfectly risen and as light as a golden brown balloon. Within seconds, though, it collapsed like it had been hit by a dart. I served it anyway, along with an explanation that the recipe called for real foie gras and I had thrown in some year-old wild goose liver. The reviews were all-around negative: "A little too strong." "It's not too strong . . . it just doesn't taste like food." "I don't like it." "It's a bit waterlogged, really." "It's like eating a plant from a swamp." Diana found the dish "too airy."

While the soufflé was being condemned, Sarah thought it would be a good time to come out swinging. "That's what you get," she said, "for eating something so fucking nasty." My brothers and Drost and Kern had begun to ignore her, so she tried to align herself with the girls at the table: "Men are such carnivores," she said reflectively. But she only isolated herself further. These girls weren't the type to respond to a girl-power campaign. From then on, our only breaks from Sarah came when she went outside to smoke cigarettes (American Spirits, of course, since they're natural).

Meanwhile, Julian and I were having a hell of a good time in the kitchen. We were cooking and drinking and making an incredible mess of ourselves. We went from Grand Marnier to bubbly to port to sherry and then back to Grand Marnier. This behavior would never have flown in Escoffier's kitchen. Escoffier wouldn't let his chefs drink any liquor at all. He devised a nonalcoholic barley beverage that he kept on the stove at all times; if his chefs were thirsty, he reasoned, they could drink that. His rule was probably a good one. I cut my hand twice while finishing up the matelote, leaving Julian to place the pieces of freshwater fish and the segments of raw eel in a large pan with onions, garlic, white wine, and a bouquet garni, while I bandaged my fingers. Julian started to pour in the brandy, but I insisted that I be the one to flame it off. When I tried, I started a small fire, which spread to a pile of greasy towels. Julian jumped in to rescue the dish, nearly singeing his pelt. When he emerged from the smoky kitchen, cradling the dish, a round of applause erupted from the dining room.

Diana, who had by this time eaten a greater variety and a greater quantity of fish and meat than she'd ever eaten in her whole life, didn't record anyone's impressions of the matelote. This may have been an oversight, or she may have already been getting woozy. Either way, she swears that she tasted the matelote and liked it.

However, she doesn't remember much about the crayfish mousse. Which is good, because the dish was a disaster. I'd begun to eye the mousse with suspicion when Julian and I first poured it into its mold. Or, I should say, I'd begun to smell it with suspicion. When we turned the mousse out of its mold, the smell hadn't improved. It was a synthetic odor, like something you might clean carpet with. Strangely, none of the constituents of the mousse—crayfish, champagne, gelatin, cream, fish stock—accounted for the stench. I tried to ignore it and breathe through my mouth.

By the time we got the thing decorated, it looked ready to melt. I entered the dining room and announced an intermission while Julian put the mousse back into the freezer for ten minutes before we served it. Kern was the only person who liked it. He even came back into the kitchen after the dish was returned to pick the bits of crayfish tail from the melting mousse and save them in a coffee mug.

By now, the meal was taking on the attributes of a Gospel sermon, with lots of ups and downs, damnation and redemption. We followed the mousse up with fried stingray. It was good—fried fish is always good—but there was an added bonus: its texture was scalloplike. It lacked the flaky grain that white-fleshed fish usually has, and it was pinker than normal fish. If Diana's nausea had indeed set in by now, she must have rallied for a minute, because she wrote down that she liked the stingray. Drost declared it "a true crowd-pleaser." Jen rebelled against the masses: "I don't think I'm very open-minded. Actually, I don't think I like meat anymore."

When I brought the rabbit pâté into the dining room, I thought that Diana looked stunned, but I figured she was just reveling in the joy of consuming mass quantities of wild game. I didn't notice that her pen was working only intermittently. She did manage to record a few quotes about the pâté, but she didn't taste it. Eric declared the pâté the best-smelling dish so far. When I sliced through the golden-brown crust and tried to remove a piece, the layers of fat and meat fell apart at the seams. Too dry, I guess. Drost said that it tasted like a piece of lunch meat that's been dropped into a vat of liquor. In a good way.

Diana's first wave of serious nausea must have hit around this time, between the rabbit pâté and the mountain goat sweet meat, because the notes about the sweet meat are in Jen's penmanship. Personally, I thought the dish was a pleasant surprise. The dome came out puffy and buttery, textured like a good croissant. Nina did a hell of a job on the decorative mountain goats that she made out of the leftover puff paste; the animals rose a quarter inch above the crust while it baked in the oven. Julian and I delivered the sweet meat to the table to show it off before slicing. Jen documented Danny's reaction. "Oh man," he said, "that is so good!" Eric concurred: "Dee-fucking-licious." Other comments followed: "You can really taste the brandy." "For a mountain goat that fell off a cliff, it tastes pretty good." "I feel so fat right now . . . Oh my God."

Once the lid of the sparrow and polenta cake was browned, we pulled it out and carefully removed it from its mold. The entire polenta case was the color of lightly toasted bread. I cut the cake in half, exposing the alternating layers of risotto and sparrow breasts. The sparrow meat came out the color of walnut shells. One of the sparrows fell out, so I popped it into my mouth. It was rich and dark, with a gizzardlike texture. The flavor was potent, like an exaggerated version of dark turkey meat. If you generally like mild food, you wouldn't like sparrow. I pried out another breast with my fingertips and popped it down. The rest went to the table with an *espagnole* sauce. Lauren didn't want to eat sparrows because she felt bad for them, so Danny tried to vilify the birds. "Sparrows are vicious,

Lauren. They kill native birds." Drost liked the sauce. "This sauce is the shit," he said. The sparrows made Nina nostalgic: "When I was a kid, my mom used to give me the heart of a chicken. I liked it. Sparrow reminds me of that."

By this point, eleven courses into the meal, Sarah was getting hungry. She asked if I had any polenta or risotto left over. "That hasn't touched meat," she clarified. I told her no. From then on, she changed her approach. She was no longer snide and judgmental; now she was bored and annoyed. She crossed her arms and scowled. Whenever I stepped out to serve a dish, I was greeted by her scowl from the head of the table. She reminded me of a chaperone at a dance.

After the sparrow was cleared from the table, Diana made a break for the bathroom. She zipped wordlessly through the kitchen, her face drained of color like a piece of meat that's been soaking in water. I followed her down the hall. The bathroom door closed in my face. I worried I'd somehow poisoned everyone with bad shellfish or tainted meat. When Diana came out, some five minutes later, I questioned her extensively but tried not to seem alarmed. "Maybe you had too much to drink? Could that be it? When did you first feel sick?"

"I think I OD'd on meat," she said. "Or I got gout. It's probably gout."

I had been talking about gout a lot lately, because Escoffier's clientele suffered from it in plaguelike proportions. It's a painful condition where uric acid crystals accumulate in joint spaces. The ailment used to be known as "the disease of kings and the king of diseases," because it's greatly exacerbated by drinking alcohol and eating purine-rich meats such as shellfish and animal organs.

"You get gout in your joints, like your ankles and toes," I said.

"Not me," Diana said. "Mine's in my gut."

Diana promised to put on a poker face and return to the table. If everyone in the living room knew she was sick, then I'd have a major crisis on my hands. When it comes to food-borne sickness, people tend to overreact. I once got sick on a pork and avocado sandwich. The pork was surely the culprit, but in my stomach's mind, the avocado was guilty by association. I couldn't eat avocado for years. A case of food poisoning at this juncture in the meal would spoil everything. I gave Diana a hug, but the hug only made her feel nauseated all over again. When that wave passed, she went back to the table and took her seat. Although she was pretty quiet from then on out, no one suspected a thing.

I was half expecting ten or twelve people to keel over with convulsions at any moment. Thankfully, I had Ray Turner's smoked eel ready. Ray Turner's smokehouse is a state-inspected facility. If we were all going to get sick anyway, we probably wouldn't get any sicker from the smoked eel. I had cut the eel into one-inch slices, saving a couple of pieces for Julian and me to share in the kitchen. We savored the smoky, slightly oily flavor of Ray's eel. It lacked the dry, aftertaste-inducing qualities of my own smoked products.

Julian and I took a brief break after the eel. I was trying to monitor the bathroom. If I thought people were using it too much, I was going to have to start worrying. But after a stretch without unusual bathroom activity, I decided that Diana's gout, or whatever it was, was an isolated case. We proceeded with the bladders.

Julian pinched the little sacks closed and I threw two half hitches on the end of each one. The sacks were sphere-shaped, the size of racquet balls. When we poached the bladders in game stock, they expanded a bit, then contracted. The leg and wing bones of the pigeons threatened to poke holes in the bladders. We consulted our resident doctor, Deirdre, about the tenacity of the organs. She glanced in the pot and surmised that a bladder should be able to withstand that level of abuse without getting punctured. As the bladders continued to cook, they turned a brilliant rainbow swirl of colors. Shades of pink, purple, black, and red spread across the bladders like motor oil on mud puddles. It was very beautiful. Julian finished the bladders with a sauce of red wine, shallots, and puréed duck liver. I assigned Danny the task of carving the birds. When he sliced through the bladder, Matt said, "Ur-*ine* there now." After tasting a piece of the poached bladder, Anna said, "It tastes the way grass smells." I took a bite and enjoyed the way the bladder resisted chewing. I eventually broke it apart a little with my teeth and swallowed it, even though I hadn't gotten it sufficiently chewed up.

The actual pigeons weren't as good as the bladders themselves. Escoffier had never said they would be. I knew I was taking a gamble by using the birds instead of ducklings, but I had hoped that the new cooking technique would render them tender and delicious. It didn't. The pigeons were as tough as I'd remembered.

The look of the bladders confirmed everything that Sarah had expected about the depravity of the meal. She resumed her that's-so-gross routine. But her running commentary about the meal had steadily lost what little bite it might have had. At first people had at least looked at her when she spoke. As the evening went along, though, she might as well have been talking to Red and Lil' Red. It was really a pathetic sight, and I couldn't help but feel a little sorry for her. Not like the sorry that you feel for a wet puppy; more like the repulsed sort of sorry you feel for a fly that's drowning in an abandoned glass of lemonade. If I were Escoffier, I guess I would have made her all kinds of delicious vegetarian stuff, if only to keep her from spoiling everyone else's time. But I guess I can't fill Escoffier's shoes on all counts. I just let Sarah suffer.

If one thing could have penetrated Sarah's veneer, it would have been the turkey galantine. It was the most visually intriguing dish of the night. After poaching the log-shaped, cloth-wrapped bird for three hours in game stock, we let it cool on a rack. The stock coagulated around the bird, forming a transparent, pinkish aspic. I demolded the package and cut the strings holding the cheesecloth, then unwrapped the bird with the care of an archaeologist unveiling a mummy. Inside, the turkey skin, which was acting as a sort of sausage casing, was firm and white. The galantine wasn't fragile at all. At the table, I sliced through the middle of the galantine with all the fanfare of a magician sawing his assistant in half. In cross section, the twirls of pistachios and sausage and morels gave the dish a kaleidoscopic effect. Even Sarah had a compliment for it: "It *looks* pretty," she said.

The galantine was supposed to be the first night's pièce de résistance, but I made a last-minute decision to give Red and Lil' Red the headlining performance of the evening. The two pigeons looked stunning, all dressed up as *pigeonneaux crapaudine*. Julian and I had to guess what Escoffier meant when he wrote, "Cut the young pigeons horizontally from the point of the breast along the top of the legs and right up to the joints of the wings but without cutting right through. Open them out, lightly flatten, season, dip in butter and grill gently." Using a heavy pair of scissors, we split the birds along their backbones, leaving a flap of flesh like a book's binding. The birds came out looking flat, but still vividly resembling themselves, the way prepared chickens at a Chinese barbecue still vividly resemble chickens. Julian finished the birds with a *diable* sauce of white wine, shallots, and cayenne. The sauce had a nice, subtle burn to it. As a garnish for the dish, Escoffier recommends gherkins, but we substituted slices of Drost's homemade pickles that he'd brought from Michigan.

Two squabs make for slim pickings when divided up by a pack of carnivores. I took my little slice and a spoonful of sauce and retreated to the kitchen to sample the dish in private. I'd never worked so hard for one little morsel in my life. I was desperately hoping it would taste good. But at the same time, I recognized that it didn't really matter whether it was good or not. The experience of collecting the birds had been such a thrill and education. A bad taste couldn't take that away. As I stood there pondering the piece of squab, the little bite of meat was getting cold. I popped it into my mouth.

I haven't been as surprised by a taste since I pressed my tongue to the points on a 9-volt battery when I was a kid. But the squab was nothing like that battery; it was delicious. The flesh was as tender as a Reese's peanut butter cup. And it was almost as sweet. I ran into the living room and most everyone in there was equally thrilled. I felt as though I had proven a point and won a bet about something that I myself hadn't even fully believed in. The squab was a new taste altogether. It was way different from regular pigeon. I wanted to shout about it. In fact, I did shout about it. "Man, it's so *different*," I said.

My one little bite of the squab didn't last long. The taste faded in my mouth as quickly as breath on a mirror. Diana didn't try the squab, but she was happy about my triumph. It was very cool of her, to be happy about something's tasting good when she didn't even want to try it. I could never be that way, so I was appreciative and impressed.

We still had two more meals and twenty-eight more courses

to go, but it was clear that my hopes of converting Diana to meat eating were dashed. By the next day, Diana had virtually no recollection of what she'd eaten. We were able to rule out gout and poison, and decided that she had overwhelmed her system with foods that she was unaccustomed to, which had caused a mental shock. Over the following weeks, I'd ask her stuff like "Hey, did you try those sparrows in the polenta cake?" She could never remember. Now she can't even remember specifics about the stuff that I *know* she ate.

"I don't know, I was sick," she always responds. Or else, "There were forty-five courses! How am I supposed to remember?"

But my assessment is that her memories are repressed. I remain hopeful that she will someday recover the memories; I hope that the tastes and flavors will come back to her and that she'll begin eating meat again. But I doubt it. She may decide to eat more meat on her own, but I've thrown in the towel on trying to force it on her. She tried wild game meat, and then she rejected it. That's better than what she was doing before: rejecting it without trying it. So there's been a small improvement. I owe Escoffier for that one.

And I guess I owe Sarah too. She probably went home and complained to her friends in Jackson Hole about the animals (people and otherwise) she'd had Thanksgiving dinner with. All in all, though, I'm glad she came. Without meaning to, she provided a great, drab backdrop against which I could see how cool my friends are. Every time I had brought a dish out to my friends, there had always been someone besides Sarah who wouldn't taste it: Lauren didn't want to eat sparrows because she likes watching them; Matt hates liver; another friend of Matt's suffered from arachnophobia and by association wouldn't eat crabs; Diana wouldn't touch wild boar because of the tenets of Judaism. People were turning down dishes right and left. But no one besides Sarah passed any kind of overriding judgment on the feast as a whole. Instead, we enjoyed discussing all our various likes and dislikes and hang-ups, because those things provided us with a way to discuss not just the food but also what food means to us.

When you go on a big trip with a group of people, you feel a bond with them that lasts for months or even years. The bond is especially strong if it's a dangerous sort of trip, like canoeing in white water or hiking into a particularly sketchy and remote piece of wilderness. I think that bond forms because the people in the group know they're doing something new and perhaps uncomfortable, and they associate their fellow participants with that great rush that comes from being brave, from going all the way out. That first day's Escoffier meal was the only time I ever felt a bond like that form inside a house. My friends felt the bond too. Our rented dinner table had been like a runaway raft, taking us into a crazy, uncharted gorge full of rare tastes and strange smells. Rather than run away, or feign lack of interest, my friends dug in and went for it. And they all came out on the other side, laughing and having a good time. And we still had two meals to go.

# CHAPTER TWENTY-ONE

# Ancient Carp

## *Le Deuxième Jour—Day Two*

*caviar*—whitefish caviar served with blinis

*huîtres*—oysters

*bouillabaisse à la parisienne*—whiting, ling cod, burbot, rockfish, flounder, and clams cooked with white wine, water, oil, onion, leek, saffron, puréed tomato, parsley, garlic, and a bouquet garni, then finished with butter and served with fresh baguettes

*crabe à l'anglaise*—Dungeness crab mixed with mustard, cayenne, and vinegar, served in its own shell with caviar and chopped egg

*brochette de foie*—skewered elk liver with duxelles sauce

*aspic de crevettes*—prawns in champagne aspic

*moules à la catalane*—glazed blue mussels with liquor of lemon and butter

*coeur de veau sauté*—elk heart with béchamel sauce

*saumon fumé*—Pooder's smoked salmon from San Juan Island

**côtelettes financières**—glazed medallions of bighorn sheep stuffed with creamed morels, partridge, and pheasant

**langue de porc choucroute**—tongue of wild boar with sauerkraut and Madeira reduction

**pâté d'abattis**—giblets of pigeon, wild turkey, Canada geese, pheasant, and mallard sautéed in bouillon fat and baked inside a puff pastry

**faisan à la georgienne**—pheasants and chukars poached with walnuts in a sauce of pressed grapes, pressed oranges, wine, green tea, and *espagnole* sauce

**écrevisses à la bordelaise**—crayfish cooked with white wine and fish stock, then flamed with brandy

**selle de chevreuil Briand**—saddle of antelope larded with bear fat and roasted on a bed of vegetables and garnished with pears poached in red wine

You can see by the above menu that Julian and Nina and I didn't skimp on the cooking for the second day's meal. Except for the caviar and oysters, we avoided repeating any of the dishes from the day before. Even though we tried to keep things new and innovative, our work was much less hectic on the second day. For one thing, we didn't need to kill anything or smuggle roadkill into town. And we had a more solid grasp on Escoffier's basic procedures. We no longer argued about how much salted bear fat was too much or too little. The bases for the sauces were all made up ahead of time and waiting in the fridge. We had a better sense of timing, so hot things were hot and cold things cold. We cranked out puff paste and short paste as casually as if we were whipping out grilled cheese sandwiches.

Also, we suffered no shortage of kitchen help. After forfeiting my battle to turn Diana into a carnivore, I no longer felt compelled to keep her out of the kitchen. What the hell did it matter now if she saw a bunch of bloody, gory stuff? If she ever wanted to try a piece of meat, I told her, just let me know. Until that day comes, I promised not to bring it up. Since she was no longer living in constant fear of having to eat some nasty piece of flesh, she had actually started to feel more comfortable around my food. Throughout the day, she came and went through the kitchen at will; she even cut a few things up and moved some pans around on the stove top. Watching her cook and hang out in the kitchen, I could visualize our future together. Who cares if I eat antelope and she eats tofu? I was ready to live and let live, as long as she was willing to do the same. After all, we wash and fold each other's clothes without wearing each other's underwear.

The second day's preparation went so smoothly, in fact, that we were basically just standing around by seven thirty. We had some things in the oven to keep an eye on, but we killed time by swigging Madeira and dredging Cool Ranch Doritos through our two-pound tub of American golden caviar. Escoffier would have disapproved of our drinking on the job, and if he'd known about Doritos, I'm pretty sure he would have disapproved of those too. However, I'm sure he would have been pleased with our efficiency. Since we'd tackled our day's workload so effortlessly, I started to fear that we'd taken all the challenge out of Escoffier. I decided to add a course to the next night's menu, just to keep things interesting.

Drost and I waited until midnight, when the meal was over and everyone was lying around in a food coma, then made a midnight run downtown. We wanted to see if we could get lucky. We did, right in the alley behind an old brick hotel that fronts on Main Street. I was showing Drost a typical covered ledge where pigeons might hang out. I shone my flashlight on the side of the building, fifteen feet up. "I've never actually surveilled that ledge," I said, "but you see that pigeon shit streaking those bricks under there? That's just the sort of thing you're looking for if you want to find a sleeping pigeon." We pulled the ladder down off the car and set it up.

When I climbed up the ladder and got to the ledge, I was greeted by two of the nicest, plumpest squabs I'd seen yet. They were still in the nest. As I lifted the squabs and tucked them into my pockets, I felt the familiar mixture of fear and excitement I got every time I went trespassing around town for pigeons in the middle of the night. I tried to come up with an appropriate thing to say if the hotel manager called the cops on us. I had a handful of different answers that I had thought up over the past year, answers tailored to appeal to other people's sensibilities: I'm living off the wild; I'm practicing a responsible utilization of a creature that most people regard as a worthless pest; I'm conserving energy by eating locally. Each answer was true, for sure, but each captured only a fraction of the total truth.

Imagine that someone invented a special brain-reading machine, with probes that go into a person's ears to determine what he or she is *primarily* thinking at any given moment. If you had plugged such a machine into my head as I collected the squabs, the meter would have read, "This person is having a hell of a lot of fun."

Fun—there are several hundred thousand words in *Le Guide Culinaire*, but not that one. Escoffier was interested in professionalism, consistency, productivity, and quality, but I don't think he was too interested in fun; that's not what he got paid for. But I can't think of a better word to describe the feeling I get from participating in the great, endless tradition of American scavenging. There I was, in the middle of the

American West, in a town that was built a hundred and some odd years ago over the decaying bones of the vanishing herds of buffalo. At the peak of their existence, the buffalo of the western plains numbered some 40 to 60 million animals. Thousands of people hunted the buffalo and lived off the meat, and then the animals were wiped out as part of some long-forgotten political and military strategy to civilize the country. And the people who killed the buffalo—or maybe their children or grandchildren—built this brick hotel. And now other people stay in the hotel and act civilized. They eat food that came in on trucks from places they've never been and will probably never go to. But there I was, beneath the stars, collecting a dinner that had never before been touched by human hands. It seemed like a miracle. At that moment, I was probably the only dude in Montana—maybe even the country—out catching squabs. That realization gave me a deep pleasure, as though I knew the greatest secret in the world.

And secrets are best when you can share them with friends. I climbed down the ladder and pulled the squabs out of my pockets. "Check these out," I said to Drost. "There's actually a recipe for squabs like these, right out of the nest."

The recipe, number 3409 in *Le Guide,* is *Pigeonneaux Gauthier au Beurre d'Ecrevisse.* Escoffier explains, "The word *Gauthier* does not indicate a particular species of pigeon but is the word once used to denote baby pigeons when they are taken from their nest." The baby birds are split in half, then covered in butter and lemon juice and cooked very slowly. The nestlings are served with a sauce of velouté thickened with egg yolks and flavored with crayfish butter.

Standing in the alleyway, we laughed about Escoffier's persnickety personality. Drost said, "I can't believe Escoffier could tell the difference between a squab that recently left the nest and a squab that's just about to leave its nest."

To Escoffier's credit, there was a difference. We ate the nestlings, or *gauthiers,* on the third and final night of the feast. Kern and Julian did me the favor of handling the last-minute preparations so I could sit at the dining room table. Even though I worked on the dishes all day, it was still exciting and suspenseful to watch the various foods come rolling through the doorway. We started with caviar and poached oysters, followed by sweetbreads in a Madeira sauce and a braised mallard with a sauce of port wine, fresh-squeezed orange juice, cinnamon, ground cloves, and poached cherries. Julian presented the squab nestlings on a dinged-up silver platter that I had found in a Dumpster in Missoula. He had cooked the nestlings in butter and lemon and brought them to the table moistened with their own cooking liquid. The meat of the hatchlings was lighter in color than the meat of the other squabs we'd eaten on the first day: Red and Lil' Red were like the color of slightly diluted blood, but these nestlings were pinkish in color. And the bones of the nestlings were softer too. You could crunch them up and eat them like al dente pasta.

After the nestlings, we experienced a series of failed dishes. The elk and antelope kidney pudding coated our mouths with a faint taste of urine; the blue mussels were so gritty I about broke a tooth; the boar's ear sausages were rubbery enough to defend themselves against the assaults of my knife and fork. Other dishes were delicious and beautiful. The frog legs from Traverse City were served on the bone; they were as light as olives on the ends of toothpicks. We had starlings stuffed and roasted inside hollowed potato casings. The birds fit as snugly as fighter pilots inside their cockpits. We had poached halibut with hollandaise; prawns and asparagus tips inside baked bowls made from creamed potatoes; black bear loin with sauerkraut; marinated roast leg of boar with plums and vegetables; and sausages of pheasant and boar tenderloin.

The snapping turtle soup was the second-to-last dish we ate. Since my first attempt at making snapping turtle soup had bombed, I was justifiably leery about how it would turn out. During the day I had colored the strips of turtle meat in butter and seasoned them with salt, pepper, and cayenne, then simmered them for thirty minutes in the cooking liquid. While I was working on the dish, I kept getting whiffs of the nasty, sea-monster smell that had permeated my initial attempt. I couldn't tell if the smell was really there or if it was all in my imagination. Once you get an odor in your nose—or even in your mind—it's hard to get away from it. The odor pops up like a psychosomatic symptom, a phantom odor.

I first discovered the existence of phantom odors when I shot a mule deer buck in the Missouri Breaks a few years ago. After it fell, the deer slid out of view down a steep, snow-covered hill. I walked to the place where I thought the deer had landed, but the animal had vanished. The trail in the snow simply ended in a patch of sagebrush. On close inspection, I found a small hole. The hole was actually the mouth of a large, bottle-shaped cave. The bottom of the cave was thirteen feet below the surface. I shone my light down there, and sure enough, there was the buck.

We didn't get the animal out until the next night. With Matt holding my ankles, I was able to hang down into the cave and get a lasso around one of its antlers. The cave had insulated the deer, so its guts had begun to spoil. It stank to high hell. We took the meat home anyway and tried to salvage some of it. It was a lost cause.

Days after messing with the meat, I still couldn't shake the odor. Even if I smelled a perfectly benign substance, such as a vodka tonic in a bar, I would get a whiff of those nasty undertones of rotten flesh. The sensation didn't pass for a week.

So when Julian came into the room with the soup, I gave it a careful smell before anyone else had a chance to taste it. Julian had finished the dish with sherry; I could smell that. I could also smell that deathly, sea-monster odor that had permeated my first turtle soup effort. I couldn't tell if it was a phantom odor or not, so I passed out the bowls. I'd let everyone else decide.

I waited and watched: the soup was received with almost universal favor. I decided to taste it myself; when I did, the nasty odor disappeared. It was like being cured of an ailment. And it wasn't that the broth was hiding the turtle, either. In fact, the broth delivered and cradled the turtle, so that the flavor of the actual meat burst right through. The meat had a little spring to it, but not too bad. It had just enough texture to let you know it was there. The broth was warm and salty and had an almost primordial quality. Elegant and primordial, all at once. It seemed like something that a turtle king might bathe in. I was astonished. I felt as though my quest to recreate *Le Guide Culinaire* had come full circle in a beautiful, brilliant way. It had begun with a turtle crossing the road; it was ending all these months later, with a turtle making its way around a table of my closest friends.

But there was still one dish left, the most beautiful of them all. Just as we finished the turtle, Julian was putting wraps on the *carpe à l'ancienne.* If Escoffier had included pictures in *Le Guide,* you'd need a team of oxen to move the book around. Still, a couple of pictures would have come in handy while we were working on the carp. It was difficult to understand what exactly Escoffier was describing. But when Julian brought out the *carpe à l'ancienne,* I was glad that I didn't have any preconceived notions of what it was supposed to look like. If I had, it might have been like reading a book after watching the movie; my imagination would have been hostage to someone else's ideal. Instead, the fish struck me as a pure surprise. Nina had molded the fish's body out of creamed carp meat and butter, then reattached the body to the carp's real head and tail. The scales were made of thinly sliced truffles, and the fish was surrounded by poached oysters, morels, and rockfish quenelles. The whole thing was floating in a bath of rich, red wine sauce. It looked like nothing I'd ever seen, but it was everything I could have hoped for. It was big. It was glorious. It was the most beautiful food item I had ever laid eyes on.

As I admired the carp, I was reminded of my dad. I think he would have gotten a big kick out of *carpe à l'ancienne.* Not that my dad liked carp. In fact, he wouldn't touch it. But he had a story about a strange run-in he'd had with a carp. After World War II, he was working for the Metropolitan Insurance Company as a door-to-door salesman on Chicago's South Side, in some of the poorer neighborhoods. Back then, you didn't need to send your monthly insurance premium through the mail; instead, a salesman like my dad would come by once a month to pick it up. Because he went to his clients' homes every month, he got to know some of them pretty well. One time he was visiting with an older woman and he noticed a big roasting pan on top of the heating pipes in her living room. The pan was steaming. My dad was curious, so he lifted the lid. He was shocked to find a gutted carp and vegetable greens cooking inside.

My dad told that story for the rest of his life. In his mind, it

318 Steven Rinella

was a story about human resilience and ingenuity. He'd say, "Hell, the heater was running anyway. Might as well cook something on there!" I eventually picked up the story for my own use. But I just told it because I thought it was weird to eat carp. I never knew what had put that in my head, but *Le Guide Culinaire* provided me with a theory. In the introduction to *Le Guide*'s fish section, Escoffier complains that many excellent fishes are considered by the public to be inferior, for no good reason. He writes, "No doubt, fashion—ever illogical and wayward—exercises her tyrannical sway here, as in other matters of opinion." When I tasted that organic, free-range, wild carp, I knew what Escoffier meant about the "illogical and wayward" tastes that we all share. It was good, some of the best fish I've eaten. I actually felt a little embarrassed about all the foods I've passed up over the years for one stupid reason or another.

When I'm about to die, I'll probably look back on my life and admire certain moments: my first sexual experience, graduating from high school, graduating from college. And if I get married and have kids, I'll surely look back on those days. Also, I think I'll always remember the day I discovered *Le Guide Culinaire*. The book is like a tangible manifestation of a recurring dream of mine. In the dream, I've been renting an apartment for a year or so. One day I notice a little door in the hallway. I haven't seen the door before, but I'm not surprised by it. I open the door, and I see that my apartment is five times bigger than I thought it was. There's a bar and bookshelves and a huge bedroom and a pool table and a balcony. The space has been there all along, waiting for me, but I just never noticed it. And that's how *Le Guide Culinaire* made me feel about the world I live in. It opened that door up and invited me to see another, bigger side of things.

In that way, I now think of *Le Guide* as a great argument for biodiversity. To preserve biodiversity, we must learn to embrace differences. And thinking about differences is what got me involved with *Le Guide* in the first place. I remember standing with my dad in his barn and marveling at *Le Guide*'s detailed description of turtle slaughtering and wondering what the difference was between fried snapping turtle and snapping turtle soup. That question led to other questions: What's the difference between a skate and a ray? What's the difference between a cliff swallow's nest and a tropical swallow's nest? What's the difference between a pig's bladder and an antelope's bladder? For some things, the differences were difficult to discern; for others, the differences were remarkable. Either way, Escoffier opened my eyes to the beauty of small differences and to the importance of variety. I want the world to be as big and glorious and varied as possible, and packed full of animals. There's that old saying, "You are what you eat." If that's the case, then I'm many of the animals that live in this world, and I don't want to give any part of myself up.